WINNING

IN LIFE AND WORK:
N E W   B E G I N N I N G S

Compiled by
Keith Blakemore-Noble

To Wilson,
long may you keep winning!
All the best,

26/ 6/15

Contributors: Christopher Howard, Keith Blakemore-Noble, Calvin Coyles, Kim Barrett, Sanja Zeman, Michelle Armstrong, Kasia Nalepa, Lourdes Katague, Duda Prestes, David Jackson, Patrick White, Ian Crawford, Colin Bennett, Heather Traeger, Candice Marie, and Jason Barrett.

Foreword by Elliot Kay.

First Printing 2015

ISBN: 978-0-9931625-0-3 (sc)
ISBN: 978-0-9931625-1-0 (e)

Library of Congress Control Number: 2014922707

Published by Be Your Change Ltd, UK – http://www.Be-Your-Change.co.uk

For more information on the Winning in Life and Work series, and for more resources, please visit http://www.WinningInLifeAndWork.com

Printed and bound by Lulu Press, Inc.

3101 Hillsborough Street Raleigh, NC 27607, USA

Lulu Publishing Services rev. date: 02/17/2015

Contents

What Others Say About New Beginnings

"I highly recommend Winning in Life and Work: New Beginnings as proof that dreams come true through massive action."
- Loren Slocum Lahav - Founder of Lobella; Author of "Life Tuneups", "Drama Free Divorce Detox" and "The Greatest Love"; Facilitator for the Anthony Robbins Companies.

'What a treasure 'Winning in Life & Work' is. I sat myself down with a lovely cup of tea on a freezing October morning in London and started reading. And reading. And reading. Not often do you get captivated by a such an inspiring selection of authors. Since running my own business, I know of the ups & downs Chris is describing and the sticky thoughts 'everyone knows you can't do that' Keith talks about. This compilation is not only a gem for your soul but also gives you a sound understanding of the personal development industry and resources for a number of challenges you might come across along the way. Expect vivid storytelling, powerful metaphors and immediate-to-implement processes to move you forward in life and beyond. This lovely cup of tea in the morning turned into four cups and a day of reading, inspiration and refreshing global insights. Back to business. It's never too late to play a bigger game. THANK YOU to 'Winning in Life & Work' for being my muse today.'
- Annik Rau, Talent Scout & Founder, PONY Express Speaker Training

Other Books

In This Series

Winning in Life and Work Volume 1 (Be Your Change, 2012)

By These Authors

Christopher Howard

- *Turning Passions into Profits*
- *Instant Wealth: Wake up Rich*

Keith Blakemore-Noble and others

- *Winning in Life and Work: Volume 1* (Be Your Change, 2012)
- *Ready, Aim, Captivate!* (Experts Insights Publishing, 2012)
- *The Inspiration Bible* (Gowor International Publishing, 2014)

Michelle Armstrong

- *Manage Your Mind, Master Your Life* (Mind Management, 2004)
- *TRANSFORM - Reclaim Your Body & Life from the Inside Out* (Morgan James, 2014)

Heather Traeger & George Faddoul

- *How to Get a Bigger Bite out of Life! – Special Edition* (Quantum Change Publishing, 2011)

Heather Traeger, George Faddoul, and Ralf Behn

- *Unlocking Your Ideal Weight – Special Edition* (Quantum Change Publishing, 2014)

Patrick White and Hannah McNamara

- *Business Cookery: Tried and Tested Recipes for Business Success* (2011).

Ian Crawford

- *Presenter / Facilitator Training Manual* (Australian Sports Commission, 2009)

Disclaimer

Every care has been taken to make the figures and specifics in this book as accurate and relevant as possible at the time of writing. However, understand that these can change dependent on market and economic forces beyond the authors' control. The content, projections, figures, and indications contained in this book are based on opinion and cannot be relied upon when making investment decisions. The authors offer this information as a guide only, and it should not be considered as financial advice in any way. Refer to your independent financial advisor to give you complete advice based on your circumstances.

The advice and strategies contained herein may not be suitable for your particular situation, and you should consult with a professional where appropriate. The authors are not qualified to give financial, medical, or health advice. Seek legal and financial advice from a qualified advisor before making commitments. The authors accept no liability for decisions made based on the content of this book.

While the publisher and authors have made their best efforts in preparing this book, they make no warranty or representation with respect to the accuracy or completeness of the contents of this book, and specifically disclaim any implied warranties of merchantability or fitness for a particular purpose. No warranty may be created or extended by sales representatives nor by written sales materials. Neither the publisher nor authors shall be liable for any loss of profit or any other commercial damages, including but not limited to special, incidental, consequential, or other damages.

Dedication

To everyone, past present and future, who has ever
faced a new beginning in life, thought "I can't do
it!" and then proceeded to do it anyway.

Foreword

Elliot Kay, the Coach with the Hat

When my good friend Keith Blakemore-Noble asked me write him an introduction, I thought to myself what an honour and quickly panicked. What do I say? How do I make it perfect? But seeing the contents of this book assured me that the very reason he is writing this book is to help people grow, be empowered, and essentially to fly with success. And this is me right now, doing something as a result of reading that book and being able to take the information that was provided in it to quiet the voices in my mind that were doubting my ability to do what I am doing right now. Being dyslexic, for me to write this is a major challenge.

My example is living evidence that what you are about to learn is going to have a major impact upon you and your life. It will help you to break through those things that might be holding you back and inform you what to do about it. What you are going to experience right now is pages and pages full of value, tips, and wisdom.

I have had the pleasure and honour of working with Keith, the main driver of this book, and it is no surprise he has attracted to so many talented authors to work with him, each bringing their own area of expertise with one common goal: to help, support, and share with you how to grow and become even greater.

As someone who has been in the personal development industry for seventeen years and worked internationally, it is my privilege to support this book and see it fly off the shelves in order to for you, the reader, to have a better quality of life.

Elliot Kay, the Coach with the Hat,

Lead facilitator of *Power to Succeed*

Preface

This book is the follow-up to the internationally bestselling book *Winning in Life and Work: Volume 1* from 2012. It follows the same premise: experts sharing their experience, skills, and knowledge in specific areas to help you to become even better at winning in life and work.

This time round, the chapters are more closely themed around the whole field of *new beginnings*, although again the content can be successfully applied to a wide range of situations in your life. After all, it has often been noted that how we do one thing is how we do everything.

It is not necessary to have read the first volume in order to get the most from this one, although perhaps after reading this book you might become inspired to seek out the guidance and suggestions offered within the first.

Introduction

We often face the prospect of new beginnings in life. Sometimes the new beginnings are planned; sometimes they are unexpected. Sometimes they are eagerly anticipated; sometimes they are viewed with dread. Sometimes they are initiated by us; sometimes they are triggered by things outside of our control.

Whatever the cause, new beginnings are a fact of life. We can either dread them or welcome them – we can't run and hide from them, at least not forever. Sometimes, despite your very best attempts and efforts, you just can't seem to find the key, that little nugget which helps you to make the most of your new opportunity or situation. You know that it's possible to win as you see many others around you doing so every day, but there are times when we could do with a little helping hand, some guidance to point us in the right direction.

That is what this book seeks to provide. Treat it as your secret weapon in the game of life – although not so secret that you won't want to tell family and friends about it, so that they too can start to win more powerfully! Read it carefully and often, for you never know when the right nugget will reveal itself at precisely the right time for you.

This volume contains the distilled wisdom from sixteen international experts in their respective fields, including how singing can improve your life; how to clear the decks for a new beginning; how to make a long-lasting transformation; social networks and dating; why you're not making money and how to start; how to excel at living in a new country; putting the WoW factor into your career – and more. Each of these experts has created a chapter specially for you, covering many key aspects and areas of life, both in your personal and professional life.

I can't emphasize enough the value to you of reading and rereading all of these chapters, even if they may not at first glance appear to be directly relevant to you. Each chapter operates at multiple levels, and while a given chapter may appear to be relevant only to a specific personal or business aspect of life, careful reading, rereading, and meditation on it may reap many benefits in other areas of your life.

Some chapters have an obviously broad appeal, while others appear to focus on a specific topic; but their content and underlying message is almost certain to be of relevance across whole sections of your life. What a discovery awaits you!

However, as the old proverb rightly puts it, "You can lead a horse to water, but you can't make it drink." Alas, simply owning or holding this book is not going to help you to make any long-term changes. Not even just reading the book is going to result in major changes to your life. You must also take action as a result of what you have read; for it is only by taking action that we begin to make the changes that we seek in our lives, and by continuing to take action that we guide our lives in the wondrous directions we choose for ourselves.

On behalf of all of the contributors, I express the hope that you enjoy this book, read it, act upon it, treasure it, and refer to it often. May doing so reward you in ways you have yet to even consider the possibility of imagining, and lead you to making your new beginning the most powerful, positive, and life-affirming experience possible.

Keith Blakemore-Noble,

October 2014

Rock Your World: Transform Your Life!

Christopher Howard

Christopher Howard has achieved extraordinary success as a social entrepreneur, transformational speaker, bestselling author, coach, and lifestyle and wealth strategist in a career spanning over two decades. Chris's lifelong mission has been to put the tools of transformation into the hands of everybody on the planet, and to create worldwide wealth through education and entrepreneurial means. On the entrepreneurial side, his seminars and products have generated well over 100 million dollars in sales globally. He has personally done million dollar sales days over and over and over again, an accomplishment which is held only by a handful of the very top 1 per cent of speakers in the personal and professional development industry, including the likes of Tony Robbins and T. Harv Eker. One of the most popular speakers in the world, Christopher has spoken in twenty-eight countries and fifty-seven cities, often to audiences of thousands. Chris has touched over a million people's lives through his teachings and programs and is known for both his heartfelt approach to transformation as well as his ability to help people to rapidly transform their businesses and their lives for the better. Chris built the largest personal and professional development presence in Australia, the second largest in the UK (behind only Tony Robbins), and he built the largest neuro-linguistic programming (NLP) training company in the world, with ten times the sales of the nearest competitor, prior to launching his latest creation, Rock House.

Chris is the author of two number one bestselling books, which capture the essence of his original philosophies: Turning Passions into Profits, *which he released in 2001, and* Instant Wealth – Wake up Rich! Discover the Secret of the New Entrepreneurial Mind, *released in 2008, both of which were published by Wiley and Sons.*

I went to bed that night as usual, with my million-dollar company running as normal; I woke up the next day and it was all gone – my business, my customers, my income – all gone, taken while I slept in an illegal hostile takeover.

What could I do now?

I could have sunk into a depression about losing it all. I could have got angry and bitter. I could have moaned about how unfair it all was. However, I knew that ultimately none of that would be helpful.

Instead, I remembered what Richard Branson had told me while we were hanging out together on Necker Island. He told me that "if anything ever happened to the Virgin companies, I'd probably just take myself off to Bali or something." Which is exactly what I did. I took myself to Bali and began to contemplate, plan, and ultimately implement the biggest new beginning I had ever undertaken in my life.

My name is Chris Howard, and I am absolutely thrilled to have the opportunity to reach out to you and connect with you. I am sharing with you some of my current thinking and ideas around the tools of transformation, how you can radically transform your life rapidly, and how you can help others to do the same thing. This is the same approach I embraced when I was moving on from perhaps the biggest professional setback I've ever experienced, and these are the thoughts and tools which enabled me to springboard back better than ever and truly embrace my heaven-sent opportunity for a new beginning.

Within this chapter you will discover my time-tested, easy-to-use system for instantly transforming the quality of both your life and the lives of others in powerful ways. Sometimes I think of it as how you create a "genie consciousness" where literally your own wish is your own command – you think it and have the ability to create it. I know that it may sound a little far-fetched, but I'm going to be sharing with you several tools, techniques, and methods that you can use to rapidly change your entire experience of life, from the amount of money you make to where you live to the career path that you're on – everything.

Can you imagine what would it be like to have the ability to shift your reality in the flash of an eye? To have the power to forge instantaneous change in anyone? A system to change their relationships, or their health, or whatever it is that they're looking to change? To have the ability to transform debt into wealth for example, or depression into fulfilment?

Can you imagine what it would be like to have the power to just snap your fingers and instantaneously have your desired lifestyle?

Again, I know that it sounds fantastical. I mean how could it possibly occur? I'm going to share with you exactly how.

One of the things that I've realize is that in today's age, times are rapidly changing. With globalization and the Internet we have the ability to make money anywhere in the world, and to spend it where it's worth a lot. This alone can radically change the quality of our lives in a flash of an eye.

There is more opportunity in the world today than ever before, and it is going to be the people that have the imagination to go out and capture the opportunities out there who will be the ones to forge that type of destiny.

As Einstein said, "All of our problems are problems of the imagination; all of our solutions are solutions of our imagination."

I invite you to join me in a journey of consciousness, and it will be a journey of consciousness that will turn your life for the better – if you'll allow it to!

Would you like me to share with you how you can become the most powerful transformational leader that you can possibly be? How you can follow a paint-by-numbers approach to growing your success so fast that it makes your head spin? How to unleash your own truly limitless potential? (You truly are limitless, you know.)

I am going to share with you the steps that you can take right now to be more fulfilled than you may have ever imagined possible, while simultaneously living your greatest dreams today.

I am going to share with you five key principles for instantly facilitating transformation for anyone, anytime, anywhere.

I am also going to share with you how to gain your freedom back by simply waking up to the unconscious forces that determine your destiny and the destinies of those around you.

We have to start with the difference between *change* and *transformation*. You've heard the statement "The more things change the more they remain the same." There is a big difference between change and transformation. To transform means to change completely – to change in composition and structure, just like when you take carbon and apply enough pressure, turning it into a diamond that, once formed, can never go back to its old form. This is the type of transformation that I'm sharing with you.

So why should you master transformation? Put simply, it is the most important skill that you can ever learn. It's about how to become a modern-day alchemist so that you can create the lifestyle that others only dream of. Just imagine how valuable you would be to the world!

Remember that money is only a measurement of the value that you create for other people. For example, Bill Gates created a lot of value for the world, and he was rewarded with a lot of money.

A wave is sweeping around the planet right now. People are diving in to learn this tool, and you know as well as I do that smart surfers have to start paddling before the wave hits. If you want to ride the crest of that wave, then you've got to start paddling right now.

The key to this is in knowing that transformation equals *freedom*.

Ask yourself: where are you in your life right now – emotionally, spiritually, financially? Where would you like to be? Would you like to be working anywhere on the planet? Would you like to be working from a beach or living a laptop lifestyle? Or maybe just hanging out spending your time in a hammock, or at the Maldives, or relaxing on your deck?

Whatever it is for you, having that is ultimate freedom, and what that is going to take is transformation.

Who am I to talk about transformation and ultimate freedom? I've been around. I'm the CEO and founder of Rock House, which is a leading provider of personal and professional development training courses, education, and media around the world. I was the founder of the Academy of Wealth and Achievement, where I generated over a hundred million dollars in sales worldwide in what was, at the time, the largest NLP education and training company in the world. I had Australia's largest personal development presence over the last decade, and I am the author of a couple of bestselling books. I've also done million-dollar sales days over and over again. But I tell you what – it wasn't always that way. There was a time when things were so bad and I was so far behind that I thought I was in first place, as my good friend Brian Tracy put it.

I lived in a torn-down house. It was literally torn down while I lived there! I had to microwave buckets of water to wash my hair with because they had cut off the gas, and I was eating only every third day because I had so little money. I had moved into the ghetto to save money, and things were desperate. I remember breaking down into tears on the floor of my apartment and trying to figure out how I was going to make my life work. I guess I needed that much pressure to get the metaphor that pressure is how the diamonds form, and that is how you get the skills for transformation. Not that I'm saying you need to move into the ghetto and eat only every third day, of course! However, it was the transformation I made which has lead me to the lifestyle I enjoy around the world today.

If you are like most people, then you may share a lot of the same challenges they have. Have a look through this list. Does any of it sound familiar?

- You feel like you're stuck and the world is against you;
- You don't believe in your ability to be wealthy or make money;
- You feel like no matter what you do, you never produce the critical results that you need;
- You don't know what to do or where to start;

- You are baffled when you see others seeming to make it all happen with ease;
- You are unhappy and unfulfilled;
- You are stressed out of your mind;
- You are binge eating or drinking or living with other addictions that numb the pain of unfulfilled expectations but also take you even further off path;
- You feel undesirable in relationships;
- Your physical health causes you to feel depressed.

Be honest, did you find several (or even all) of these feel like they apply to you right now, even though you have perhaps done a lot of work already? It is common for most people to feel at least some of these apply to them – I know I can certainly relate to each and every one of them in the past!

The good news is that it doesn't have to be like that for you; I'll come on to why that is so in a moment.

First, I want to share with you some common myths many people hold about life:

- That if you don't have cash in the bank you have no money;
- That if you don't know the right people you can't succeed;
- That if you keep chasing away relationships you aren't good enough to keep one;
- That if you're overweight you're out of shape and fat;
- That if you don't make X amount of money you aren't successful or wealthy;
- That if you don't have savings or investments you can't live your dream lifestyle today;
- That if every waking moment of the day is taken up just for you to survive, you don't have the time to transform your life.

These myths are so commonly held that most people have bought into them and believe them to be true. Yet, the reality is that none of them is true! When Richard Branson bought Necker Island, he had no money in the bank, yet he didn't let that stop him! It is never a question of resources, it is only ever a question of resourcefulness.

It's time for you to make a decision. Do you remember the movie *The Matrix?* Morpheus came to Neo and said: "I am only trying to expand your mind," at which point he offered him a choice – take the red pill or the blue pill. If you take the blue pill, then you go back to the way you've been living, complete with all of its limitations and all of its illusions. However, if you take the red pill, then it's going to open and expand your mind to new possibilities beyond anything you can possibly imagine. The only problem is that once you take that red pill you can never go back again.

Right now I'm offering the same choice. I'd like to suggest that it's time to take that *red* pill. It's time to expand your mind, to expand your thinking, and to wake up to the true possibility that you have in your life. Realize this is your opportunity.

But you have to act now!

Maybe you've heard before that the past and the future don't exist, that they are just constructs in your imagination. It's true. The only time that you can change your life is right here, right now, in the moment. You've been boxed in and limited. So have I. We all have – by our past programming and past conditioning.

How often have you heard yourself say "Someday I'll…"? The reality is that someday never comes – it's a figment of your imagination. You won't act ever unless you act now – you'll stay stuck where you are if you don't act now!

I'm going to share with you the five steps to transformation that you can embrace right now, today, this minute, to radically change everything.

Step 1 – Take the red pill say "I'm in."
Step 2 – Take charge of your creation.
Step 3 – Expand your maps.
Step 4 – Chart a new course.
Step 5 – Magnetize and optimize.

Let's take a closer look at each of these steps.

The first step to transformation is to take that red pill – to wake up and realize that when you look around the world, people are living like sheep; literally living like sheep. They do what they're told, they stand in line, they go in and work jobs…

Now, I don't mean anything critical by that. There's nothing wrong with a job. A lot of people demonize having a job; I don't. However, I always say that you should never work for what you make, rather you should work for who you become. That way, every moment of every day becomes an investment spent in the greatest future that you are looking to create, while you are enjoying every inch and every moment of every day.

The universe is commonly defined as the totality of everything – planets, stars, galaxies, the contents of intergalactic space, all of matter and energy. So when we think of the universe, this is what we are thinking of. However, I want you to consider that perhaps what you experience in the universe is not all that it seems. Perhaps the universe is different than you and I think. Perhaps reality is just an illusion. Let me explain.

As far back as sixth century BC, the Greek philosophers developed the earliest known philosophical models of the universe. They admitted that appearances can be deceiving, and they looked to understand what's beyond the appearances. They noted particularly the ability of matter to change forms. Ice changes to water, water changes to steam. So several philosophers proposed that apparently different materials of the world are not different but are one single primordial material. For example, Pythagoras and Plato both believed that all things are composed of numbers.

Hermes Trismegistus wrote on the Emerald Tablet what was supposed to be all the secrets of the known universe. Isaac Newton translated it as follows:

Tis true without lying, certain & most true.
That which is below is like that which is above &
that which is above is like that which is below to do the
miracles of one only thing

And as all things have been & arose from one by the mediation of one: so all things have their birth from this one thing by adaptation.

The Sun is its father, the moon its mother, the wind hath carried it in its belly, the earth is its nurse.

The father of all perfection in the whole world is here.

Its force or power is entire if it be converted into earth.

Separate thou the earth from the fire, the subtle from the gross sweetly with great industry.

It ascends from the earth to the heaven & again it descends to the earth & receives the force of things superior & inferior.

By this means you shall have the glory of the whole world & thereby all obscurity shall fly from you.

Its force is above all force. For it vanquishes every subtle thing & penetrates every solid thing.

So was the world created.

From this are & do come admirable adaptations whereof the means (or process) is here in this. Hence I am called Hermes Trismegist, having the three parts of the philosophy of the whole world

That which I have said of the operation of the Sun is accomplished & ended.

Essentially, he is saying that all things are one, that there is no difference between you and that which you perceive outside of you.

We know today that if we were to look at your body, or this book, or anything at all, through a high-powered electron microscope, then we would see far more space than solid matter. The solidity of matter is just an illusion! In fact, if you were able to suck out all of the space in between, you could put the entire world on a single teaspoon. All of the atoms and molecules are constantly in motion, flowing and rearranging. Everything is in a constant state of change. Take your stomach, for example. Did you know you have a new stomach lining every seven days? The Greek philosopher Heraclitus said that you can't step in the same river in the same place twice, because the second time you step in it, the river has moved on, the water you first stepped in has gone, the river is not the same.

We talked about the universe a moment ago. I'd like to suggest that perhaps we actually have seven billion different universes. There are seven billion individuals on the planet right now, and the concept of the subjectivity of perception of reality implies that the perception of everything differs for each individual. We all live in different universes. We may have some things in common; that's our common reality. But we all have our own individual experiences and perceptions which are not true or real for others. Indeed, until you have personally experienced something, it may not even be true for you in your life!

Before you judge others or claim any absolute truth, consider this. You can see less than 1 per cent of the electromagnetic spectrum, and hear less than 1 per cent of the acoustic spectrum. As you read this, you are travelling at 220 kilometres per second across the galaxy. 90 per cent of the cells in your body carry their own microbial DNA and are not "you." The atoms in your body are 99.99999999999% empty space, and none of them are the ones you were born with, but they all originated in the belly of a star. Human beings have 46 chromosomes, 2 fewer than the common potato. The existence of the rainbow depends upon the conical photoreceptors in your eye; to animals without cones, the rainbow does not exist. This is pretty amazing, especially considering that all the beautiful colours you see represent less than 1 per cent of the electromagnetic spectrum.

Reality is very different from what you think it has been. You might look out the window and thinks that is reality, which in a way it is, but it is all inside your mind. The reality that we perceive does not take the shape it does until it passes through our perceptual filters, which are unique to each and every one of us, and to us as a species. For example, think about how different reality is for a bat, who perceives the world through sonar – do you think the bat perceives the world as a different place? Absolutely, it does.

If you are finding this a strange concept to grasp, then you are not alone – it used to bug Einstein! He asked: "You mean to say that the Moon doesn't exist as anything other than a probability until I look for it to exist? And that by looking for it to exist I actually bring it into existence through my observation?" Yet, that is the reality. The Moon is just a bunch of atoms and molecules, but it takes its form inside your mind as you look for it and observe it. As does everything else. That's why Einstein also said that imagination is more important than knowledge.

So if the world around us is not the reality we take it to be, then where does reality take place? It takes place inside your head! You create your own internal representation of reality, upon which is based everything you do. We don't see the world as it is; we see the world as we perceive it. How we perceive it is based upon who we are and the components of our personality.

In 1933, Alfred Korzybski said that the map is not the territory. You wouldn't go to a restaurant and eat the menu! Yet people still take their internal representation of reality, based upon our own unique filters, as being reality. It's like we each have our own maps of reality. The problem is, so many navigate their way through life with poor-quality maps which show the way only to things like depression or sadness or poverty or being overwhelmed or anger or poor relationships instead of where those using them actually want to go. The problem is, they mistake the map for the territory all the time. For example, they think that if they keep getting poor relationships then it means they weren't meant to have a great relationship because the map says so.

Reality is merely an illusion, albeit a persistent one. That was our friend Einstein again. We each live in our own unique illusion of reality.

Yet all possibilities are out there for us – the possibility of richness, the possibility of poverty, the possibility of great relationships, the possibility of poor relationships. If we continue to focus our reality based on our poor map, however, then we will continue to experience poor outcomes. When we wake up to the fact that we can adjust our own reality and not rely on the poor map, then it's like waking up to realize that we've been sitting and watching just one channel on our TV. There are a huge number of channels out there that we could watch if we would just tune them in and change the channel.

Just as the TV tuner creates what you see, so your own thoughts create your own reality.

The human brain produces approximately 70,000 thoughts on an average day. There are 86,400 seconds in a 24-hour day, which means that you have a different thought every 1.2 seconds. Those thoughts are habituated based on your past programming and conditioning and are expressed and defined in relationship to your values, beliefs, and other filters. In other words, you think about the same stuff all the time! It's those very thoughts which trap you in your own personal world and cause you to keep getting those results you keep getting. It's all a result of your thoughts.

If your thoughts create your reality, then what creates your thoughts? They are the result of your personality, past programming, and conditioning. What if we just changed our thoughts? That's the basis behind the law of attraction. Change your thoughts and change your results. But what people find is that they change their thoughts without changing themselves (the very thing which creates their thoughts), and pretty quickly those same old thoughts come rushing back with the same old results.

The good news is that the human mind is malleable. We can change. When we change who we are at the unconscious level, we change the way we think and thus the results which we get. It takes the desire to and the realization that you can expand your mind. Whatever has been your reality because of your past programming and past conditioning up until now was just the starting point. You may not realize it yet, but as you read this chapter you have already begun to shake up your old models of the world and to expand your thinking so that you can embrace new realities and make new beginnings.

The second step to transformation is to take charge of your creation. We are constantly creating our future. So why not take charge of that creation process and start creating the future you want, not the future that old map said you had to have? The way you do this is by taking charge of what you are doing, what you are thinking, what you are believing, and what you are valuing in the here and now.

As His Holiness the fourteenth Dalai Lama said, "Ultimately, the creator is one's own mind." That is true for the creation of anything. Disneyland, before it was created, first had to exist inside Walt Disney's mind.

So how do we start to take charge? We do it by first beginning to realize that perception is projection. What we perceive in the world, our reality, is a projection of our internal thoughts, beliefs, values, and judgements. The world as we see it is simply a reflection of ourself. We don't see the world as it is, we see the world as we are.

So the question is what do *you* see in the mirror? In the mirror of your bank account, the mirror of your relationships, the mirror of your business, the mirror of your happiness?

An atom is the smallest particle of matter which exists, yet you cannot prove that it exists as anything other than a quantum probability until you actually look for it. By looking for it to exist we collapse the probability function and bring it into being.

Do you know how many pages there are on the World Wide Web? If you answered "a lot," then you are pretty close! There are pages out there covering everything you could possibly think of and many more things beyond that. However, if you take your favourite search engine and tell it to search for poverty, what are you going to find? Nothing but pages dealing with poverty. Someone seeing that might conclude that poverty is all that exists, yet if you next searched for abundance, you would be flooded with nothing but pages dealing with abundance. We find what we search for. If you are searching for obstacles, you will find obstacles. What if instead you searched for opportunities and success? What do you think you might start to find?

So many people go through life with their own internal search engine tuned in to poverty or failure or poor relationships, and then wonder why that is all they find and they then assume that is all there is. The reality is that there is so much more. We live in a quantum soup of pure potentiality where nothing exists until we look for it to exist. The way we see reality is how we create reality.

So how do we change the reality we see? How do we change our perceptions, our models of the world? How do we take charge of our maps and our search engine? It all starts from within. Where does reality take place? Inside our minds. We don't even react with people the way they are. We react with our own internal representations of them.

What you expect is what you get; expectation rules outcome. Yet our expectations are largely unconscious. It is our own unconscious expectations of the future which create our future.

What you focus on expands. Oprah Winfrey said that when she was growing up, she would have never even dreamed that there was anything to live other than the poverty in which she was growing up, if it weren't for the books that she read. Reading those books changed her focus, allowing her to imagine whole new possibilities which she went on to create. What she focused on expanded.

Wealth is a state of mind. That is true of wealth in all of its forms – spiritual, emotional, financial, mental. It is nothing more than a state of mind. It is a reflection of your thinking, which is a reflection of your values and your beliefs. As Henry Ford said, "Whether you think you can, or you think you can't – you're right." When Richard Branson wanted to buy Necker Island, he didn't have the money in the bank. Did that mean he wasn't wealthy? Did he focus on how much money he didn't have? No! He focused on his desire – buying the island – and on finding ways to be able to do it.

Everything that exists in your universe stems from you. You are the creator of your own reality in your own personal universe.

What determines your thinking? It's your values, which is what is important to you. It is your beliefs, your feelings or convictions of what is true, right, or real. It is your attitudes, which are a collection of values and beliefs around a subject. It is your meta-programs which are the collection of unconscious switches. It is the decisions that you made and make in your life, your memories, your references, your driving force, your language, and your traits. Wittgenstein said "Whereof one cannot think one cannot speak, and whereof one cannot speak one cannot think." Warren Buffett reads around 3,000 annual reports a year, which is how he gets his knowledge of which companies are good investments. He can do this because he has the financial language to be able to interpret what he is reading. All of these components drive our thinking, which drives our outcomes.

Remember, your thoughts create your reality, and you have on average a different thought every 1.2 seconds. What are those thoughts creating? Look at your reality to find out. As you change what drives your thoughts, you change the outcomes you get. Take charge of your creation.

The third step to transformation is to expand your maps. If you are living with a poor-quality map, one that shows poverty as the only destination, it's time to get a new map!

Remember, wealth is just a state of mind. Everything starts off in the mind. One of the big things which drives those states of minds and emotions is your set of values – what's important to you. Think of them as the major *keywords*. Some of the values common to nearly all of those we might consider to be the super wealthy include:

- Something grander than the money
- Passion
- Desire to *succeed* in the realm of business
- Preternatural ability to watch bottom line results
- Competitive drive; desire to be the best in the industry
- Obsession with expansion
- Pursuing the money in ideas

When you start to embrace and embody the values of the super wealthy, do you think you might start to think the way the super wealthy think? Of course you will! Remember that our values are part of what drives our thinking, they are part of the filters in the search engine of our own life. And when you start to think the way the super wealthy think, what kind of results are you going to start to get?

It is our sense of identity which determines our actions, which in turn is what drives our results. If we have conditioned ourselves to believe that we will never amount to much, then what will happen? We won't amount to much. When we change our values, our beliefs, our decisions about ourselves, when we expand our maps to include success and wealth and happiness, that's when we really start to make change in our actions which changes the results we get.

Perhaps the two most important words we can use are "I am," for it is what we place after them which truly defines the outcomes we get. What do you tell yourself you are?

The fourth step to transformation is to chart a new course. Now that you have expanded your maps, you have new routes, pathways, and options available to you. So it is time to chart your new course! If you want a different result, you have to do something different. With your new expanded map, you can now chart that new course, a different course leading to a different destination.

So what is your new destination? What is it that you want to create for your life? What do you want your life to be in ten years time?

It's all about your vision, mission, goals, and values.

Your vision is your ultimate destination. It's where you want to go, what you ultimately what to be, do, and have. If you don't have a clear vision of where you want to go, how can you even begin to plot a course? It would be like getting into your car, turning on the sat nav, and expecting it to take you somewhere without telling it where!

Your mission is the path you take to get there, it's the route you follow, it's how you are going to meet your vision. The clearer and more well-defined your mission, the greater your ability to know that you are on course.

Goals. People often talk a lot about goals as if they are the most important aspect, but that's not true. Goals are simply the signposts along the way. They are important to have, so that you know you are following the path, they let you know you are on the path, but if you miss a goal it is not the end of the world. What happens if you are supposed to take a turn and you miss it? You simply note that you missed the turn, plot a new route to bring you back on course, and continue on your way.

So it is with goals – if you miss a goal, and you will – we all do at times – then simply note that you missed that goal and plot the new goals you need to bring you back to your path, to your mission.

Your values are like your compass that keep you on track and guide your way.

The fifth step to transformation is to *magnetize* and *optimize*. This is my favourite one. It's who you are and who you become that is more important than any goal. Indeed, it is who you are which determines those goals. When you magnetize yourself and optimize your performance, this makes you more powerful than you could possibly imagine. When you magnetize yourself, it enables you to bring teams together to conspire to help you to achieve your goals and vision.

To start this, I would like you to take a few moments to create your *circle of influence*. List the twenty people you want to be a part of your circle, to help you to achieve your vision. They can be anybody; you don't have to know them personally at this point. Who would be the twenty best people who could help you with your vision? When I created my first list, I had no idea how I would ever get to reach those people, yet within six months of creating it, ten of them had become close personal friends or business associates, and that included billionaires and leaders in my field. It was this circle of influence which changed everything. So write out your list of the twenty people you would want and need to best help you to fulfil your mission.

You now have in your hands and your mind the five powerful steps for creating long-lasting transformation. These are the same tools I have successfully used over and over again throughout my life, as have countless others I've had the privilege to train. Now it's your turn. And it can all be yours, provided you act and act now!

Remember, too, that it takes teamwork to make the dream work. Who do you want on your team to help you to make the best new beginning possible, to solidify your transformation, and to fulfil your mission?

Until we meet again, love deeply, shine brightly, and make every day an extraordinary adventure!

Let Go to Begin

Keith Blakemore-Noble

Keith Blakemore-Noble, FRI, FBCS, CITP, also known as the Confidence Alchemist, is an international bestselling author, international speaker, coach, trainer, and mind changer. From paralyzing shyness to teaching on stages in the UK, USA, Indonesia, Vietnam, Malaysia, and Singapore, Keith has come far from a life that is just a distant memory now. Keith, who has been working closely alongside Chris Howard for over four years and with whom he now travels the world sharing these tools and technologies, brings a natural humour and wit to the stage, and has a captivating presence, allowing you to learn from him with ease as he shares with you the same tools which he used to make massive transformations in his own lives and those of his clients.

Through the use of his unique Ultimate Confidence system, which he has carefully developed and refined and continues to enhance as brain and behavioural sciences evolve, he helps people to conquer their shyness and to unmask their confidence. This helps them to find their voice – be it for speaking from a stage, speaking in team meetings, or just having the confidence to raise their hand and ask questions in seminars – and ensures that his clients are in a far better place to be able to connect with other people in social and business situations, resulting in them leading happier and more fulfilling lives. And who doesn't want that?

A living embodiment of the cutting-edge sciences and tools he employs, he has used them all on himself first, so he knows how well they work and also understands how the processes feel from your perspective.

Prior to moving full-time into helping people, he spent thirteen successful years in IT, including leading a team with members in the UK, Norway, and New Zealand. He has gone from reprogramming and upgrading computers to reprogramming and upgrading people's minds! The latter is infinitely more rewarding, it has to be said.

A strong believer that change is always possible, he invites you to change your mind, change your life.

You can't start the next chapter of your life if
you keep rereading the last one.
– Whoever Saidit

You are reading this book because you are planning a new beginning in some area of your life, or because you have already started one. Either way, it is a very exciting thing to do! At the same time, it is challenging. There are so many things to be considered, and so many things that could go wrong. That thought alone can be enough to put many people off, which is a great pity because if we continue to allow our fears to hold us back then we will always remain where we are.

Very often, the greatest thing holding us back is not the fear of failure, or even the fear of success, which, surprisingly, is nearly always the bigger of the two fears. Success will bring new things, and people worry about how they will ever cope with them. No, there is something far greater which holds us back, causing far too many of us to fail to realize our dreams, to give up on our new beginnings before we even started.

It doesn't have to be this way!

To help us explore and better learn how we to give ourselves the absolute best starting point for our new beginning, let's follow the story of a monk and his apprentice on their journey from their comfortable monastery in a village into the wilds and, for at least one of them, an unknown destination.

Wait a minute. Unknown destination? Yes! For sometimes, no matter how much planning and preparation we undertake, our destination can turn out to be a surprise when we finally get there. It is as much about enjoying what we learn on our journey as it is about reaching our destination. Indeed, all too often we can be in such a hurry to "get there" that we miss the wonderful opportunities that present themselves along the way. In life there is always something to learn if we would only open ourselves to the possibility.

Some of the situations the monk and his apprentice experience along the way may have a ring of familiarity about them, for some of them are oft-told tales. But you are encouraged to read them, be it for the first time or once again, for within them you may yet uncover some hitherto unseen secret or some subtle new insight you were previously unaware of.

Are you sitting comfortably? Then I'll begin.

It was the first day of their great journey. A younger monk, who had grown up in the monastery and knew nothing other than the monastery and the small village of which it was part, had wanted to explore the world and journey to a new monastery, but was a bit hesitant, not knowing the way, and was apprehensive about what he might find in the outside world. Therefore, an elder monk had agreed to accompany the younger on his journey, to help him find his way safely and to help him to experience the best of his journey. The elder monk was doing this out of kindness to the younger, but also for his own reason. For he had been in his monastery for a great many years, and whilst life was good there, he felt he had learned all he could, and he wanted not only to explore the world but to perhaps seek a new phase in his life. It was time to let go of the old and familiar and to seek new horizons, new challenges, new opportunities for him to grow. It was time for his own new beginning. Quite what that was to be he was not yet certain, but he knew that if he looked at the world with a ferocious curiosity then he would spot the opportunities as they presented themselves.

The two monks had agreed to meet at the top of the road just outside the village, and so it was that the elder monk sat at the point where the village road met the larger road and quietly waited for the younger monk to join him.

As he sat there contemplating what the road ahead might bring, he spotted a stranger walking towards him, greeted the stranger with a friendly hello, and asked where he was going. The stranger said that he had come from another village down the road but was looking for a new place to live, and asked whether this village might be suitable.

"What did you think about your last home?" asked the elder monk.

The stranger replied, sourly and with barely concealed anger, "Oh, it was an awful place. Everyone was always sticking their nose into each other's business. The shopkeeper was always looking for ways to cheat me, and the bar was disgusting and full of scum and villains. What's this place like?"

His face filled with sadness, the elder monk replied, "Then you had best keep on walking, my friend, for you will find this village to be the same," and the stranger went on his way.

Soon, along came another traveller, who greeted the monk with a friendly wave and explained that he, too, was from the village down the road and was looking for a new home, so he enquired about this village. Again, the monk asked what the traveller had thought of his previous home.

"Oh, it is a wonderful place!" exclaimed the traveller. "The people are friendly, always looking out for each other, making sure nobody felt left out. The shopkeeper was always looking for the best bargains for us, and the bar was filled with bright and colourful characters from all around, always with an exciting tale to share!"

The monk smiled and beckoned the traveller to head to his village, explaining that the traveller would find this village to be the same.

The monk wisely realized that what we perceive of any situation is less about the reality, and more about ourselves and what is going on inside. All too often, when someone wants to make a new beginning, it is not the old situation they are running away from, but themselves, and pretty soon they find the new place is just as bad or good as the old one was.

I certainly found this out in my own career. In my first job, I was thrilled and excited at the start, but quickly started to find fault with the work, the company, and some of the employees. After a year or so I decided this was not the place for me and I found a new job. Well! The new job was fantastic – thrilling and exciting! But, sure enough, after a while I started to find fault with the work, the company, and some of the employees, and after a couple of years I resolved to find a better job elsewhere. And so the same pattern continued for my first five jobs. (You could say that in some things I was clearly a slow learner!) It wasn't until my sixth job that I began to realize that the problems were not with the job or the company or the employees, but within me – my expectations, how I handled situations, what I was looking for. So in my sixth job, having realized this, I began to change myself. I started to look for other explanations for situations, to explore how I was contributing to things, looking to see if there might be other more benign reasons for people's behaviours. And as a result of letting go of things over which I had no control, of looking for the positive in things, of adapting and taking responsibility for how I was choosing to feel (for we are all responsible ultimately for how we choose to feel and react to anything), I was able to continue to enjoy my job. Indeed, I spent longer there than I had in my five previous jobs put together because I had realized that no matter how many new beginnings I had, it was always me and my own baggage that I was taking with me!

The younger monk joined the elder, and soon they were on their way. These monks belonged to an order which forbade contact with any sort with women, so in order to avoid potentially embarrassing encounters, the elder monk led them along the back roads, avoiding the villages and towns on the way. Instead, they took a little-used path which wound its way through the forests.

After many hours of walking together in silence through the forests, enjoying the beautiful trees and listening to the enchanting sound of the birds singing overhead, they came upon a clearing.

In this clearing were a team of wood cutters and their elephant. These woodcutters would cut down the trees, and use their elephant to drag the trees away to be chopped up and sold for their timber.

The younger monk wondered how the woodcutters stopped the elephant from just running away at night, so he asked the head woodcutter how they did it.

"You see that peg in the ground?" said the head woodcutter, pointing to beside the elephant. "All we do each night is take this small pink rope, tie one loop around the elephant's back leg, and tie the other end of the rope to the peg. The elephant, knowing the rope is there, doesn't make any attempt to run away."

The young monk looked at the rope and, noticing that it wasn't a very strong one, was puzzled. After the head woodcutter had wandered off, the young monk turned to the elder monk and asked, "That rope is very thin and not very strong. Surely the rope is not enough to stop an elephant?"

The elder monk replied to the young monk, "Study the rope carefully. What else can you tell me about it?" After studying the rope for a few minutes, the younger monk replied that the only other thing he could notice about the rope was that it was pink. "But how does that make it strong enough to stop the elephant from running away?" he asked the elder monk.

"My brother, the rope doesn't have to be strong! The colour alone is enough to let the elephant know that there is no point in trying to escape," replied the elder.

Noticing the look of puzzlement on his young companion's face, he went on to explain, "It all starts when the elephant is very young. When the elephant is small and young, this rope is certainly strong enough to hold it. So the woodcutter tied the rope around the elephant's leg and tied the other end to the peg driven into the ground. At some point in the night, the elephant tries to escape, but no matter how hard it pulls, it can't break the rope. Every night the woodcutters tie the elephant's leg to the stake in the ground, and every night the young elephant tries to escape, but every night it is unable to break the rope. After a while," continued the monk, "the elephant realises that the pink rope is just too strong and it can never break the bond. So the young elephant comes to associate the pink rope with being unable to escape and knows there is no point in trying. As the elephant grows bigger and stronger and older, it still remembers that the pink rope was unbreakable. No matter how many times it tried to escape as a young elephant, it never could, so it learned that the pink rope is unbreakable. Of course, you and I both know that the elephant, who is now fully grown and big and strong, could easily break the rope if it tried, but the elephant simply sees the pink rope and remembers that every time it tried in the past it failed to break it, and so it assumes that if it were to try now it would also fail to break the rope. So you see, the elephant is stuck. It's tied to where it is. Even though you and I can both see the elephant is strong enough to break the rope and to escape to its freedom, the elephant doesn't believe it can escape because of the fact that the pink rope was unbreakable in the past."

And so, having paused to rest a while and eat a light meal, the two monks continued on their journey through the forest. The younger monk looked back at the elephant and felt a pang of sorrow; for this magnificent beast, this powerful and strong beast, was allowing itself to be held back and stopped from living the life it wanted to live, because it didn't realise that the pink rope which held it back when it was young was now so easy to break. If only the elephant could realise how foolish it was to allow its experience in the past to stop it from doing what it wanted to now.

What's your pink rope?

We all have them. We all have something that is holding us back from achieving our full potential. Something which a life experience in the past showed we couldn't do, so we assume that we will never be able to do it, and have long since given up even thinking about attempting to do it. Yet today we are not the same person we were five years ago. We're not even the same person we were last year or even last month. We are constantly growing, learning, developing new skills and abilities and strengths. Just because something didn't work in the past, or just because we weren't able to do something in the past doesn't mean that we can't succeed now!

The tricky part is realising this. And it's not always easy to spot where we're allowing a pink rope to hold us back.

So what is holding you back? What is it that you want to do, you know you want to do, but that little voice at the back of your mind is saying, "You can't do that. Remember what happened years ago when you tried? You failed then, and you'll fail now, so there's no point in even trying."

But what if you did try? What if, over the years, as you've grown and learned and developed, you have grown strong enough to break that pink rope? Wouldn't it be a shame to stop yourself from doing the things you want to do simply because of something that happened in the past?

So the next time you find yourself contemplating some new project or some course of action and that voice starts up telling you that you can't do it because you weren't able to do it in the past, rather than give in, what would happen if you paused and really considered, and I mean *really* considered how things have changed since then? Of course, we must always learn from the past, but we don't have to be ruled by the past. Learning from the past can mean realising that a failure years ago was simply because we didn't have knowledge, strength, or skill which we have subsequently developed. Could it be possible that we can break that pink rope now?

Oh, just imagine the possibilities!

But back to our monks.

They continued journeying through the forest, and presently the trees started to thin out as they reached the edge. They emerged looking over a beautiful, lush valley, the big river flowing through the middle. The elder monk knew that in order to reach the monastery that was their destination, they would have to cross the river. The river was deep and flowing quite fast, but the old monk knew that there was a jetty with a rowboat tied to the jetty which they might use to row across the river. So the two monks wandered down from the forest, down the hill, and through the valley, heading toward the jetty. What the elder monk hadn't known was that days before, the river had been flooded. It was such a strong flood that it tore the rowboat away from its moorings and washed it way downstream. As they approached the jetty, they spotted a young woman standing at the side, looking forlornly at the bank on the other side of the river.

The young lady spotted them as they approached and said excitedly, "Ah! Thank goodness you are here! I need to get to the other side of the river, but the boat has gone, and the river is too deep and too fast for me to cross. I fear I may be swept away if I try. Perhaps you might be kind enough to carry me upon your back across the river?"

The younger monk, knowing that their order forbade all contact with women, ignored her and looked down at his feet. Meanwhile, the elder monk, without saying a word, scooped the young woman up, placed her on his shoulders, and waded into the river.

The young monk looked on aghast but followed, wading through the deep fast river. The monks reached the other side and the elder monk set the young woman down on the bank. The young woman thanked him profusely and headed off on her way as the two monks headed off on their way in the other direction.

The young monk was astounded! He couldn't believe it. They weren't allowed contact with women! Here the elder monk carried the woman across the river! How could he have done such a thing? How could he have gone against their order?

As they continued their journey, the young monk couldn't get the river crossing out of his mind. He couldn't understand why the elder monk had carried this woman when he knew they were forbidden contact with women. He kept thinking about it over and over and over again. Why did it happen? What was the elder monk thinking?

After a while, the elder monk indicated it was time for them to sit down for a rest and to have a bite to eat before making camp for the night. He could see the younger monk was troubled and asked him if all was well.

The younger monk could contain himself no longer. "Why did you carry that woman across the river? Why did you do it when you know we're not allowed contact with women?" he blurted out.

The elder monk studied the younger monk with wide eyes tinged with a hint of sadness and replied, "Brother, I set the woman down when we reached the other side of the river many hours ago. It is you who still carries her."

What are *you* still carrying? Often we carry all manner of resentment about people and situations from the past. We cling to it, holding it tight, and using it to justify anything and everything that goes wrong. "I would have succeeded if it weren't for that thing someone said or did years ago." How often have we heard others use that old excuse? And being honest (for it is only through total honesty with ourselves that we can move forward), how often have we used that excuse ourselves?

The problem with carrying such resentment is that it only ever harms us; it doesn't affect the object of our resentment. It has been said that holding a grudge is like drinking poison in the hopes that the other person will die.

Let's think about the monks for a moment. What might have happened had the younger monk continued to carry his feelings about the older monk's actions? Certainly they would not have affected the older monk, but the younger may well have found that they started eating away at him, clouding his judgment, perhaps even turning into feelings of resentment toward the older monk until he felt that he could no longer trust him or his teachings, guidance, and advice. Maybe even to the point that his feelings poisoned the esteem in which he once held the other, damaging their friendship and ultimately hindering his own growth and development. As long as he carried those thoughts and feelings, they would have clouded his ability to evaluate current situations, lessening his ability to spot his own opportunities.

All this could have happened because he was still carrying those thoughts and feelings over something which was long ago finished and had no bearing on his world.

I have a wonderful tool which I use with some of my clients (and yes, I also use it regularly with myself) called Forward through Forgiveness. You can get hold of a free copy at the back of the book. It's all about letting go by forgiving – forgiving others for what they've done, and ultimately forgiving ourselves; forgiving ourselves for clinging on to those old grudges; forgiving ourselves for reacting the way we did; forgiving ourselves for holding ourselves back.

I recall one particular situation where I found it very helpful, and which is closely related to new beginnings. I was in employment, and the US director of our division decided for financial reasons that my job had to go, so my role was to be made redundant, putting me out of work. I was based in the UK, so although I had a US manager, I spent a lot of my time indirectly reporting to our local UK site director, with whom I'd built up a good working relationship over the years. However, when this situation arose, whereas I'd expected he might fight for a change or at the least might offer some words of support, he was notable by his absence. He hardly said anything to me, keeping himself to himself. I must admit, I felt rather let down by this. How dare he treat me this way after everything I'd done for him over the years? The more I dwelled on it, the angrier I got. It was clouding my own judgment and my ability to think clearly. Because I was then setting up my own business, that was the last thing I needed. If I was to make a success of my new beginning, I needed to let go of feelings about the past so I could free my mind up to focus on the real challenges I needed to address. But *no* – I kept dwelling on what had happened, getting more and more angry. I'd show him! If I ever saw him in town, I'd cross the street to avoid him. That would show him! How dare he? And so it went.

In the end, I remembered my own advice to others, and I used my Forward through Forgiveness process to allow me to let go of it all, to stop carrying all those feelings of resentment. As always, it was a really refreshing experience.

Did it work? Well, three days later I invited him to meet up in the pub for a drink over lunch. We had a great chat about all manner of things, and I felt wonderful. Even better, I was no longer consumed by the burden of the anger I was carrying, my mind was a lot clearer, and I was able to focus fully on the creation of my own business and get my new beginning off to a wonderful start. There is no doubt in my mind that had I been unable to let it go, I would not have had the successes I have enjoyed. My mind would not have allowed me to focus.

The next morning, feeling refreshed after their rest, the monks continued their journey. The new monastery was less than a day's walk away now, so they set off in good spirits, eager to see what they would find.

As they drew closer to the monastery, they came upon a monkey sanctuary. This was where some of the monks from the nearby monastery would take in injured monkeys and look after them while they healed before releasing them back to the wild. The monks had heard about this place, and were pleased to be able to visit it on their way. The head of the sanctuary welcomed them and offered to show them around.

He showed them the hospital where they treated the sick and the injured, and finally showed them where they kept the monkeys while they recovered. It was a large, beautiful area, with plenty for the monkeys to do and shelter for them to rest. The younger monk couldn't help but notice, however, that although there were bars around the edge, there was no roof to stop the animals from escaping.

The young monk became curious about this and, realizing that a ferocious curiosity about the world is the best way to develop a deeper understanding of it, asked the head of the sanctuary about it.

"What is to stop the monkeys from just climbing up the sides and escaping?" he asked.

"Ah," replied the head of the sanctuary, "there is a very interesting story there. You see, the first monkeys we got were all rescued from a zoo where the keepers were rather cruel. Every time one of their monkeys tried to climb out, they sprayed all of them with water. This made the others shriek and yell and leap about. When the climbing monkey stopped and went back down, they stopped spraying them.

"They did this each time a monkey tried to escape, and pretty soon none of them tried."

The head went on, "Then we rescued those poor creatures and looked after them here, and even though our bars and walls are a lot lower, none of the monkeys ever tried to climb out.

"And then, an interesting thing happened. We had a new monkey come to us, and we put him in with all the others. Sure enough, he went to climb out, but before we could do anything, all of the others were shrieking and yelling and leaping about and they pulled him back down, all without any water being used."

"That's strange," said the younger monk, fascinated by the tale.

"Yes," continued the head of the sanctuary, "and we found this happened every time, even though we were never going to spray them with water.

"But then it got even more interesting. You see, we had another monkey come to us, and while he was recuperating, we put him in with the others. Of course, he went to climb out and all the others stopped him, including the one who had never been in the zoo where they used the water!"

29

"You mean he was stopping the new monkey from escaping even though he knew nothing about the water?" asked the young monk, wide-eyed with intrigue.

"That's right. And then it got even more strange, because as you know, when our guests are fully recovered, we release them back into the wild. So now, none of the monkeys you see have ever experienced the water, but they all join in to stop any new arrivals from escaping!" finished the head of the sanctuary.

"So," said the older monk, *"You mean they all stop each other from escaping, even though none of them know why?"*

"Exactly!"

Sometimes this story (or one like it) is told and ends with the punch line "and that, ladies and gentlemen, is how company policy is created."

The thing is, while that makes for an amusing poke at some incomprehensible aspect of company policy at whichever organization the storyteller happens to work, the reality is that many of us use this exact process to define and create policies which govern our own personal behaviour.

We allow something that happened to us in the past, even as a one-off, to control how we behave now, even though the situation is completely different.

"I can't do anything, because look what happened years ago, the last time I attempted to do something. It all went disastrously wrong, so there is no point in me doing anything about it now." Of course, you have never thought that way, dear reader, have you? However, you may know others who have.

Worse still, we allow other people's old experiences in other situations to stop us. "Everyone knows you can't do that!" How many times have we allowed what "everyone knows" to stop us? Even though we have no idea what "everyone knows" ourselves. Usually it is hearsay at best or even urban legend. Someone knows a friend of a friend who once heard of someone who did what we wanted to do and they could not, so of course there is no reason to think we could possibly succeed.

Right?

Wrong!

Conventional wisdom, the name usually given to "everyone knows" to make it sound a little more legitimate, is generally anything but wise. It is based on third-hand information from people about situations that are usually never explained. It is invariably unrelated to you and your situation.

Yet we allow these stories of other people's problems to stop us from ever getting started.

At one time, "everyone knew" it was impossible for humans to fly. "Everyone knew" you could not sail around the world. "Everyone knew" it was impossible to run a mile in under four minutes, until Roger Bannister ignored what "everyone knew" and proceeded to run a mile in under four minutes. The interesting thing is, barely two months later, two more runners also did a mile in under four minutes, and today four-minute miles have become commonplace in athletics.

Next time you hear someone dismiss your plans because "everyone knows" it can't be done, or the next time you start thinking back to your own past attempts which did not work out, just remember that "everyone else's" situation is not your situation. Your current situation is not even the same as it was the last time you attempted!

Does this mean you should just ignore everyone's advice, throw caution to the wind, and jump in blind? Not at all. It makes sense to learn from what has gone before and to incorporate what you learn to further improve your chances of succeeding in your new beginning whilst also recognizing the differences in the situations, in your abilities, and in the possible successful outcomes. What does not make sense is to give up before you even start because "everyone knows" it will not work.

Later that day, the monks finally reached the new monastery, where they were welcomed warmly. It was time for them to go their separate ways. The younger monk was introduced to several of the monks, and one was assigned to be his mentor for his stay. As the two monks who had journeyed so far together made their farewells, the older monk whispered something into the younger's ear, and then smiling, walked off.

The older monk, who was looking for something new to occupy him, had noticed some building work was going on just outside the monastery and asked the abbot if he might take a look. The abbot was delighted by his interest and invited him to go for a good look around and introduce himself to some of the workers.

He came upon a man who was laying stones, placing them down and slapping the mortar on before quickly moving to the next stone, resulting in a wall that, although it looked pretty strong, looked sloppy and uneven.

"What are you doing?" asked the older monk.

"I'm laying stones," replied the worker. "I've got a family to feed, and the pay here lets me keep them fed and clothed."

The older monk moved on and came upon another man who was also laying bricks, but with painstaking attention to detail. He made sure every brick was just perfect, chiselling off any rough spots, making sure they lined up perfectly, and making sure he used exactly the right amount of mortar for each one, smoothing it in place. The small wall looked stunning.

"What are you doing?" asked the older monk.

"I am building the most perfect wall it is possible to build. People will look at this wall and know that it was built by me, for they will admire its perfection and they will say that it was built by the best builder in the land." And with that, he went back to slowly laying each stone.

Sure enough, the small wall looked good, but the time taken was so long that the older monk knew this wall itself would probably never be finished, let alone the rest of the project.

Finally, he came to another man who was building another wall. He was making sure the bricks fitted together, placing everything correctly, and doing it with such speed and finesse that the older monk was impressed.

"What are you doing?" he enquired.

"Brother, I am building a cathedral!" exclaimed the craftsman.

"A cathedral!" said the older monk. "But brother, won't you be long dead before it is anywhere near finished?"

"It is certain that I will not live to see this cathedral completed. Nor will my children. However," the craftsman went on, "perhaps their children will see it completed, and people from far and wide across this great land will

be able to come and worship in this magnificent cathedral. That is why I am working, so I can help to build this for generations to come, even though I will not see it complete."

And with that, the older monk knew he had found what he was looking for. He had found something into which he could pour his heart and soul. He knew that had found the right person to learn from as he began his new life. And with that, the older monk apprenticed himself there and then to the craftsman.

Meanwhile, elsewhere in the monastery, the younger monk was settling in to his new surroundings. As he sat eating his meal, his mentor said, "Forgive me, but I couldn't help noticing as you and your friend were saying goodbye, he whispered something in your ear. The look on your face told me that it was something profound. Could I ask – What were his words that caused you to experience such revelation?"

The younger monk replied, "My friend the older monk said to me, 'What have you learned from this, our journey together? How is what we discovered together going to help you to make the best of your new beginning?'"

Make a Fortune Making a Difference

Calvin Coyles

Calvin Coyles is an award-winning social entrepreneur and international speaker who believes that if you're not making someone else's life better then you're wasting your time!

Regarded as Australia's leading peak performance strategist, Calvin has extensive experience working with entrepreneurs at every level of business, from start-ups to Fortune 500.

Having worked with and transformed the lives of over 50,000 people in sixty-four countries, Calvin has led change everywhere, from the desert of Australia to the slums of Kenya and throughout rural India.

His vision is to eradicate extreme poverty by developing 100,000 Warriors of Light around the world, and to collectively change the lives of one billion people during his lifetime.

As a keynote speaker and seminar leader, Calvin has shared the stage with industry leaders, including Christopher Howard (international bestselling author of Turning Passions into Profits *and* Instant Wealth: Wake up Rich), *Nik Halik (thrillianaire, astranaught, and bestselling author), Pat Mesiti (mindset coach and bestselling author) and Lisa Haisha (life coach to Hollywood's A-list and creator of Soul Blazing).*

In 2010, Calvin led Australia to the top sixteen of the World Championships of Social Enterprise, and in 2011, flew to Africa to establish a microfinance program in Kenya. In 2013, Calvin was named a finalist for the Young Entrepreneur of the Year award.

Now 24, Calvin is the CEO of Young & Wildly Successful, Australia's fastest-growing personal and professional development company. He runs four companies and advises over a dozen others.

Live Life on Your Terms.

If you're not making someone else's life better,
then you're wasting your time!
– Calvin Coyles

A prized back stallion wrestled with the master, fighting, struggling, and resisting with every muscle in his body the pressure to conform and be tamed. After hours of thrashing around the courtyard, the master gave up and approached the king, who oversaw the proceedings from the courtyard steps.

"My King, this horse cannot be tamed. He is too strong and too stubborn; he refuses to bend to the pressure of the whip. He is of no use to you, my King," said the master.

The king replied, "Very well. Have him taken away."

"No!" shouted the king's son. "I'll tame him, Father." The whole courtyard burst into laughter at the prince's statement.

"What do you know about taming horses son? You are but 7 years old. What do you know that these masters of the horse and whip do not?" said the king.

As the prince rose to his feet and approached the stallion, the courtyard fell silent, fearing that the horse would thrash once more. The prince, with eyes locked on his target, approached the horse and in one fluid movement launched himself bareback onto the horse.

Upon mounting the beast, the prince proceeded to ride him out of the courtyard and out into the open fields with every ounce of passion the horse had displayed before. Upon retuning with the stallion, the courtyard erupted into celebrations for the prince's tenacity. Belief had prevailed.

His father, the king, raced down the courtyard steps to greet his son. After embracing him in a crushing hug, he said, "My son, Macedonia is too small for your gifts and talents, go out and find a kingdom worthy of thee."

The young price was named Alexander. Before he was 30 years old, he had conquered half of the known world with an army often a fifth to a seventh the size of his enemies' armies. This was the story of Alexander the Great!

Why did Alexander and those that have come after him achieve so much with so little, while others do so little with so much? Why do many possess the same gifts and talents Alexander's father talked of, yet do nothing with them? How are the Bonos, Bransons, Oprahs, Jay Zs and the Obamas different from everyone else? What makes them exceptional, and how can we reach the same if not greater heights?

Welcome to Young & Wildly Successful

The world needs leaders who will rise up against the adversity of the average, challenge the plague of mediocrity, and overcome the barriers of failure to show others what's possible. Will your life be a line in the sand of future generations or a message hidden within the vast sea of forgotten dreams? I challenge you to make today, this year, and this life a testimony to all that it possible. If you believe, you will achieve. You are too smart to let *you* stand in your way. If not now, then when? Yesterday you said tomorrow!

We both agree that all these things are true. This chapter will show you the *exact* steps that you need to take to become wildly successful in any area of your life. I used these exact steps to build a public company from a staff of none to 120 in six months; to establish microfinance organizations in East Africa; to lead Australia to the top sixteen of the social enterprise world championship; to propose to the love of my life; to build a company from nothing to $100,000 in ninety days; and to teach over 50,000 entrepreneurs from sixty-four countries around the world how to do what they love and make a fortune.

The only thing stopping you from becoming wildly successful is a proven plan and massive action. This chapter is designed to be a workbook for your life. I would encourage you to approach these pages with the following quote in mind:

Explore life and cooking with reckless abandon.
– HH XIV Dali Llama

Below are the seven steps to make a fortune making a difference. Whilst they appear simple, they are masterful, in that they create a simple solution to the often complex problem of pursuing your dreams and making a fortune doing so.

Redefine Success

What do you desire? Ask yourself what would you do if money were no object, and then do that, and the money will take care of itself.
– Alan Watts

Today more than ever we are bombarded by other people's views of success. It is for this exact reason that I don't own a TV. (Also because there's a direct correlation between unsuccessful people and watching vast amounts of TV.) If you simply turn on your TV, you'll see twenty minutes of brainwashing crap telling you what success is in every area of life: health, beauty, cars, money, houses, lifestyle, sex, money, and the celebrity scandals you need to know about. Everything down to what snack to give your kid for lunch to be a good mother has been chosen for us and served to us without us knowing.

Sorry for the rant, but when did we forget that beauty is on the inside, love is universal, health is more than whether you look like a model on a catwalk, being wealthy has nothing to do with money, and that what you get doesn't make you happy, but who you become will make you either very happy or very sad? The very fact you're reading this book means you're one of the few who are willing to do things differently.

Eight key areas of life are shown below. These areas are what I call the *wheel of life*. They depict the areas of mastery that you and I must pursue and one day master for ultimate happiness and profound joy. Unless we consciously seek the fulfilment of these areas, then no amount of money will ever satisfy our need to be successful.

How to Define Success

Let me tell you, money's pretty nice. But having a lot of money does not automatically make you a successful person. What you want is money and meaning. You want your work to be meaningful, because meaning is what brings the real richness to your life.
– Oprah Winfrey

You can change the world with a single idea. The world belongs to the learners. Victims love entertainment. Leaders love education. Victims love leisure. Leaders love learning. So I ask you, what is success to you? How do you measure a life spent doing what you love? I wish for you every abundance in the world. I, too, wish for a life rich with material possessions and the "good life." I just refuse to allow my happiness to be dependent upon such unstable things.

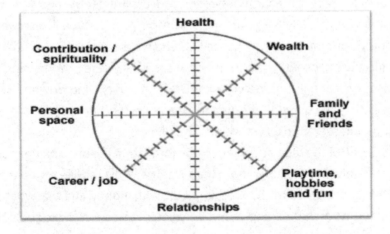

So take some time and ask yourself: What brings you joy, fulfilment, and positively affects the world you live in? No accomplishment is insignificant. We should take inventory of the small things we do every day and realize that without those small achievements larger ones would not be possible. And even if an accomplishment seems small to you, you never know how large of an impact that accomplishment may have on someone else. Even if you, too, are the random mentor person.

Redefine Success in Your Own Life with the Following Steps

- Complete the Wheel of Life chart above based on how you view *your* life – *not* someone else's view!
- In what areas of life are you successful, and what areas need improvement?
- Write a list of five awesome things you can do in the next five days to improve the areas of improvement and celebrate the areas where you rock!

Ignite Passion

Dedicate your life to a cause greater than yourself, and your life will become a glorious adventure.
– Mark Douglas

In 2010, I had just come back from East Africa, having helped establish a microfinance organization in the heart of the Korogocho slums. This was a profound experience where I was able to help a group of impoverished women with no education beyond the fourth grade learn how to start up successful companies. Not long after my arrival back into Australia, famine hit Ethiopia, Kenya, and the rest of the region. A full-page report in the national news told the story of how thousands of families were leaving everything behind to walk across the Ethiopian desert in search of refuge in Kenya.

As I read this story, my heart broke. Just a month before I had spent time with these families, and now their worlds were being torn apart. One woman had left Ethiopia with her two sons but arrived with only one as she was not strong enough to carry both over the fourteen-day journey without water or food.

I was immediately flooded with so many emotions: devastation, anger, hurt, and grief for her loss. Then my mind immediately shifted to asking the question: How can I help? I was inspired by a project that needed my help, and it was something I was deeply passionate about. Within a month we had a charity night and raised over $10,000 for the cause with Oxfam and Rotary.

Do what stirs your heart, challenges your mind, and calls your body to action.

– Calvin Coyles

I believe we all have a passion in our life that consumes us if we embrace it. Some call it our life's work. Others call it our calling. All I know is that when you ignite this passion deep within, your life takes on a whole new sense of meaning. Passion is a contagious and dangerous experience. It causes people to attempt things that they otherwise wouldn't and succeed in the process. Think about the last time you were "out of your skin" passionate about something. What was that like? Amazing, I bet. We have the capacity to feel so much more than our conditioned lives allow for. I want to know what lights your fire inside.

Write below a list of twenty things you're passionate about.

1.
2.
3.
4.
5.
6.
7.
8.
9.
10.
11.

12.

13.

14.

15.

16.

17.

18.

19.

20.

*Don't start a company unless it's an obsession and something
you love. If you have an exit strategy, it's not an obsession.*
– Mark Cuban

If you want to live a life of passion, simply ensure that you live at least three of these things on a daily basis. Success is not difficult – it's just different. Most people have none of their passion lists in their daily lives. This is why you and I must be different from the public. You and I have the opportunity to do what few would dream of: to live all twenty items on our passion list every day of our lives. Celebrate this and recognize that even if you have a few areas to improve you're still much further ahead of everyone sitting at home watching their TVs.

Model Success

Success leaves clues.
– Tony Robbins

When Henry Ford was growing up, he served his apprenticeship with none other than Thomas Edison. At GE, Henry learned from the father of invention in America, and the skills and abilities he learned there served him well when he launched the Ford Motor Company some years later. Would Henry have been as successful had he not had this experience and the opportunity to learn from the best?

There are three ways to learn and grow. The easy way, where you learn from other people's mistakes and victories; the hard way, where you learn from your own mistakes; and the suicidal way, where you don't learn at all. The only reason why I can write this chapter at the age of 24 and spend my life changing people's lives around the world is because I'm standing on the shoulders of giants.

Leaders like Tony Robbins, Chris Howard, Robin Sharma, Nelson Mandela, Leonardo da Vinci, Les Brown, and Oprah Winfrey are just some of the men and women I've sought to work with, learn from, and model. The more we learn, the faster we grow. The path to becoming young and wildly successful is meant to be travelled at a supercharged pace.

As leaders, entrepreneurs, and high achievers we have the desire to create things on our own, without help, support, and guidance from others. Why do we make things harder for ourselves than they need to be? We become emotionally attached to our own ability to do things no one else can do, and we try to reinvent the wheel. This is a sure-fire path to failure. If you want to achieve success rapidly, seek out the best in your field of endeavour, learn from them, study them, and repeat everything they do. Once you understand exactly their proven strategy for success, don't change a thing. Take massive action, then review your results and change accordingly.

Seek out the best and model them. Then repeat the
process until you have achieved your desired result.
– Calvin Coyles

Steps for modelling excellence in any area:

1. Find the best in your field of endeavour.
2. Become ferociously curious as to *why* and *how* they became the best.
3. Discover what their drivers of success are.
4. Take massive action to apply those drivers into your own life.
5. Review your results and repeat the process until you win!

Craft Your Strategy

If you're unhappy for even half a second doing something, stop it! You can lose just as much money doing what you love.
– Gary Veynerchuck

"Yes, but I can't make money doing that" are words I hear more times that I care to share. Once people arrive at this destination with a clear sense of their purpose and an understanding of what drives them and what fuels their life and their own ideas of success, they inevitably turn to thinking about money and how little they believe they can make doing what they love. I've seen people with less passion and fewer skills or talents make far more money than those with all of the God-given ability one could ask for.

Think about your own industry. Do you know someone who is less skilled at what they do but makes far more money than you? Chances are the answer is yes. There is a reason for this, and when you understand it, you will fast-track your financial success and industry ascension.

There are two types of skills required to succeed in life: technical skills and business skills. Technical skills are those required to do your job, career, or profession. A plumber must know how to change a leaky tap and build the piping infrastructure for a new home. These skills alone are insufficient for success in business and will limit any plumber's ability to leverage their business and make a difference.

Traditional forms of education in the world today are designed to make you an employee, not an employer. As an employee, you must discover the skills to be an employer outside of the traditional mainstream system. Business skills can be broken down into five key areas. I encourage you to master each of these.

1. Sales and marketing
2. Finance
3. People
4. Operations
5. Business development

There comes a time when you ought to start doing what you want. Take a job that you love. You will jump out of bed in the morning. I think you are out of your mind if you keep taking jobs that you don't like because you think it will look good on your resume. Isn't that a little like saving up sex for your old age?
– Warren Buffett

If we are to make a fortune, making a difference we must master these five areas of business. Now how do these concepts fit into our understanding of strategy?

Most traditional courses will teach you to find a gap in the market that you can exploit by creating a product or service. I've never been a subscriber to this line of thinking. I think we'd all agree that money is only one of the reasons that one would launch a business. Passion and your core competencies must also be considered. Throughout my work with business owners around the world, I always advise on creating a Competency Driven Strategy (CDS). This means that instead of looking at the industry or market for your *gap*, you look at yourself and discover who you are and what you can do that no one else can even dream of doing.

We all have our own unique greatness.
– Jay Z

From this place we can craft a strategy to address market needs and wants based on our core ability to do great work. When we align our core passions, competencies, and business ideas, we have a tremendous chance at success because our ideas are fuelled by love. The world craves authenticity and truth.

I had no idea that I would make as much money as I have from being my genuine authentic self. If I had, I would have done it long ago.
– Oprah Winfrey

We're swimming in oceans of information but thirsty for wisdom and truth. Now is the time to share yours with the world.

How to Discover Your Competence Driven Strategy

1. What are your key strengths?
2. What are your key aspirations or goals?
3. What opportunities exist within your industry?
4. What would be the three to five core things you do better than anyone else?
5. What products and services can you design to align with those capabilities?

Immerse in Success

If you're the smartest person on your team, then
there is something wrong with your team!
– Robert Kyosaki

It is often said that your success or failure is directly proportionate to the number of successful people you surround yourself with on a daily basis. When I discovered that I was the average one of the five people closest to me, I started to kick people out of my friendship circle. Oprah Winfrey has on her office door at Harpo Studios the following sign: "Be aware of the energy you bring into this room." I love this, because it reminds me that we all have a vibration and that in order to have long-term sustained success in our lives, we must maintain a positive, vibrant, and abundant energy. Don't let those who think so little of you have such a large hold on your future. You are the master of your own destiny, the captain of your ship. Chart your own territory and set sail for a new adventure.

It is vital that we understand that environment trumps willpower. We understand from the latest research in the field of human potential that environment governs an individual to a greater extent than willpower can withstand. Willpower is a myth. It is a muscle that wears down over time when overused. Therefore, willpower fatigue exists. Yes, this is why you come home from a big day at work and eat the whole block of Cadbury fruit and nut… well at least I do.

If you want to succeed even when you're low on willpower, there is a secret key to success that hides in plain sight – accountability! Having a team of people to help you and hold you accountable for your success in life is a sure-fire way to achieve success. Without accountability, most people stumble and fall along the path to greatness. Don't be one of them.

Instead, write down a list of five amazing people in your life who you want to spend more time with and go do it! If you're really struggling to find people, this is a perfect opportunity to change things up and extend yourself. Write a fresh list of five types of people you'd like to connect with and set yourself a target to meet five new people per week for five weeks. The law of averages suggests that you'll make find one great friend a week.

How to Immerse in Success

Ask yourself:

1. Who among my current friends are making me better, and who do I want to be surrounded by on a daily basis?
2. Who can I surround myself with that will take me to the next level?
3. How will my life improve by having great people around me?
4. What can I share with them so we all grow together?

Invest in Yourself

Investing in yourself is the best thing you can do. Anything that improves your own talents, nobody can tax it or take it away from you. They can run up huge deficits and the dollar can become

46

*worth far less. You can have all kinds of things happen. But if
you've got talent yourself, and you've maximized your talent,
you've got a tremendous asset that can return ten-fold.*
– Warren Buffet

In 1980 Oprah was earning $22,000 and her male co-anchor was earning $53,000 for the same role. When she asked her boss for equal pay, his response was, "Why should you get paid the same as he does?" Her response: "I'll show ya'."

When she launched the *Oprah Winfrey Show* in 1985, her team of women were being paid so little that she approached her new boss and asked for more money for the team. His response: "No; they're all women."

This was a turning point in Winfrey's life, where she decided to launch Harpo Enterprises, and in 1997 took ownership of the show. She invested in herself and her brand, and the program became the most successful TV show of all time.

I would not be where I am today without investing in myself. I've spent tens of thousands on my own education, learning, and growth. If you want to reach the height of success, you must be willing to grow and outlearn your competition. We don't fully appreciate the amazing life-changing opportunities we have available. Can you fully comprehend that twenty years ago, the president of the United States didn't have access to the technology that we now have on every computer across the world?

Your success can grow only to the level you grow yourself.
– Calvin Coyles

Look at the areas of your life that are not succeeding in the way you would like and ask yourself "Who is the best in the world at this area?" Then invest whatever it costs to work with the best. The money you spend will return tenfold. Education is always less than the cost of ignorance; you pay for education once and you pay for ignorance over and over again.

Below are some simple steps to help you invest in yourself:

Create your own personal development plan: Come up with a plan that defines your desired future or life's purpose, evaluates your current reality, sets well-defined goals, and creates a specific plan of action.

Be a lifelong learner: Take classes, read good books, etc., and apply what you've learned in real life.

Improve your communication skills: It is extremely important to learn how to be a good speaker as well as a good listener.

Create a personal development budget: Take money out of your weekly earnings to invest in yourself.

Hustle

> *Work every day like someone is working 24/7*
> *trying to take it all away from you!*
> – Mark Cuban

One of my favourite hustle stories is Mr Soichiro Honda, founder of the corporation that bears his name. Like all companies, no matter how large, Honda Corporation began with a decision and a passionate desire to produce a result. In 1938, while he was still in school, Mr Honda took everything he owned and invested it in a little workshop, where he began to develop his concept of a piston ring. He wanted to sell his work to Toyota Corporation, so he laboured day and night, up to his elbows in grease, sleeping in the machine shop, always believing he could produce the result.

He even pawned his wife's jewellery to stay in business. But when he finally completed the piston rings and presented them to Toyota, he was told they didn't meet Toyota's standards. He was sent back to school for two years, where he heard the derisive laughter of his instructors and fellow students as they talked about how absurd his designs were.

But rather than focusing on the pain of the experience, he decided to continue to focus on his goal. Finally, after two more years, Toyota gave Mr Honda the contract he'd dreamed of.

His passion and belief paid off because he had known what he wanted, taken action, noticed what was working, and kept changing his approach until he got what he wanted.

Then a new problem arose. The Japanese government was gearing up for war, and they refused to give him the concrete that was necessary to build his factory. Did he quit there? No. Did he focus on how unfair this was? Did it mean to him that his dream had died? Absolutely not. Again, he decided to make use of the experience, and developed another strategy. He and his team invented a process for creating their own concrete and then built their factory.

During the war, it was bombed twice, destroying major portions of the manufacturing facility. Honda's response? He immediately rallied his team, and they picked up the extra gasoline cans that the US fighters had discarded. He called them "gifts from President Truman" because they provided him with the raw materials he needed for his manufacturing process – materials that were unavailable at the time in Japan.

Finally, after surviving all of this, an earthquake levelled his factory. Honda decided to sell his piston operation to Toyota.

Here is a man who clearly made strong decisions to succeed. He had a passion for and belief in what he was doing. He had a great strategy. He took massive action.

He kept changing his approach, but still he'd not produced the results that he was committed to. Yet he decided to persevere. After the war, a tremendous gasoline shortage hit Japan, and Mr Honda couldn't even drive his car to get food for his family. Finally, in desperation, he attached a small motor to his bicycle. The next thing he knew, his neighbours were asking if he could make one of his motorized bikes for them. One after another, they jumped on the bandwagon until he ran out of motors. He decided to build a plant that would manufacture motors for his new invention, but unfortunately he didn't have the capital. As before, he made the decision to find a way no matter what!

His solution was to appeal to the 18,000 bicycle shop owners in Japan by writing them each a personal letter. He told them how they could play a role in revitalizing Japan through the mobility that his invention could provide, and convinced 5,000 of them to advance the capital he needed. Still, his motorbike sold to only the most hard-core bicycle fans because it was too big and bulky. So he made one final adjustment and created a much lighter, scaled-down version of his motorbike. He christened it the Super Cub, and it became an overnight success, earning him the emperor's award.

Later, he began to export his motorbikes to the baby boomers of Europe and the United States, following up in the seventies with the cars that have become so popular. Today, the Honda Corporation employs over 100,000 people in the United States and Japan and is one of the biggest car-making empires in Japan, outselling all but Toyota in the United States. It succeeds because one man understood the power of a truly committed decision that is acted upon, no matter what the conditions, on a continuous basis. What a tremendous story of overcoming adversity and hustling to make your dream become a reality!

If there is one word that determines the success or failure of a dream, it is *hustle*. Without it you have nothing; with it you are capable of achieving greatness. What does hustle mean? It's a process of relentless hard work with the street smarts to do things in an innovative, cutting edge and outside of the box way.

Don't be afraid to be unconventional. You're a gifted and talented leader. People expect you to shake things up and challenge the status quo.

Consider that where you are today is a direct reflection of the level you have been hustling up until this point. A mentor of mine once shared that life is much like a refrigerator – you get out of it what you put into it. This being the case, how can we really extend ourselves and make sure we have a consistent and never-ending drive to succeed?

Your inner drive or hustle, is determined by three core pillars:

1. Focus
2. Meaning
3. Alignment

Focus: What we focus upon we get more of. It's the same in every facet of life. If you want more success, focus on success and not failure. If you want better health, focus on vitality and not obesity. Easily said, harder to do. As leaders we have many demands on our focus. Don't be reactive and quick to change course. Successful people make decisions quickly and change them slowly.

Meaning: Simon Sinek has a phenomenal TED Talk called "How Leaders Inspire Change." In this talk Simon shares the following insights:

"The ability to motivate people is, in itself, not difficult. It is usually tied to some external factor. Great leaders, in contrast, are able to inspire people to act. Those who are able to inspire give people a sense of purpose or belonging that has little to do with any external incentive or benefit to be gained. Those who truly lead are able to create a following of people who act not because they were swayed, but because they were inspired.

"For those who are inspired, the motivation to act is deeply personal. They are less likely to be swayed by incentives. Those who are inspired are willing to pay a premium or endure inconvenience, even personal suffering. Those who are able to inspire will create a following of people – supporters, voters, customers, and workers – who act for the good of the whole not because they have to, but because they want to. People who love going to work are more productive and creative. They go home happier and have happier families. They treat their colleagues and clients and customers better. Inspired employees make for stronger companies and stronger economies."

A key distinction is that when we communicate why we do what we do, also known as the meaning behind our work, people connect in a powerful way and will take massive action towards making your business and mission successful. The same goes for your own goals and dreams. Have you ever set a goal without the key emotional drivers needed for success? If you're like me, then the action and motivation to succeed would have been short-lived. If you want long-term consistent results in life, you need long-term consistent action. And all action is bred from an emotional alignment between your conscious and unconscious minds.

Alignment: According to the famed hypnotherapist Dr Milton Erickson, "People are walking around in a trance of disempowerment, projecting their unresolved limiting beliefs and emotional baggage onto others." Why do so many people talk the talk but fail to walk the walk? The answer is *alignment* – specifically the alignment between their actions and subconscious conditioning.

Consider a young woman who has had an abusive father and struggles to maintain a relationship with men later in life. She may say she wants to be in a relationship every day of the week, but until she releases the emotional trauma and blockages from the past, she'll never open her heart and allow a partner in. This is obviously a simplistic example; however it is one I see too often today with coaching clients. People are not yet aware of their own limiting beliefs. They believe that everyone is the way they are, an exciting prospect for positive, optimistic, and open-minded people.

A great example of the power of self-sabotage is recorded in this "three feet from gold" excerpt by Napoleon Hill:

One of the most common causes of failure is the habit of quitting when one is overtaken by temporary defeat. Every person is guilty of this mistake at one time or another. An uncle of R. U. Darby was caught by the gold fever in the gold rush days, and went west to dig and grow rich. He had never heard that more gold has been mined from the brains of men than has ever been taken from the earth. He staked a claim and went to work with pick and shovel. The going was hard, but his lust for gold was definite.

After weeks of labour, he was rewarded by the discovery of the shining ore. He needed machinery to bring the ore to the surface. Quietly, he covered up the mine, retraced his footsteps to his home in Williamsburg, Maryland, and told his relatives and a few neighbours of the strike. They got together money for the needed machinery, [and] had it shipped. The uncle and Darby went back to work the mine.

The first car of ore was mined and shipped to a smelter. The returns proved they had one of the richest mines in Colorado! A few more cars of that ore would clear the debts. Then would come the big killing in profits.

Down went the drills. Up went the hopes of Darby and Uncle. Then something happened. The vein of gold ore disappeared! They had come to the end of the rainbow, and the pot of gold was no longer there! They drilled on, desperately trying to pick up the vein again, all to no avail.

Finally, they decided to *quit*. They sold the machinery to a junk man for a few hundred dollars, and took the train back home. Some junk men are dumb, but not this one! He called in a mining engineer to look at the mine and do a little calculating. The engineer advised that the project had failed, because the owners were not familiar with fault lines. His calculations showed that the vein would be found just *three feet* from where the Darbys had stopped drilling! That is exactly where it was found.

The junk man took millions of dollars in ore from the mine, because he knew enough to seek expert counsel before giving up. Most of the money, which went into the machinery, was procured through the efforts of R. U. Darby, who was then a very young man. The money came from his relatives and neighbours because of their faith in him. He paid back every dollar of it, although he was years in doing so.

Long afterward, Mr Darby recouped his loss many times over when he made the discovery that *desire* can be transmuted into gold. The discovery came after he went into the business of selling life insurance.

Remembering that he lost a huge fortune, because he *stopped* three feet from gold, Darby profited by the experience in his chosen work by the simple method of saying to himself, "I stopped three feet from gold, but I will never stop because men say no when I ask them to buy insurance."

Darby is one of a small group of fewer than fifty men who sell more than a million dollars in life insurance annually. He owes his "stick ability" to the lesson he learned from his "quit ability" in the gold mining business.

Before success comes in any man's life, he is sure to meet with much temporary defeat and perhaps some failure. When defeat overtakes a man, the easiest and most logical thing to do is to *quit*. That is exactly what the majority of men do.

More than five hundred of the most successful men this country has ever known told the author their greatest success came just one step beyond the point at which defeat had overtaken them. Failure is a trickster with a keen sense of irony and cunning.

It takes great delight in tripping one when success is almost within reach.

The lesson:

Never, never, never give in!
– Sir Winston Churchill

You are now at a blessed point in the development of your calling. You have a deep understanding of the things that drive you and an understanding of what you need to discover in the areas of life and business to bring them to the world. It was once said that the future is to rely on you. The only thing standing between you and greatness is time. Enjoy the journey and live each moment like it is your last.

Until we have the opportunity to meet in person, at one of my seminars or live events:

Live strong.
Live with passion.
Make today and every day a phenomenal life-
changing adventure, and remember
to live life on your terms.

The Business of Social Media

Kim Barrett

Kim Barrett is a successful entrepreneur, and is passionate about health and fitness and developing an international thriving health and wellness business. Working with businesses around the world to help them achieve their goals, from start-ups to multi-million dollar companies, Kim has led the way in state of the art strategies and marketing concepts, taking businesses to the next level.

Using the newest strategies combining social media and marketing concepts to drive growth, Kim has enabled business owners from around the world to develop.

We live in a crazy world. You can access all the information in the world with a click of a button, and you can find nearly anyone without even breaking a sweat. It's a world where we can start again and begin a new business venture without even leaving the house.

Social media has been at the forefront for the last few years. It is allowing businesses new and old to get a new beginning and to engage with their customers in new and funky ways. Whereas before, businesses would spend countless marketing dollars to connect with their target market, business leaders of today can do it ridiculously cheaply or free if they know how.

Three or four years ago, people thought search engine optimization (SEO) was a fad and that it would pass. Now you can't be found on Google unless your site uses SEO. That's where social media is heading at the moment, and most businesses don't realise that if they aren't on social media and connecting with their customers, they are quickly becoming irrelevant to their client base.

Social media encompasses platforms like the ever popular Facebook, the powerhouse social media platform that dominates over all the rest. It allows you to connect with schoolmates, friends, co-workers, family, and people from all over the globe. Businesses have stepped up to Facebook. Today you will find the vast majority are building a presence there, some better than others. This platform allows you to share ideas, words, pictures, and videos with each other with just the click of a button.

Twitter is the second or third largest, with people tweeting anything and everything, with only 140 characters to express their thoughts and feelings. This was taken mainstream by the Hollywood A-list, with many of them carrying millions and millions of followers, people that connect with you and have access to read what you write.

Other than the two aforementioned staples, there is also Instagram, which is a photo-sharing, video-sharing and social networking service that enables its users to take pictures and videos, apply digital filters to them, and share them on a variety of other social media sites, such as Facebook, Twitter, Tumblr, and Flickr. A distinctive feature is that it confines photos to a square shape, similar to a Polaroid picture.

Pinterest is a visual discovery tool, quite similar to vision boarding, that people use to collect ideas in the form of photos for their different projects and interests. People create and share their own personal collections (called *boards*) of visual bookmarks and images (called *pins*) that they use to do things like plan trips and projects, organize events, or save articles and recipes. This platform is huge for women planning weddings and large-scale events.

Tumblr, stylized in its logo as *tumblr.*, is a micro-blogging platform and social networking website that allows users to post multimedia and other content to a short-form blog. Users can follow other users' blogs as well as make their blogs private.

Snapchat is a photo messaging application developed by Stanford University students. Using the app, users can take photos, record videos, add text and drawings, and send them to a controlled list of recipients. These sent photographs and videos are known as *snaps*.

Google+ is a social networking and identity service that is owned and operated by Google. Google has described Google+ as a *social layer* that enhances many of its online properties. It is not simply a social networking website, but also an authorship tool that associates web content directly with its owner and author. It is the second-largest social networking site in the world after Facebook.

The platforms mentioned above are just a few. These platforms are becoming more and more popular, with each having its own unique opportunity to share your story and your business's story.

Facebook is king currently, and as business leaders we need to be where the people are. This chapter covers five secrets of using Facebook to connect with your clients on social media so you can build your business. These are also core business principles that can be mapped across to your business in general, not just social media.

Facebook is not only a popular location for social interactions, but is very quickly becoming a fiercely competitive marketing tool for many business owners. Business leaders are beginning to use this new method of generating leads and sales for their businesses. Current research shows that most people will spend six hours a month on Facebook, double that of the next closest competitor. Fifty per cent or more of consumers are accessing Facebook from a mobile device, over 543 million people around the world looking for products and services. Every day more than three billion items are liked or commented on Facebook pages, and that means that it's proving to be a powerful mode of advertising for any business. Advertising campaigns on Facebook, if set up correctly, are currently achieving up to a five-fold return on any investment because of the ability to target audiences with laser precision. Customers are recognising brands they see regularly on Facebook more than any other online methods. Facebook advertising is the catalyst for more positive conversations about businesses as well, due to a 47 per cent trust rate of Facebook advertising.

Secret 1

The first and most important secret is finding your customer avatar. I always get told by business owners that they know who their customer avatar is, but in reality people have no idea, and they know nowhere near enough detail. If you can get laser-targeted on who your customer avatar is, you can take your business to a whole new level, lower your marketing costs, increase your company turnover, and increase profit. Age, gender, and location are just a few of the criteria you need to know, and would be enough for traditional forms of marketing. In today's online world, as a business leader you need to know age, location, gender, likes, relationship status, schooling ... you can even get as specific as name! All the traits and details about them. It's the process of uncovering this information and then using it to convert more leads into customers and clients.

It's important to remember that it's not the employer who pays the wages. Employers only handle the money. It is the customer who pays wages. And I didn't say that – Henry Ford did. If you want your wages, rent, and expenses to be paid, then you better know who your customer is!

One of the most important points is understanding what platform your customer avatar is on. If they are on Twitter, why are you on Facebook? If they are on Instagram, there is no point tweeting at them to try and connect. The list below should be addressed as a minimum to ascertain who your customer avatar is.

- Age bracket
- Gender
- Location (city, state, country)
- Likes (competitors, music, fashion, food)
- Platform (Facebook, Twitter, Instagram, Pinterest, etc.)

The questions above are a good starting point, but we need to get deeper to gain even more clarity. If you combined all of your perfect clients into one super-client, what would that client look like? What traits would it have? These questions should get your brain running.

- What clubs, associations, and groups would they be a part of?
- Where would they spend the most of their money?
- What is their income?
- Where would they hang out for fun and leisure?

A more detailed list is available on our website, which you can find in the Contact section at the back of this book.

Once you have accumulated all that information, do a collation to determine what your clients have in common. You will find as your customer avatar becomes clearer and clearer that you will be crafting a distinctive image.

You may find that your customers have their own buzz words – almost their own language. Make sure that all of your communication is at their level to start building rapport and connection with them. Don't start talking – *like diz coz they use abrv words lol*. Keep your professionalism, but if they talk about Miley Cyrus twerking, feel free to talk about that too!

Now that you have your customer avatar, you can laser-target your marketing through Facebook's advertising tools, and you can use lead generation software as well. Understanding where your customer avatar hangs out, what they like, and what they are doing, you can connect with them on Facebook in other groups, other pages, and even their own profiles to start providing them with content and value. The more you put value and content on Facebook, the more responses you will be getting when you look to ask for a sale, promote a product, or start to look to capitalise from your social media marketing campaigns.

Secret 2

In business and also in social media, knowing your *outcome* is a key problem that always needs to be addressed. Most people start business and don't not know what outcome they are looking for. This is even more evident in social media. If you are starting a social media profile, you need to know what outcome you are looking for, especially when you are doing paid marketing. If you *don't* know what outcome you are aiming for, you will pour marketing money down the drain, and you won't be able to get maximum results or maximise profits.

Let's use an example of using paid marketing on Facebook so you can see how this works in real life.

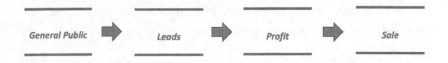

General Public → Leads → Profit → Sale

Sale – $1,500 product
Profit – $750 (50 per cent of our product is profit)
Leads – 1:10 Buys our product
General public – Customer avatar

This is where it gets exiting, where we look at reengineering success. If you don't know what your cost per product item produced is, and how many leads it takes for you to get one sale (how many people come to you directly via phone, email, or in person, and how many buy) you need to work this out ASAP! This need is monumental in developing a strong business and social media marketing strategy.

The model above shows a theoretical product, one that costs the buyer $1,500. If we know what outcome we desire (to sell as many of that product as possible), we need to work out what is the profit that we keep per product item that we sell. In this model we assume that 50 per cent of our product is cost and 50 per cent is our profit, so per product item we sell we make $750.

If we know that it will take ten leads (ten clients watching our webinar, calling us, emailing us, or visiting us in person) before we get one sale, then for us to break even we can spend a maximum of $75 ($750/10) per lead. The cheaper our cost per lead is, the more profit we can make overall.

When running Facebook marketing campaigns, we are shown how much we spend and how many people are clicking through to our offer. If, for example, we get 1,000 clicks on our advert and from that we get 100 leads (phone calls, emails, in person contacts) and that costs us $1,000, our cost per lead is only $10. Then we know we are making $65 profit *per lead*, regardless of whether they buy from us.

Looking at business from this angle allows us to understand how much revenue each part of our marketing campaign is earning us each step of the way. If we understand how to start with the end in mind, knowing what outcome we are aiming for, as Stephen Covey (a great mentor of ours) says, we can ensure that we are maximising our profit across all areas of the business.

In social media we need to have absolute clarity about what our outcome is for each platform. Facebook may be your platform for providing value and then asking for the sale, or it may be YouTube. Twitter is more of a customer relations platform, where you can connect closely with your clients and potential client base to address issues, concerns, complaints, praises or whatever comes up for you. It is important, however, to put a cap on your communication, so that clients know when they can and can't expect responses from you. An amazing example of this is Scott Stratten, author of *QR Codes Kill Kittens*, and voted as one of the most influential persons on social media, who shared a story about communicating on Twitter around 12 a.m. and then fell asleep. He had two tweets when he woke up. The first said "Scott Stratten is awesome love his work and his book, Scott what makes you so successful?" One hour later he had another saying "Scott is a scammer he doesn't even respond to his customers wtf!?" This just goes to show that you need to know what your outcome is with communication. If you or your staff are connecting with clients, make sure you set your communication parameters, for example "We are live between 9 a.m. and 5 p.m.," or "We respond to all questions within twelve hours."

Secret 3

Once you have established your customer avatar and know your outcome, it's time to increase your online presence. It's time to let your customer avatar know that you're ready and open for business.

Some people (I'm sure none of you reading this) think that this means just setting up a business page, putting your logo on it, and letting it take off. This is old school methodology, the process for making your business *redundant* on social media. Building your online presence requires providing your customers with tangible value, content that relates to your field of business, so that when it comes to doing business with your clients, you are in the front of their minds. Jim Rohn always said that you don't get paid what you are worth, you get paid for the value you bring to the marketplace. Want to get paid more? Provide the marketplace with more value!

To give your business the best chance of going viral, you need to stay ahead of the curve when it comes to celebrity news. If a celebrity does something in relation to your product or service, this is something you need to be sharing ASAP. Let's use the example of a shoe designer. When it's award season and the outfits of celebrities and their shoes are hitting headlines, assess what they look like, relate it to your business, and make sure you hashtag (#) the celebrity's name, the awards, and whatever you can think of that's relatable so that when people are searching for information in the news headlines, you will come up in the relevant posts.

Some people may have said to themselves, *What the hell is a hashtag?* A hashtag allows all the related posts on a particular topic, person, or event to be linked together so that you can see everything that relates to it. It's huge for getting your business out there and also allows you to connect with clients that are interested in your product or service. It allows you to connect with potential joint venture partners, and also to connect with competitors so you can see exactly what is going on in your industry. Less is definitely more when it comes to hashtags. Using a few is more powerful than using twenty different hashtags. The staples are usually your business name, your product or service, location, and anything that ties in to the story that you are telling at the time with your social media strategy.

Facebook, being the authority site that it is, allows you to build your online presence not just on Facebook, but across the Internet as a whole, but most people do not realise that Facebook has this ability. There are a few authority sites on the internet that Google absolutely loves! Facebook is a big one, as is YouTube, and if you are providing your clients and customer avatar with value, you are killing two birds with one stone, making your clients happy and increasing your online influence as well. If you are writing blogs on your website (quick tip: write blogs on your website), you can share the link on Facebook with all your fans and followers, and the more Google sees links to your website on Facebook popping up regularly, your website will automatically start jumping ranks on Google, and you will see it skyrocket through the pages all the way to number one.

Facebook assesses pages influence through a system called *edge rank* (check *your* website's edge rank at http://www.edgerankchecker.com), which lets you check to see how you are engaging with your customer avatar on Facebook. This assesses how viral your content goes (how many times it is shared, commented, and liked) and many other factors to see how your business's website is going.

One of the number one questions we are asked is how to increase this – how do I boost my edge rank and my influence online? The answer is simple, so if you take anything away from this whole chapter, write this down: *Give value!* Give your customer avatar so much value, such engaging content that they can't not share what you give to them. To quote a great mentor of mine, Zig Ziglar, "Help enough other people get what they want and you will get everything you want." So don't be afraid to share. The more valuable and engaging content that you share with them, the more likely they are to share, like, and comment on your posts and spread your message.

Second, if you want someone to like, share, or comment on your content, you need to ask for it. You need to give them a call to action (CTA). Writing a CTA on your post in all CAPITALS will get you better response than using lowercase.

If you are now thinking "OK, I get it, I've written it down – I need to give content; but how much content is too much?" – good question! For most of my clients I recommend as a principle two to five posts per day giving content, providing value, and if you are in a personal services business, where you are the face of your company, share some of your personal experiences. Don't take this too far and share all the most intimate moments of your life, but a few parts of your personal life allows people to connect with you and see that you are a real human being, someone they can connect with, and that will help increase your online presence. This will make a huge difference to your existing influence, and by doing something as simple as scheduling your post (look for the little timer symbol when you post on your page), you can do it in as little as five minutes a day.

Tip: To take this to *legendary* status, start commenting and connecting through your page in groups and on other people's pages, which gets you more exposure and allows you to provide value as your business to your customer avatar.

Secret 4

This next secret may be *the* most valuable part of this chapter, if not the entire book, namely: *take action*. So many people will hesitate. Be honest with yourself. Have you ever said to yourself "Oh, I'll do it tomorrow"? We all have, but it's getting over that mindset and actually taking action that separates bad business from good, and also good from great.

Napoleon Hill, the compiler of *Think and Grow Rich*, the book that has created the most millionaires and billionaires, found from Henry Ford that his most outstanding quality was his *habit* of reaching decisions quickly and definitely, and changing them slowly – essentially taking action! He also found those that failed to accumulate money reached decisions slowly. Make it a habit to start taking more action, and do it daily. It may be something as simple as scheduling some posts now that you know how to do it. Make your first Facebook ad. You might spend $10 or $20 and not get any leads, but you will be learning and you will have taken action.

In marketing and business there is a process called *testing and measuring*. So many people miss this essential piece of the pie, for if you're not testing and measuring your progress, how do you know the results you are getting? If you're running a Facebook ad campaign, you need to be testing and measuring your results so that you can go back, make the necessary changes, and ensure that you are getting the optimal results.

This is where some people let taking action stop them. What if I run a Facebook ad and it fails and it costs me thousands of dollars? If you are testing and measuring the results, and you are not getting the desired outcome, you can pause the ads, or stop them completely. You don't have to wait until you have spent your whole $1,000 marketing budget before you take action and make the adjustments. Too many people will sit and wait till they find the perfect image, the perfect text font, the perfect font size, and the perfect colour border to catch the reader's attention. In a perfect world we would wait and wait and wait until we have everything set up, but we don't want perfect to get in the way of better. If we don't get our ad out, our marketing campaign, our social media strategy, out and in front of our customer avatars, we won't know what the market wants.

Start small and build your way up to taking action daily. Do something as simple as listening to a new podcast, looking at a new website, or checking out a new business opportunity.

The other day someone recommended a new podcast to me. As soon as I finished the meeting, I jumped on, downloaded the latest episodes, and started listening to them straight away. (I'm even listening and taking notes as I'm writing this now.)

I have built this up so that now I take action on opportunities as soon as they come. My sister told me that I could get a new Apple MacBook Air interest free if I called Apple. Guess what I did that day? I called Apple. I needed a secondary travel laptop, as I have so many different pieces of software running and need to be accessing so many different online platforms that I have the need for two. I have built up my ability to take action where I do it daily straight away without even hesitating. I still assess if it's something that I need, and I needed a new laptop. If I didn't need a new laptop, I wouldn't have called. I did it because I've trained myself to go take action, and if I need to, I can change my mind later. This has been how I have been able to gain success in social media. When I first started running Facebook ads, I had no idea how to make it happen, but I put them up, found out what the response was, and tested and measured what I was doing so that I could build an optimised business.

Take a moment and write down how can you start taking action today – now. Are you going to run a Facebook ad? Set up a Snapchat account? Maybe it's just going for a walk and working on your health and fitness. Write down a list of three to five things you can do each day to start taking action, in your personal life, business life, even your relationship. It's been proven over and over again – how we do *anything* is how we do *everything*. Start taking action across all facets of your life and business and notice how the results start increasing. Now *please* don't blame me if your personal life and business start skyrocketing just from starting to take action daily.

Secret 5

One truth at the core of all business, marketing, social media, or anything to do with building your business is that there is always more to learn. You cannot keep growing your business unless you continually learn and grow. I learned from listening to Arnold Schwarzenegger's speeches and talks over the years that this was instrumental to his success. He put down his success to finding a mentor, passing him up, finding another mentor, passing that one up, until he was the best in the world. This technique he applied throughout his bodybuilding career and into his movie career.

Social media is growing and moving constantly. Just today, while writing this chapter, my news feed on Facebook changed and I got an email advising me on new ad guidelines and marketing techniques. If you aren't continuing to learn, continuing to expand your awareness in your business and the landscape your business is a part of, you *will* fall behind. And in business, if you aren't ahead of the curve you're making your chances of success dwindle. Keeping up with what is happening on social media is easy if you keep an eye out for updates and also watch your emails so you're in front of any changes and can make sure that you as a business leader are using the changes to your benefit.

I personally like to make sure that I am learning every day, for I truly believe that if you're not growing, you're dying. This book has some amazing people in the field of personal and professional development contributing to it. Some of the people that I like to learn from daily include the greats Chris Howard and Calvin Coyles. Even though I'm in a business not directly correlated to it, if I personally grow my knowledge daily my business can't help but grow as well. People like Les Brown, Brian Tracey, Jim Rohn, and Zig Ziglar are all informal mentors of mine that allow me to grow my business daily. I also learn from the titans in my industry. Some people think that it's not beneficial to connect with your competitors, but if they are in business and doing better than you, you should be learning from them. In business we all have an ego, but to be a *success* in business, in social media, in anything, we need to check our egos at the door and take a beginner's mindset. I connect with local businesses in Perth that are in the same industry so we can share tools, stories, and techniques that can help each of our businesses grow. If there is nothing like this in your area, your best friend is http://www.meetup.com. Look for people in your area that are in the same or a similar field and connect with them, share value with them, and help each other grow your businesses. If there isn't a group yet, then create one! Don't let perfect get in the way of better, and start learning more from people around you.

Connecting with leaders in your field is easier than you think. Just doing something as easy as sending them an email, a Facebook message, or a tweet can have you connecting with some of the largest players in your industry.

A good friend of mine runs a business called MMA Seminars, and the largest player in the Mixed Martial Arts (MMA) scene is the Ultimate Fighting Championship (UFC). He was able to send a tweet to the head of the UFC (Dana White) and had a response almost straight away. Social media lets you get access to those people easily and effortlessly. But they aren't going to contact you; you still need to take action: pick up the phone, send that email, or send those messages on Facebook.

A hindrance to some people is the cost of continuing to learn, realising that there is always more to learn. A lot of small business owners in particular don't want to spend the money on more books (you obviously value learning, so well done), courses, training (live and online), mentors, and the cost to learn by doing. But the cost of education is always going to be less than the cost of ignorance. Take a moment and just think: if you had a mentor that was going to show you how to take your business to seven figures, but that mentor cost $35,000 per year would it be worth it? What's the cost? Well, every moment you *don't* take up their mentorship it's costing you seven figures per year! It might cost you more than $300,000 in profit if you don't take action and get yourself a mentor. That $35,000 up front looks pretty small if your return is over $300,000, doesn't it? This is something that a lot of business leaders don't take into consideration, not only for themselves but also for their staff. Imagine if all of your staff were being trained by the world's best, like Chris Howard, Calvin Coyles, and everyone else in this book, how much more would they be producing?

A lot of people come from a scarcity mindset. What happens if my staff are trained up and they leave? You cannot live your life on what-ifs, though. What if you're hit by a bus tomorrow (God forbid)? As long as we are coming from a mindset of abundance, the more we help people get what they want, the more we can have everything we want in turn. You might find that by training a staff member, that person can help systemise your business and then move on as the position that employee held becomes redundant, so your business's efficiency goes up and costs go down. How much better would that be?

We have had the ability to help so many businesses create an online presence and connect with their audiences on social media that previously had no idea what they were doing, which is what really makes us happy. We have been working closely with Australia's fastest-growing personal and professional development company. In one weekend we were able to set up a new Facebook page for their business, and we generated over 400 likes and followers in two days, whereas their previous page had been active for over six months and had only recently cracked the 500 likes mark.

Business owners starting from a standing start think that they may have missed the boat. However, they can still get on the various social media platforms and start building band awareness and connection with their market. We work directly with a real estate company here in Perth that had *zero* social media knowledge or recognition. Through engaging with us and using some of the social media strategies available in our free ebook (see http://www.yoursocialvoice.com.au), they have over 400 likes with great engagement and now have a great following and can connect with their audience with ease.

In the lead-up to events, social media can have a hugely positive effect on your business and exposure. We worked with an amazing fashion designer (Gorge Design) in the lead-up to their charity fashion event, and through just using some of the speakers from the event, the charity prizes, and the charity profile that they were working with, we were able to increase engagement on their page by over 700 per cent, which is *huge*. We didn't do anything fancy, crazy, or special. We just asked people to like and share the content (gave them a call to action) and we used parts of the event that would engage with an audience.

It's not because I'm so good or my teams are so good that we can achieve these results. It's because the strategies that we have in place are so good! If you combine strategy with execution, you will get amazing results.

While I'm sure that everyone can take their social media management and marketing and turn it into a strategy that works for their clients and for their bottom line, it will still overwhelm even the savviest of business owners. This is why I do what I do, why I write books, do seminars, and run a team of people that do this at the highest level, to alleviate the stress for business owners. To create a strategy that works for your clients and for you. Please *take action* on what you have read, and reach out to us (find me on social media!) if you need some more guidance. I look forward to seeing you and your businesses creating an amazing presence on social media.

Driving Your McLaren: Autism, Formula 1, Lasting Change

Sanja Zeman

Sanja Zeman is an industry leader in the neuroplasticity, wellness, and functional improvement arenas. With a background in occupational therapy and over twenty-five years experience as a medico-legal adviser and consultant to business, the legal fraternity, insurance industry, and health care professionals, she has tuned that wealth of knowledge and experience to everyday people wanting to better their lives. She is also an inspiring teacher and influential keynote speaker.

Sanja seeks to inspire and advise businesses and individuals on how to harness best practice thinking to the management of function, and how to tune in to your unique bandwidth to create your best life. She provides a compelling perspective that challenges traditional thinking, surrounding the physical, emotional, sensory, cognitive, and social components of function. Her modern thinking and best practice ideas bridge the gap between perception and reality, building on a sensory integration approach to create the foundation for brilliance in achieving wealth and success.

I have just been pulled over by an officious highway patrolman – speeding again. Rushing to get to that next appointment; scrambling to cram just one more task into my frenetic day; juggling the multiple balls of my life and constantly stooping to pick up the ones I drop, only to start the discordant juggle again. As I contemplate losing three points on my license and a $250 fine, I wonder why? What on earth is going wrong? Nothing seems to be going my way. The positive side of me visualizes the law of reciprocity in action. What goes around comes around; there is an equal and opposite reaction to every action. Given that the highway patrolman just booked me, I visualize what might reciprocally happen to him? But my cheeky smirk suddenly furrows into a contemplative frown as I realize it doesn't quite work like that. I inwardly reflect on what it is about me that is creating all of this drama, busyness, havoc, and quiet destruction in my world.

Have you ever felt like that? Have you ever felt that things are just stacking up against you; that the domino effect is entrenched and all your dominoes are tumbling down at once – and not in any nice orderly, synchronized pattern, but a somewhat rough and tumble scuffle? Have you ever felt that your life is like one giant crisis aversion, with you constantly juggling to make ends meet, create stability, and in that process simply producing stimulus packages to dig yourself out of one hole, only to be dragged into the next?

Did you survive the last global financial crisis with a silent sigh of relief that its cyclonic power swept past you, leaving some messy carnage but an intact bottom line, allowing you to regroup and rebuild, only to find yourself wondering whether you could survive such a cyclone another time around; whether you have sufficient reserves to weather out the storm; whether in fact you want to be weathering storms such as these in your life, work, and business with the ongoing sense of haunting uncertainty that presents like a cataract, blurring the clarity of your vision?

My story begins in 2008, in the middle of the global financial crisis that was absolutely, unequivocally, not going to impact on me. Sure, it might cause us to batten down the hatches a little tighter, but that's all it could possibly do. After all, I had a strong business as a medical professional, employing a staff of thirty, and working in shiny, sleek, state-of-the-art offices with everything that we needed at our fingertips. My world seemed invincible, until all of a sudden things started to fall apart, slowly at first, but with the rising tide of momentum, increasing in intensity, ferocity, and power. In the carnage that resulted, I learnt a lot. Lessons about diversifying risk and not keeping all of my eggs in one basket; letting go of control – let's face it, what is that beast anyway? Lessons about loyalty, purpose, belief, and values. But most importantly, lessons about using character and my underlying unique neurological blueprint to drive success and architect my life according to my design.

Having been brought up in a first-generation Australian family with my parents migrating from Eastern Europe, I had an extremely strong work ethic, and believed that with hard work I could create anything. I had done it before and I would do it again.

When I lost consultancy contracts when my customers were affected by the global downturn, I too downsized my business and knuckled down to rebuild and secure new contracts within the changing financial marketplace. What happened as a result was more than I could imagine. I secured new contracts and got the work that I needed, but it was unmanageable. There were not enough hours in the day for me to do the jobs that I needed to do in order to service my liabilities. I was stuck. Too much work; not enough hours; and still not enough dollars to service my debt. I had a downsized business with insufficient resources to operate successfully, and more work than I could manage, thus a perfect environment to bake an unpalatable meal of failure, achieved by destabilizing the very foundation of my business.

As a result, I decided to sell my beautifully manicured five-acre property in Sydney's Hill's District, having fully renovated it with every contraption known to mankind, and to relocate to a small investment property that I was building on the north coast of New South Wales. I figured this would be a great tree change and sea change. I figured that downsizing would decrease my liabilities and allow me to work less, but still allow me to manage my own financial needs and those of my family.

What seemed like a great idea brought its own whirlwind of challenges, not least of all relocating my 14-year-old son to a new school and moving into a property with no running water, power, or kitchen. I recall accepting invitations to dinner with friends, only to turn up twenty minutes early with a towel and a plea to borrow a hot shower, having been forced to use those beach showers, which initially seemed like a fun, glam camping idea, but which rapidly made the descent from glamming to scramming. The relocation of the business entrails didn't even figure into the difficulties I faced, nor did I contemplate the fact that in this monumental move, I would lose my social support network due to distance.

I was the eternal optimist who made things happen, suddenly turned into the single mum trying to survive with no support and an endless barrage of uncertainty. The support network that I had previously taken for granted was gone – friends, acquaintances, even the network of local services such as the staff at the local post office, my bank manager, my accountant, my greengrocer. People that in their own way provided me with a sense of security when I went down the street to complete everyday tasks simply vanished like a puff of smoke into thin, thin air. I felt like an inexperienced climber on Everest, facing hurdles I was ill-equipped to face, and without an oxygen supply.

I felt totally out of control. I felt an overwhelming sense of responsibility. I knew that things had to change, and that although I had changed location, it was not enough to create the lasting change that I needed in my world. People have always told me I work far too hard, that I am dedicated, and that I make things happen, but all of those qualities were no longer working for me. Downsizing had not been enough. I questioned whether a simple relocation with decreased overheads would be sufficient to bring everything back in place and rebuild. All I had left going for me were twenty-four hours a day – shame, I so wanted eighty-four hours a day; a brain that worked; and a resilience that was going to allow me to bounce back no matter what.

As I sat on the beach watching the sunrise early one morning, I contemplated what it really was that made an individual manifest their best and achieve lasting change. I reflected on beauty, success, power, and the creation of something unique. I reflected on the challenges many of the bravest individuals I had worked with faced in their lives. I reflected on the McLaren motor car and the world of autism.

At this point I can see you jerking awake from your quiet reverie in my somewhat interesting but nothing new story and wondering what on earth a McLaren motor car and the world of autism have in common? More importantly, what does either of these things have to do with new beginnings and sustaining positive change in life, aside from one representing a good opportunity to enjoy the thrill of a ride, and the other representing something most of us know little about? For me, it was about what each could teach us about life, people, and creating sustainable success with what you uniquely own.

I recall watching the movie *Rush* and wondering not only about the factors that drove both Niki Lauda and James Hunt to succeed, but also about the vehicles they used to get there, their expectations of themselves, their team, their machines, and ultimately what drove their success, or ultimate demise.

The McLaren is known as an *unobtanium* car. Although technically produced as a commercial vehicle, the reality is that this is a motor car that uses the best Formula One technology and applies it to the commercial market. It is technologically advanced. It is beautiful. It is all about performance. But technology, beauty, and performance come at a price.

The price of driving a McLaren, and I'm not talking about the actual ticket dollar value, is that it's not the easiest car to drive. Its hard suspension, constant clutching, and shifting gears is described as tiresome in rush hour traffic. But this also allows it to be the best that it can be in perfect conditions. Never yet having had the opportunity to drive one myself, I have only been told that in order to drive a McLaren, you need to be a skilled and proficient driver; a driver that understands all aspects of both driving and of the vehicle itself; a driver that is not scared to apply skill and knowledge dependent on circumstances; and one that is well able to manage contingencies using the power and strength of this amazing vehicle to get the most out of it.

As I began to understand what it is that car buffs love about this McLaren motor car, I understood that it is only with a certain set of skills, sheer determination, will power, and a trust in yourself to use those skills that you could master the art of driving a McLaren. This is not a car that you could simply jump into for a casual drive to the corner store to get the milk you forgot for your morning coffee; neither is it safe to drive down any road. I pictured driving it down the back roads in Bali, navigating the sleepy, mangy dog sunning itself in the middle of the narrow, bumpy road; the pedestrian tourists taking in the scenery while avoiding near death caused by the multitude of scooters careening around the blind corners. I just couldn't imagine any mangy dogs, pedestrians, or scooters left standing as the McLaren circumvented those corners, leaving a cacophony of chickens and roosters in its trail.

This is a car that you would need to be vigilant in driving; to understand and work in synchronicity with the vehicle to get the most out of the driving experience. It is a car that could give you the thrill of a lifetime; however, it's up to you to create that thrill and to use your own unique skills to manifest and manage it.

As I pondered the question of performance and the McLaren, I drew an analogy to the individual powers of people and our ability to be aware of our own strengths; to be aware of our idiosyncrasies that make us unique. I began to think about how we use that knowledge about ourselves in relating to ourselves and to others. What became apparent as I was pondering the McLaren was that I was in fact looking at an object of desire, which in its own right does not understand its strengths, weaknesses, and idiosyncrasies, and relies on the driver to sort it out. If the McLaren has a competent driver who understands his own capabilities; his own strengths; how to get the most out of the McLaren motor car; how to drive that car in all conditions, not only on an unrestricted autobahn, that driver would be able to bring out the best in the McLaren. Ultimately it's up to the driver.

The issue for many of us in our quest for achievement and success in any part of our life is that we navigate and commandeer our own life without a clear understanding of ourselves, our uniqueness, or our strengths and weaknesses. As a result, we spend countless amounts of money, energy, and time trying to develop strategies which will allow us to succeed in fitting a mould of what society, community, family, and others picture is right for us. It strikes me that when we do this we are actually building a personality rather than character.

I think about character in terms of the values that inherently belong to us as individuals, with our idiosyncrasies being the spices that bring out the flavour. If we possess core character traits, which include honesty, integrity, transparency, generosity of spirit, and loving kindness, our idiosyncrasies will simply spice us up. They make us unique in our expression of character, and they are the things that attract others to us, and ultimately drive success.

The question may be pondered as to why it is that we allow personality, expectations, and attitudes to override our character, and in so doing, to make us no different from others and prone to fail in our quest for the manifestation of brilliance. When we succumb to challenges and are unable to stay on the spicy character trail, we are simply manifesting a lack of clear understanding about ourselves.

At this point you are probably thinking, "Great, I need to understand myself. How do I do that? I have read every self-help book I can get. I have gone to every therapist under the sun. I have done every spiritual course and healing ceremony that I can do. I have drawn from Eastern and Western medicine, and every complementary thing in between. Lovely to talk about, but how do I achieve in this endless quest?"

In my world it's really simple; it's where the world of autism intersects the McLaren motor car. It's only when we look at extremes of behaviour, wellness, success, and function, that we can really learn about who we are, and how we become our best. In the world of autism and related disorders, we see individuals who live more intense and less moderated lives. By exploring the experiences of these individuals and trying to join them in whatever way we can to relate inside their world, we can gain a unique understanding of the extremes of experience and how these relate to behaviour. What a gift they bring to all of us, by allowing us to look at extremes, identify our strengths, and thereby develop means of moderating our own world to create lasting change.

Scrutinising in Pit Lane

Let's look at who we are and perhaps treat ourselves to some objective scrutiny as we would a machine. The McLaren is a brilliant machine that needs input – fuel, something to make it run, something to turn it on, and someone to control it.

As humans, we can draw the analogy that as a machine, our body is the motor and moving parts, and we each have a driver with a central processing unit – our brain. The human brain is the fastest computer in the world. It houses the best operating system known to mankind, incorporating over a billion nerve cells, each linked to as many as ten thousand others. Our brain processes input, and creates an output. Understanding how to manage our inputs allows us as individuals to navigate and perform at our best, producing the brilliance we are capable of in a sustained way.

In my personal journey, I started to explore what I had always done in business. In my professional career I had allowed my analytical, problem-solving, and mapping skills to provide an overview of an individual's life. What I needed to do was exactly the same for myself. It was a ruthless exercise as I mapped out the strengths that I had, the weaknesses that I stringently avoided, and the systems that supported me. What became apparent was that I was not actually using my strengths. I was using certain skills, and I had been doing that for a very long time. I went to university and completed an undergraduate degree, followed by postgraduate studies, a masters degree, and extensive, specific skill acquisition in my chosen field. Thereafter, like a lot of people in similar situations, I continued to tweak and refine my skills. At no point did I actually stop to assess my strengths. That was the revelation for me.

Not having a lot of active business contracts, largely because of the global economic downturn, I started to take on more clinical work with individuals that needed to get their life back on track. After all, that was my expertise in the medical-legal arena; so why not apply these skills to everyday people that want to create lasting change and new beginnings?

After having made this decision, one of the first clients that I worked with came to me after several sessions and said, "I have seen so many therapists, so many medical practitioners, so many business coaches. I have done so much training and self-development. I have read book after book after book. Until now, nothing has moved or shifted for me. Do you know what the difference is in what you have done for me?"

Naturally, I asked what, and her response was, "You helped me differentiate between my strengths and weaknesses. Rather than listening to me talk about my problems and working on trying to fix these problems, which were in fact manifestations of weakness, you set about giving me confidence and improving my strengths, allowing me to see my brilliance within. I was able to see what I was truly brilliant at, and how I could use that in a variety of situations depending on my goals. Previously, I had been looking at where my skills were, what skills I needed to develop, and how I would go about that. I was looking at skill acquisition to bridge my gaps. What you did for me was move my focus right away from skill acquisition. You helped me understand that skills can be learned, but strengths are what we need to steer us in the direction of achieving our goals and staying on track."

As I listened to her, I found myself thinking that what she was voicing was exactly the process I had recently been through myself, when I had started to analyse what I needed in order to rebuild my business and generate sustainable, long-lasting change that works for me.

Understanding the Machine to Tune the Results

The model which underpins understanding your unique sensory blueprint is based on extensive scientific research that has been tried and tested over time and that has been used in the therapeutic and medical arenas, along with other research that has been used in the business world. In a nutshell, it's like this.

Everything that we do as humans has to be processed by this wonderful organ that we all possess; it's called our brain. In some of us, that brain allows us to be resilient and bounce back when hardship strikes. In others, it gets bogged down. Why is it that we differ in our ability to find solutions, to keep going, to structure goals, to create pathways around life events that are not working for us, and to develop solutions which support us? The reason that we differ has everything to do with how we process the information that comes into our brain, with respect to our individual tolerances and preferences.

I draw on the analogy of the brain being like a computer. In order for a computer to operate, buttons have to be pressed and data has to be entered. Data can then be retrieved when it is required, processed, routed, and used in different ways. The brain is absolutely no different. As a human being, every single thing that we process in our world comes into our brain through our senses. If we have lost our sense of smell, we will be unable to smell a gas leak and understand an associated risk, or smell a rose and revel in its sweet perfume. If we cannot feel the heat as we touch a hot stove, we cannot assess that we are actually burning. If we cannot interpret the sensation of touch, we will never know what comfort feels like. If we cannot see a car coming towards us, we have no awareness that we should stop and avoid walking in front of it, nor will we be struck with awe and wonder as we witness a beautiful sunrise. All of the understanding, decisions, and actions that happen more or less instantaneously in our world, are the result of our brain processing information.

Information enters our brain through our senses, either externally from our environment, or internally from our body. We gather input from our senses – vision, our eyes; hearing, our ears; taste, our mouth; smell, our nose; touch, the receptors all over our body; balance, the equilibrium-based receptors in our vestibular system; and our perception of body and space which relates to the proprioceptive receptors in our muscles and joints. We all receive these inputs differently and uniquely.

Sensory information is converted into an electrical impulse, which enters our nervous system for processing. Each of us possesses individual thresholds for how much sensory input we can manage. This relates to sensory input as a whole, and to individual senses. Some of us can manage a lot of visual input, loving and seeking an abundance of bright colours, bright lights, and competing visual demands. Others of us can manage only a little before we become overwhelmed. The issue for most of us is that we do not understand what our tolerances are. We do not understand where we have a large capacity and where, conversely, we have a minute capacity. As a result, we fail to architect our environment, our world, our decisions, and our goals to meet our neurological thresholds and requirements for peak performance.

Have you ever been in a situation where you have walked into a crowded room with a multitude of people conversing, music playing, and miscellaneous background noise? As you join a group and engage in conversation, other people in the group start talking to each other. You try to focus on the person that you started talking to, but you find this increasingly difficult, becoming acutely aware of everybody else talking around you, the music slicing through your thoughts and distracting you, the noise suddenly feeling as though it has escalated. You start to feel discomfort because you cannot hear clearly, but you see all these other people around you that appear to be coping really well in this environment. It doesn't seem to faze them that there are sixteen people talking at once, and you wonder what is wrong with your hearing, questioning whether you should go and get that hearing test so you don't turn out just like your deaf uncle. That is the process of auditory processing. That instant when you feel discomfort is when you fail to filter extraneous information that is not important to you at that moment in time. That capacity, timing, and intensity is unique to you.

This is a simple example of one of your senses integrating and providing information to your brain for it to use in a structured, organized, and synchronized manner, to direct the orchestra of your brain and produce a brilliant symphony. Consider how much more special you are when all of your senses start to integrate as a whole. This combination makes each and every one of us extraordinary. In understanding ourselves, we need to grasp our uniqueness. We need to understand neurologically who we are, and cognitively how we can manage that. In so doing, we become the most competent drivers of our own machine.

Neurologically, we each process sensory input along a threshold continuum, high to low. Cognitively, we employ active management strategies to control that input, or we manage it passively, reactively in fact. If we start to understand these factors, we start to become more and more aware of our uniqueness. If we lack an awareness of what we can manage as an individual and what works best for us, we will have no idea how far to safely stretch ourselves in life and business. Some of us will be under-stretched and fail to gain sufficient motivation to achieve our goals. Others may become so over-stretched, that they create a constant and perpetual state of anxiety within themselves, as they cram in too much neurologically, failing to put controls in place to manage their optimum input.

When we understand our overall individual neurological blueprint, only then can we understand exactly how to structure success. I liken this to building a house. If we have a clear idea of what we want, we are going to know what we need to do in relation to the foundation. If we want to build a three-story building, we can architect a foundation to meet our needs. The part that is missing though, is giving consideration to the site. In this case, the site is our brain and our body. If we understand that we want to build a three-story building on the edge of a cliff that has an unstable geological structure, we are better able to architect appropriate foundations to support the building.

I, too, have been to a lot of seminars. I have read lots of books. I have done lots of study and research, and one of the things that often strikes me is the individuals who we refer to as *seminar junkies*. I remember a young lady speaking to me on a flight, saying, "You know, I go to seminars and get so excited about what I am going to do with my business. I come out with a clear idea of the steps I need to take. I am on fire. I am going for it. I am revved up and three weeks later, it's gone. Why?"

The why relates to her failing to understand her individual strengths. What she was seeking was skills. She wanted to know what she needed to do to build her dream business, but she had not taken even a moment to think about her individual blueprint, and to understand the foundation that she was building on. When I talked to her and we explored her individual strengths and weaknesses, it became apparent that she had an extremely high neurological threshold to a range of inputs, and needed to meet that threshold consistently so as to enable her to stay in her peak performance zone. She rarely became overwhelmed. However, she frequently failed to act and to achieve her goals. By understanding what she needed to allow her to be within her peak performance zone, we were very quickly able to come up with strategies which enabled her to remain in that state without burnout. The next seminar she went to she applied her strengths to her decision making. She created a blueprint for success, and when I contacted her three weeks later, she was still going strong. She could not believe how easy it was. The skills that she had acquired on this occasion stuck, because her individual blueprint for success was set.

If many years ago I had understood my extremely low threshold to visual input, I would never have been offended by the boyfriend who criticized me for being too neat, too organized, too tidy. I would not have tried to undo what I inherently was, because I would have understood myself, my strengths. As a result I would have had compassion towards myself and compassion towards him, understanding that perhaps this was not one of his strengths. Rather than trying to change to fit a mould of somebody else's expectations, I would have learned how to be the best I could be in that environment, in that team; how to use my strengths to bring out not only my best, but the best of those around me. I would have taken over the organizational components of tasks. I would have taken over the neatness and the tidiness, the keeping things together, and allowed him to manage other areas that were not my strength.

Only by understanding our own strengths and weaknesses can we maintain the integrity of our whole. The issue is ultimately one of understanding ourselves, understanding our uniqueness, and building our character. We must allow our idiosyncrasies to create a unique manifestation of our character traits instead of trying to fit a mould of personality dictated by others.

So for those of you like me that have been challenged at some point in their life about making wrong choices, about how to build a life and business that supports and sustains yourself and others, rather than constantly presenting challenges in a seemingly endless vortex which increases with speed and power, I challenge you to ask yourself why. Is the foundation of that answer as simple as understanding your strengths and working with these, rather than continually facing the uphill climb to develop skills to bridge your weaknesses?

At the end of the day, if we are going to master the art of driving a McLaren, we have to realize that this is a vehicle worth cherishing. This is something special and unique. It is perfection, and like everything that is perfect, it can always do with a tweak – but it is about the tweak, not about being pulled apart and deconstructed. So how do we do it?

Using Neurology to Drive Character

Right now you are probably asking yourself what you need to do to create your individual blueprint. For now, I would like to take the opportunity to ask you to complete a short exercise which will help you understand exactly what it feels like to know and to have a blueprint of yourself.

Take five minutes to write down all the things that you can think of quickly about *what you don't want*. It doesn't matter what they are. No one else is ever going to see this list. Don't think too much about it. Don't contemplate it. Just start writing. Let me help you.

Don't want to worry about money.

Don't want to feel alone.

Don't want to be single.

Your turn. Keep going.

Look at the list and think about it. In fact, I want you to look at it for the next five minutes. Re-read it. Embed it in your consciousness, and then do something, anything that you find relaxing. For some of you, it might be going for a jog. For others, it might be lying down in a darkened room with a scented candle. The only stipulation is that you are not to be doing any reading or listening. You are to be either engaging in something active, because you find that relaxing; or something extremely passive such as lying down, sitting in a comfortable chair, or meditating.

Engage in this activity for twenty to thirty minutes. It doesn't matter what it is. While you are doing this activity, reflect on your list of *don't wants*. As your mind's eye works through that list, feel what it would be like if those things were in your world and continued in your world today, tomorrow, and five years from now. How would you feel if in five years you were still struggling for money? How would you feel if in five years you were still single? How would you feel if in five years you were still complaining to your friends about the lack of good staff and not being able to find good support? How would you feel if in five years you ran into me and you said: "I'm still struggling because I trust people too much and I get into bad situations that are not good for me, that are not aligned with me." *Feel* your *don't wants*; don't *think* them.

You have completed your activity, either passive or active, whatever works for you. You felt the experience of *living a life you don't want*. Now, having felt it, write down what it is that you *do* want.

So how can you achieve these goals and make lasting change? Here's a part of the missing link: a corner of your neurological blueprint. Take the following quiz:

	Yes	No
Do you become frustrated if you are looking for something in a messy drawer or crowded cupboard?		
Does having a crowded, messy desk bother you at work?		
Do you prefer a screensaver with a static image rather than rapid visual transitions?		
Do you prefer large open spaces to a bustling city environment?		

Do you prefer interacting in small groups rather than in large groups or parties?		
Do you prefer calm tonal, colours to bright colours?		
Do you often notice things that others don't?		
Are you good at following maps and visual directions?		
Can you pay good attention to detail?		

Scoring:

Mostly yes: You have a low threshold for visual sensory input. You are finely attuned to receiving visual input, and don't need a lot of this type of sensory input to reach your peak performance zone. Too much will overwhelm you and impact your productivity. You will function at your optimum in a calm, organized environment. Use cupboards to store items away, out of direct sight. Limit the number of visual distractions that occur simultaneously. Remove clutter. Performance will be improved by maintaining visual organization, but this should be integrated with other sensory preferences.

Mostly no: You have a high threshold for visual sensory input. You need a lot of visual stimuli to kick-start you into action and keep you in your peak performance zone. Not enough will result in you failing to take action and sustain momentum. You will function at your optimum in a busy, changing environment. Use open shelving and work in an open plan office to be at your best. Use bright colours and moving images to keep you in your peak visual performance zone, but this should be integrated with other sensory preferences.

Some of the most enlightened people are not those who have achieved academic excellence or had shamanic healings, but people that truly understand who they are, who are not trying to be something that fits a mould. These are people that understand their inputs and use that knowledge to create a brilliance of output according to their own design.

When I talk about understanding ourselves and understanding our strengths, building on strengths rather than trying to build on weaknesses, I'm talking about being your own architect, creating a blueprint, understanding where you have a lot of capacity and where you have diminished capacity. That's not about skill. It is about neurology – about your brain. It's about knowing where you can stretch yourself and how much you need to stretch yourself to get the best and most sustainable outcome.

Life is about riding the waves. With every peak there is a trough; and with every trough there comes a peak. Sometimes you're in a trough, and there's a really big wave about to come crashing down, but you are unprepared. It's about knowing when to dive through the bottom of that wave to come out into calm water on the other side.

Life brings its challenges, but if you truly understand yourself, you can understand your unique strengths. You can build on those strengths to create brilliance. And you can ensure that you allow yourself, as the driver of your unique machine, to take the wheel with exceptional competence and the skill to recognize your strength and your uniqueness and to use that to manifest and sustain your best performance. You then become a driver that can react to adverse weather and road conditions; a surfer that knows when to dive through silently rather than ride the wave; an exceptional individual who creates brilliance by your own design.

Embracing Change

Michelle Armstrong

Michelle Armstrong, MM, CPT is the Life Renovator and creator of the Renovate Your Life programs and retreats. Armstrong is a published author and writer, board certified holistic health practitioner, published fitness model and competitor, television personality, radio host, and an internationally recognized motivational speaker and mind-body coach. Michelle has spoken to thousands worldwide about how to improve their health and lives by applying the practices and principles from her unique transformation program, The Armstrong Method.

Change in life is not happening to harm you. It's
happening in order to reveal you.

When the idea of this book was presented to me, my heart immediately leapt at the opportunity to submit a chapter about *change,* and how we can learn to navigate through the changes in our lives with greater ease and understanding.

Change has been a constant companion in my life, just like it is for us all. Via the last decade of witnessing my clients go through change in their lives as well as in my own, I've come to discover a new and empowering approach to managing change more effectively in our lives.

In this chapter, I'd like to share five empowering mindsets that may make change a little easier for you, particularly if you are in the process of change right now or are still perhaps holding on to the past in some way, and finding it difficult to let go. These mindsets are new perspectives – new ways of choosing to believe, view, and experience the world – that can propel you into a life more aligned with who you are capable of becoming and with your purpose in the world.

Before I begin, I want to share with you a story that gave me a clear picture of what change can be.

The Dandelion

The other day I was picking dandelions from my front lawn. I live in a beautiful court with spectacular neighbours who each year diligently remove all their dandelions from their gardens and lawns so as not to turn their lawns (and their fellow neighbours' lawns) into a carpet of crabgrass.

While I was bent down, picking the dandelions from my lawn, simultaneously apologizing profusely to each dandelion for ending the course of its short, beautiful, yellow life, I noticed to my right my neighbours' little girl – 9 years of age – blowing the one dandelion that has bloomed into "fairy seed" (which is what my five-year old son calls it) all over my lawn and onto the lawn of my immediate neighbour. I just about had a heart attack! Once those fairy seeds take flight, they could land anywhere, and the last thing I wanted was the seeds to take root in my neighbours' lawns.

Despite my mother's thumb being greener than Ireland, this particular DNA code has either not been handed down to me or has yet to awaken and reveal itself. Therefore, because I am almost always the last in my court to tend to my dandelions, I felt somewhat responsible for the potential demise of my neighbours' lawn. So somewhat reluctantly, yet dutifully, I decided to chase down all the fairy seeds blowing in the wind, in hopes of stopping as many as possible from making their new home at my neighbours.

But the panic of chasing the fairy seeds lasted only a brief moment as my eyes were drawn to the drifting of one particular dandelion seed that was being carried high up into the sky and off into an unknown distance by the magical pull of an unseen force. It looked so peaceful and serene as it floated through the air at an angle that made it look like it was being gently pulled and cradled. It showed no resistance whatsoever and didn't look back once to where it had been rooted to the ground with all the other fairy seeds. It was as though it had fully embraced its new journey and destiny, and it almost seemed to smile back at me before it vanished from my sight. It was in this very moment I thought, *Ah yes, this is how we should all experience change. Detaching, allowing, releasing, and floating. Just like a dandelion seed in the wind.*

Change Is Continuous

When I look back over the course of the last forty years of my life, not very much has stayed the same for me. I have had several different significant relationships, multiple careers within varying industries, many different friendships and connections, and multiple shifts in perception. I have lived in four different countries and over twenty different homes. I've stepped off the ledge and into the unknown on so many different occasions that I've lost count. Change for me is natural. Change to me means, "I'm *alive*."

But for many people, and maybe it is the case for you, change is something that sends them spiralling down into a pit of fear and anxiety. Many people I know – family, friends, and clients – associate change with much fear, trepidation, and panic. Next to death and public speaking, change is what many fear most.

But why is this? Why is it so difficult to just let go, and go with the flow?

Rooted in Our Stories

As we age we accumulate experiences, including what we do at our jobs, the roles we play for others (wife, stepmother, father, brother, son, boss), the events we have experienced (bankruptcy, divorce, death, abuse). It's easy to begin identifying with these roles and events to the point that we think they are *who we are*, not simply things we do or have experienced. Even those some of these roles and stories may no longer serve who we are destined to become in the world. We can still hold on to them so tightly that our knuckles turn white – fearing that if we release them, we will no longer know who we are. This fear of losing our sense of identity can cause a sense of deep anxiety, as our identity is how we determine not only our significance in life, but life's meaning as well.

Yet think back now to when you were a child. How often did you think about the future? How often did you think about your past? Do you recall getting up on titles? Did it matter to you that things changed around you, or was change simply a part of who you were?

When we can let go of our stories, of who we *think* we are, we create an open space – a blank canvas – a stage on which to re-enter the world in a new and different way that better supports who we want to be. Our souls don't change, just the costumes we choose to wear.

Five Empowering Mindsets to Support You through Change

Ultimately, the way we experience change in our lives comes down to the way we *think*, what we choose to *believe*, and how we manage our *emotions* during the process of change.

So sit back and relax, clear your mind just for a moment, and take a personal journey with me, where you will discover the five empowering mindsets I use to process change in my life, and to help my clients do the same. These are not listed in any particular order, as there is no linear order to this process, and nor does there need to be.

Empowering Mindset #1: Surrender Control

*The only way to make sense out of change is to plunge
into it, move with it, and join the dance.*
– Alan Watts

When the brain enters into unknown territory and it doesn't know what is going to happen next, it automatically activates the flight-fight response and sends messages to the rest of the body to prepare to attack or get ready to run. This is the state of fear.

When fear arises, most of us panic as we feel something terrible is about to happen and we may no longer have control over our circumstances.

When change happens, we often do lose our reins of control. But this is essential and necessary and part of a purposeful and divine plan. There are *reasons* for why we experience change at various times in our lives, and it's important if we want to experience change powerfully that we *believe* those reasons are positive, and for our highest good. Yet many of us, I for one, have been guilty many times of doing this, of trying to hold on to the reins of life so tightly, believing that we can somehow prevent or delay a change from happening and avoid an unknown but feared outcome.

The challenge with this pathway, though, is that the tighter we hold on to the reins, the more difficult and painful our lives become. It's a lot like stepping out on a rainy day and wishing it were a blazing hot day. The desire to change what you cannot change will only leave you feeling helpless, depressed, angry, and frustrated. Have you heard of the serenity prayer? It's the one that goes: *God grant me the serenity to accept the things I cannot change, courage to the change the things I can, and the wisdom to know the difference.* We don't have the power to influence the weather, just like we don't always have the power to influence every circumstance of our lives. Some things are going to occur whether we like it or not and it's our choice how we choose to experience it. But where we *do* hold significant power is in how we choose to manage and respond to those circumstances through our thoughts, beliefs, emotions, and actions.

What thoughts we choose to entertain and focus on, what we choose to believe and perceive, and where we choose to direct our emotional energy are what determine the quality of our changing experiences and ultimately our lives. They also determine the degree of suffering we experience when change in our lives kicks in.

When uncontrollable and unforeseeable change takes place in my life, the first thing I like to do is stop, recognize the change that is taking place, and then become aware of what I do and don't have the power to influence. Where I do have power to influence, I act accordingly, and where I don't, I accept *without question* what I cannot change. How am I able to do this? Because I *believe* with every fibre of my being that all change beyond my control is for my highest good and is coming from a higher source much wiser and more aware than myself. This belief fuels positive and empowering thoughts in me like "This is happening for a reason I just can't see yet, or I don't need to see the reasons but they are necessary and positive." "This is for my highest good." "Even though I am uncertain of the outcome, I know I am being taken care of. I am loved and supported – I am safe."

Then, usually thoughts like these arise next as I start to feel pleasantly curious: "Something amazing is about to happen in my life!" "It's time for me to get excited!" "I can't wait to see what new doors are about to open!" I go from states of acceptance to states of excitement and a joyful curiosity. So, too, do my clients. It's wonderfully freeing and liberating.

Suggested Practice

Every day write down as many thoughts as you can that you are aware of. Circle the thoughts that fuel resistance and spark limiting emotions such as anger, fear, guilt, and shame as it relates to the changes you are experiencing. Write down new thoughts you could have that evoke positive feelings and actions.

Next, notice and journal your beliefs. Do your beliefs support or resist what's happening in your life? Do they empower you or disempower you? Do they lift you emotionally or pull you down? What do you believe about change? How does this belief influence you? What are you most afraid will happen as a result of this change? Where did this idea come from? How would things be different for you if you didn't have this fear and what would you be free to experience instead?

Empowering Mindset #2: Let Go

Be still, and know that I am God.
– Psalm 46:10

When I was in my twenties, I got sucked under a series of massive waves while swimming at a beach in Sydney, Australia. As I got tossed around in the blue water without any air for what felt like eternity, I had no choice but to surrender to the flow of the waves and simply wait until the time arrived when I would be able to stand back up and take a new breath.

My approach to change now is much the same. Resisting change is just as futile as trying to fight the waves would've been. There is a much larger force at work in our lives, and at times we just need to stop trying to control our lives and simply allow what is happening and let go. Like the dandelion, there is value is simply detaching and allowing ourselves to float. So when I see change looming on the horizon, approaching me at an alarming rate, or it suddenly overtakes me, I immediately relax my mind and quiet my thoughts. I know my thoughts could rage out of control, so by intentionally turning down the volume of my thoughts, this instantly quells my fears and any instinctive panic. I simply *choose* to let go of how I *expect* things should go, based on my impenetrable faith that I will once again stand strong and everything will be alright – in fact, it will be even better than it was before. *What we believe is what we'll experience.*

Just as the year cycles through the seasons of winter, spring, summer, and fall, our lives also experience seasons of change. I know without doubt that divine timing is at work in our lives, and even though some days I want to shake my fists at God and tear out my hair at what feels like an unacceptably uncomfortable, or inordinately inappropriate and unsatisfactory snail's pace manifestation of a new door opening, I also know in that deep, quiet, still, and peaceful place within me that the creator of the universe is much wiser than me and has a greater plan in store for me and you that will be revealed at a the appropriate time.

Suggested Practice

Every day, engage in the practice of meditation and prayer (if you pray). Practice quiet, stillness, surrender, and peacefulness. The goal of these practices is to quiet your mind, help you let go and allow truth and wisdom to manifest through you. Fear also gets released when we quiet our mind and connect with the oneness that's all around and within us. Mindfulness practices like prayer and meditation also reduce depression and anxiety, and instead fill us with a quiet knowing that everything is happening exactly as it's meant to and it will be OK.

Empowering Mindset #3: Release Emotion

All changes, even the most longed for, have their melancholy;
for what we leave behind us is a part of ourselves; we
must die to one life before we can enter another.
– Anatole France

In her pioneering book *On Death and Dying,* Swiss-American psychiatrist Elizabeth Kubler-Ross reveals the five stages of grief she witnessed in her work with terminally ill patients: denial, anger, bargaining, depression, and acceptance.

I've seen these same five stages at work when change occurs in my life and when I witness it in my clients. When clients resist emotionally expressing any one of these stages, their process of change gets delayed and becomes uncomfortable, if not unbearable. In my own life, I can attest to the importance of fully expressing the emotion of each of these five stages in order to emerge with joy and a greater level of awareness on the other side.

In 2008, my beautiful son was born. At that time I was married to a Canadian man and living in the United States, and so we decided we would relocate to Canada to raise our family. I applied for permanent residency and was granted six months in Canada while I waited for permanent status. However, six months came and went – and no confirmation of residency. My lawyers suggested I return with my son to the United States to wait possibly a few weeks, maybe more, for my status to be finalized. To make a long story short, two years went by before my son and I were reunited with his father. To say I experienced significant change in my life during those two years would be a massive understatement.

Because I didn't return to the place I had previously lived in the States – I didn't think I needed to, as I was only intending to stay a few weeks – I ended up bouncing around from a friend's house to a hotel and then finally to a small condo unit with my infant son, never knowing from one day to the next when I'd be able to plant roots again, let alone join my husband and build the family life I had envisioned. The life and career I had previously not only disappeared, but for two years I was unable to create anything new to replace it. It was terribly frustrating and disheartening at times. But it was one of those times when I had no power to influence anything different except how I chose to experience it. I simply went from day to day, doing the best I could to care for my little guy, whose destiny at the time was uncertain. And, boy, did I go through all of Elizabeth Kubler-Ross's five stages of grief.

When I drove across the border from Canada back to the United States, I was definitely in *denial* – likely because I had to keep myself from falling apart. I needed to stay strong for my child. I was basically driving into the unknown with a baby and no family or support around me. I recall praying like crazy as I drove the long distance from Vancouver back to Los Angeles.

By the time I reached my destination, I was definitely in the stage of *anger*. I remember having thoughts like *How could this be happening to me?* and *Why, when I did everything right* (referring to the immigration process), *should I have to endure this challenge?* These thoughts seemed to serve no purpose at all until I saw them for what they were – my anger was just masking my fear and sadness. My dreams and expectations were not manifesting as I had thought. I was experiencing the loss of these expectations.

For the next six months, I toppled back and forth between *bargaining* and even bouts of *depression*. Some days I could see the light at the end of the tunnel, and other days it seemed the tunnel had closed up and no light was present. But through it all, I never gave up the hope of reconnecting my family, and I prayed and I prayed and I prayed. I also let my feelings fly. I bawled my eyes out when I needed to, and I wrote down words of frustration when they arose. I grieved the loss of the life I'd had before, and I grieved the loss of the life I expected to have. The more I expressed and released my emotions as they arose, the quicker and easier it became to accept my circumstances and respect what I could not change. As soon I came to *accept* my circumstances, a space got cleared for a new life to emerge – one, by the way, that is far more fantastic than I could've possibly dreamed or imagined.

For the next eighteen months, my son and I spent every waking (and even sleeping) moment together before we were finally reunited with his father. As hard as those times might have been for me, they were also times of significant transformation that have shaped me in a way for which I will forever be grateful. The same will transpire for you, too, if you let it.

Empowering Practice

When your emotions arise, give yourself space to release them. Share your authentic feelings in the pages of a journal, with a trusted friend, with a family member, or with a professional, and recognize your choice about the thoughts you entertain.

I like to share my emotions directly with God. I will say things like, "God, today I just feel so sad and I thank you for being with me and helping me to release this feeling of sadness." Or "God, today I am feeling supremely frustrated and impatient!! Thank you for letting me vent my true feelings and for helping me to release these feelings so I can return to my natural states of peace, love, and serenity."

You can also listen to music that moves you emotionally or watch movies that help you release your feelings. I use all of these practices frequently and recommend them to my clients. Eventually you'll reach a place of acceptance about the change in your life, and from this place of acceptance, a new awareness will arise within you and you will see the new doorways life has in store for you begin to open.

Empowering Mindset #4: Express Gratitude

While I am certainly grateful in retrospect for that time with my son apart from his father now that I realize how significantly and positively it has transformed and shaped me and prepared me for the life I now experience, I practiced gratitude *during* my experience as well. Daily, I would thank God for the challenges I was experiencing. I believed and still believe without question that life presents us only with experiences and challenges we are capable of overcoming and that will produce positive results in our lives.

The challenges we face are really *opportunities in disguise*, which we need to experience to awaken our true potential, grow into our finest selves, and discover our true gifts and purpose.

During my time of change, I would thank God daily for the incredible strength and courage that allowed me to function as a mom, catching maybe one or two hours of sleep in a week in order to care for my child. My little guy very rarely slept, and on many occasions I can recall rocking him in my arms for sometimes more than sixty minutes, not once being able to put him down and not having slept myself for days.

To this day I am still in awe of my capabilities during those times. There is no doubt in my mind I was surrounded by a powerful and loving force as I underwent this significant time of challenge, transformation, and change. We are never left alone to bear change and challenge on our own. We are *always* being taken care of, loved, and supported. We just don't always realize it.

On the days I felt I could not stay awake when I needed to, or the frustration of my experience would get the better of me, I would start a list in my head of all the things I had to be grateful for. My health, my son, the health of my son, a roof over my head, my family, enough money to pay for the roof over my head, food, sunshine, quality time with my son, God as my source of comfort, the car I drove, air conditioning, my strength, my fortitude, my endless and unconditional love for my son, his smile, his sounds, the small pockets of time he did finally sleep, a fantastic lip gloss I had at the time (yup, even lip gloss made the list), and so on.

Gratitude helps us endure tremendous challenge and change, and empowers us to overcome significant hurdles regardless of how high they may appear before us. Gratitude also keeps us in a positive and encouraged frame of mind and spirit that in turn evokes positive action and behaviour. It reminds us how fortunate we really are to live this life, and what a miracle of beauty life is, even in the midst of challenge.

By the time I completed my gratitude list, I would feel like I was the luckiest person in the world and would believe the life that I'd had before would not be lost, but would in fact morph into something greater – which, of course, it absolutely has. My practice of gratitude was giving my spirit a cleansing shower, washing away all signs of negativity.

My clients who participate in a regular practice of gratitude also speak of the positivity it brings to their lives and how it greatly empowers them to remain in states of happiness and peace no matter what is being presented in their lives.

Empowering Practice

Every day, make a list of everything you have to be grateful for. Keep adding to your list and read it over and over until feelings of peace, love, and deep gratitude sink in. Be grateful for the little things in your life as well as the big things. Be grateful for your sight, your sense of taste, your body, your breath. Be grateful for it all, and note the joyful shift that arises within you.

Empowering Mindset #5: Get Excited!

Your living is determined not so much by what life brings to you
as the attitude you bring to life, not so much by what happens
to you, as by the way your mind looks at what happens.
– Khalil Gibran

I am currently working with a client who recently lost her job. Having loyally worked for twenty-one years with an organization that had felt like family to her, she was suddenly called into work one day and told, "We are letting you go." Naturally, at first my client was shocked. Then she was angry, then sad and devastated, but by the time we got together a few days later to discuss the event, her perspective on the situation had transformed.

"I'm no longer shocked or angry," she said. "In fact, I think it's quite possible I manifested this change at some level within myself without being totally aware of it. For the last few years my final thoughts before my head hit the pillow have been, *My career no longer fulfils me – not at the deeper level of what I really want in my life. Yet I don't know how to change my circumstances.*" She went on to say, "I believe this change has happened now because I realize I am ready. Although I'm scared at times and sometimes wonder how I will recreate the same income I once received and I don't know what's to come in my future, I also have this wave of childlike excitement and curiosity rippling through me, as I feel like I'm now free to choose and experience something new and wonderful – something perhaps I have always wanted to experience. I don't know what that wonderful thing is yet, but I am excited to find out."

Her perspective on her situation was so empowering for her that we spent the rest of our session together chatting about what she may want to do with her life in the future. What does she *value* in life? What *excites* her? What is she *drawn* to? What *matters* to her? What type of *legacy* does she want to leave? What sort of *impact* does she want to make in the world? What awakens a childlike curiosity and energy in her that causes her eyes to widen, her speech to quicken with joy, and her heart to beat just a little bit more quickly? What, when she visualizes herself doing it, ignites expansive feelings of love, joy, passion, purpose, and motivation? If she had a blank canvas and could start her life all again, where money was no object, fear was non-existent, and she could create a life according to what mattered most to her, what would that life look like?

By the time my client left our session she was grinning from ear to ear, and so was I! She hugged me like a gleeful child and her eyes sparkled like moist, radiant diamonds. "I'm so excited!" she squeaked. "I can't wait to see what my new life has to offer me!" Her smile was wide and she had a new lightness and youthfulness about her. I could see in that moment her body was filled with light, her heart had opened, and she was already stepping through unseen doorways and onto the pathway of her new life and destiny. At 53 years of age, my client had just been reborn! And you, my friend, through this change you are experiencing, you too are about to be reborn!

Empowering Practice

When change occurs, the first thing many of us do is to begin to focus on *what we feel we are losing or going lose*. But what if instead we shifted our focus to what we stand to gain and what we can create now as a result of what's being swept away?

In this practice, I invite you to put on your creativity hat and engage in the practice of creative and heartfelt expression. Using either a journal or a large piece of white card, use words and images to begin creating the life you want to experience. (You can draw, paint, or cut out pictures from magazines.) Before you begin this process I suggest you start with a meditation and set the intention to come at this practice from your heart-centre and not your head. Let whatever wisdom and truth that wants to naturally arise from within you find its way to either words on your page or journal or images. Begin to imagine that a new doorway is now opening up for you to step into an incredible and amazing new life. The life perhaps you've always wanted… What do you want to see and experience beyond that door? Who do you want to now know yourself as? What do you want to feel?

Allow Your Life to Unfold

> *You must take personal responsibility. You cannot change*
> *the circumstances, the seasons, or the wind, but you can*
> *change yourself. That is something you have charge of.*
> – Jim Rohn

Change is an inevitable part of life. It is one of the few things in life that won't change. Life is a constant ebb and flow of vibrating particles, molecules, and atoms. Spring, summer, autumn, and winter form a constant cycle of change, from birth to death to rebirth. The sun comes up, and the sun goes down. Flowers begin as tiny seeds and then sprout into physical and spectacular manifestations of colour and beauty for fleeting moments before they fade, wilt, and return to the dust. Babies are created and first live in a bubble of liquid – a few months later, they are rolling about on the floor, breathing the air, cooing, talking, pooping, and eating. Twenty years later they are driving a car and applying for a job. Nothing in life stays the same, nor is it supposed to.

To be honest, I could write an entire book about change, but it would only elaborate further on the essence of what's already been shared in this chapter. Change does not need to be scary or something you need to run from. Change is necessary and exciting, and it's what life is all about – experiencing, releasing, growing, discovering, applying, learning, loving, creating, and doing all of it all over again, each time perhaps a little wiser, more present, and hopefully with a lot more love, peace, grace, creativity, and compassion.

While you may not be able to see it clearly yet, in the midst of your current change, a grand plan and bigger picture for your life is rapidly unfolding for you. Don't be concerned if you cannot see the grander vision just yet – there's a reason for this, too. Just like a puzzle, we start with only pieces of the big picture until eventually the entire picture is revealed. You're being given an incredible opportunity to trust and have faith that everything will be revealed to you in a perfect time and place.

You do not need to control everything, my friend, nor do you need to feel afraid. Life will take care of you so long as you let it. All you need to do is have faith, trust, believe, and let go. Imagine you are floating on your back in the waves of the ocean. Simply relax, look up at the sky, and wait.

There is a magical, loving, and beautiful reason for why you are experiencing this change in your life, and I assure you it's not to punish or hurt you. It's to empower you to grow and discover what you are truly capable of. It's to awaken your tremendous, unique gifts and limitless potential inside you.

It's so you can become the person you most want to be.

It may be hard for an egg to turn into a bird: it would be a jolly sight harder for it to learn to fly while remaining an egg. We are like eggs at present. And you cannot go on indefinitely being just an ordinary, decent egg. We must be hatched or go bad.
– C. S. Lewis

Break The Rules. Find Your Freedom. Live Your Life.

Kasia Nalepa

A professional and business woman with an analytical mind and an artistic soul, Kasia is a person of integrity and a volcano of energy – a free spirit.

With an extensive educational background in business studies, she has pursued careers in auditing, consulting, banking, and advisory roles. She has run her own businesses in financial services and property investment. She is a strong believer in investment in tangible assets, such as precious metals, land, and property. Currently she has been developing her interest in diamond trade. She feels strongly about changing the financial industry for the better.

Kasia is a hypnotherapist certified by the National Guild of Hypnotists, Inc., the oldest and largest hypnosis organisation in the world, based in the USA. She is a member of several other hypnotherapy and complementary medicine associations in the UK. She has developed her own unique style, constantly seeking to improve her therapeutic practise by integrating a wide range of established and experimental techniques. She has been accumulating experience and knowledge in the pursuit of optimal wellness in herself and others by taking the holistic approach.

Kasia is also a master practitioner of transformational leadership, transformational coaching, next generation NLP, and a certified professional speaker.

Kasia loves travelling around the world and other adventures, art, antiques, nature, and water. She loves to mingle with like-minded people who do their best to make their dreams come true.

Her personal objective is to become financially free and to live the life of her dreams filled with purpose and meaning. She has a strong desire to leave a legacy for future generations.

Her destiny is to bring out the best in people and to change the world for the better.

Her ultimate goal is to write books and to speak from stages in order to inspire people around the world and to motivate them to transform their lives.

Originally from Poland, Kasia has travelled the world and for the past ten years she has been living in London. She envisions herself having a holistic retreat on the ocean side for mind, body, and soul.

"What I am going to talk to you about today is *freedom* – my freedom. What does freedom mean? Well, probably all different things to all of us. I am going to tell you two stories from my life describing my journey to freedom.

I come from a beautiful and mysterious part of Poland called Lower Silesia, a region full of castles, spas, and secret military installations, remains of World War II.

I am a child of the Solidarity movement. My first memory of political awareness comes from 13 December 1981, when I was a small child. That particular Sunday morning I was awaiting my favourite kids' TV programme, called 'Teleranek'. Imagine my disappointment, when I saw a man wearing funny glasses and the army uniform instead. I saw images of tanks on the streets on the television screen. It made me very upset. Of course I did not understand at that time that martial law had just started in Poland. It became clearer over the years what was going on, when my family used to gather and listen to the radio station called 'Radio Free Europe'.

You would think that my childhood and adolescence must have been difficult. Well, in a way… but not really. We were studying hard and playing hard. We used to study between eight and ten hours a day. I used to practice sports and athletics as well. But we were outdoors all the time. We were pretty rebellious. We spoke out our mind. What I remember from that time the most was constantly observing or participating in all kinds of demonstrations, strikes, or peaceful manifestations. Also going to the various live concerts and singing to the words of my favourite song: 'This is my piece of the floor. Don't you dare to tell me what to do.'

I have been always fascinated by the world we live in. I started to travel extensively during my university days, and I have been travelling since.

My first job was a position in a consulting company. For nearly three years I audited and took part in privatisation and restructuring of companies. I saw a negative face of a new capitalism, for instance wilfully dilapidated factories being sold to foreign 'investors' for next to nothing, and corruption. I didn't like it. That's why I left my job and started to travel.

Finally I settled in London, and seven years ago I started to work for a bank. Almost from the very beginning I noticed various acts of wrongdoing, and at times also mis-selling or bullying. As a former auditor I could not look at it. I also could not believe that such things were taking place in one of the longest established democracies in the world. I wanted to discuss it. I wanted to bring it to people's attention. I even used to approach certain individuals in question and ask them: 'Please don't do that. This is wrong!' Oh, my naivety! But I have never followed the crowd. I have always followed 'gut feeling', intuition, and my heart. That's for sure.

Over the years I went through all stages: from the very bottom to the very top. In 2009 I also wrote to the executives of the bank for the first time. My colleagues kept warning me: 'Kasia, stop it! You are risking your career. You put yourself in danger.' But I kept going as I could not turn a blind eye on wrongdoing. I have been in trouble all the time, but – even though only on a part-time basis – I am still there. I reckon I still cannot let go. I still hope that the bank is going to apologise to me and thank me for my commitment one day. Sometimes I am surprised how naive I could be at times as this is probably not going to happen.

On 21 December 2012, I wrote a long email to the new senior executives, in which I expressed at greater length what needs to be changed, how to change it, and my vision for the bank. 'I have been endeavouring to create an atmosphere in which both customers and colleagues are comfortable. By doing this I have been transparent in everything I do, treating customers and my colleagues fairly, always having their interest at the top of my agenda, always ensuring they are fully aware of what I am doing for them and of the consequences of my actions. I always strive to bring the best out of people. My goal is to see my vision being implemented throughout the whole bank.'

Well, everyone is saying that it's going to be the end of the world today, so let's just go for it, I joked to myself with encouragement.

Do I really agitate to break the rules no matter what? The answer is: *absolutely not.* I seek the judgement of a reasonable person. What actually happens? Most people keep their heads down; most people keep quiet because they are scared of losing their job, which may result in losing their home.

I have to admit that things are improving these days. Also, the problem is not about one bank. It is about all banks and financial institutions. It is about the financial industry as a whole, and it will take years to change the culture for the better. But there is a light at the end of a tunnel.

In August 2012, I woke up one day and asked myself this very weird direct question: *Kasia, what would you really like to do in your life?* All these strange answers started to come up out of the blue: hypnotherapy, energy healing, writing my books, speaking from the stages around the world, inspiring and transforming people's lives, having my holistic retreat on the ocean side. Well, I am well on my way. In 2013 I qualified as a Certified Consulting Hypnotherapist and also in Reiki energy healing. Due to the large number of letters I have produced over the years, I have material for several books. Public speaking? Well, this is a tricky one, but here I am. Freedom, sweet freedom. Ladies and gentlemen, what I want you to take away from my speech today is: Break the rules. Find your freedom. Live your life."

Just to let you know, dear friend, the text above has been taken from my 'Ice Breaker' speech, which I did on 15 October 2013.

Prior to that I was so scared of public speaking. And then I came across this absolutely incredible person, George, who I met at a birthday party in August 2013. At the beginning of the party I overheard this distinguished gentleman, talking to another person about coaching. I joined the conversation because I am deeply interested in personal development and changing people's lives for the better. We started to chat about hypnotherapy, about coaching, about helping others, and about public speaking. George told me the story of how he became a patient of Lionel Logue, the speech therapist to King George, made famous in *The King's Speech*. I told him that I am totally scared of public speaking. He started to laugh and told me that I must attend a Toastmasters Club meeting. George relocated outside of London shortly after, but I never would have started public speaking if not for his encouragement.

He invited me for the first meeting on 29 August 2013. The first thing I told him after saying *hello* was, *George, I'm so scared! Please make sure that nobody asks me any questions; anything at all!* I was dead serious, I was absolutely petrified, and felt intimidated after listening to such advanced speakers. I managed to introduce myself after all, but my heart was beating like crazy. Why I am not surprised the *fear* of *public speaking* is found to be a more pressing concern than *death*, according to a ranking of society's most pervasive *fears*?

Well, it was a very special day for me to say the least. Not only did I have a serious encounter with public speaking and professional public speakers, but it also just happened to be the seventh anniversary of my accident.

In the early afternoon, I headed to the Liberty department store, the place where seven years before I was almost killed by scaffolding. I spent some time just being there, taking photos, observing. I used to avoid that place in the past. When I went there for the first time the year before, I pretended that nothing happened, that it did not affect me in any way. I paid particular attention to Liberty's beautiful historic clock this time. Above the clock is an opening where St George can be seen on his white horse. He is wearing gold armour and is carrying a lance. To the right of St George is a dragon that has green wings and its head is tuned to face the saint with fire coming from its mouth. On the quarter hours St George chases the dragon. As the hour chimes, brave St George once more slays the dragon from his valiant steed. At 1 p.m., I started to film it. Imagine my shock when I noticed the words beneath the clock in gold lettering with a black background and the inscription: "No minute gone comes ever back again, take heed and see ye nothing do in vain." Tears came to my eyes. I sat on a pavement and cried, cried my eyes out. I grieved for the first time.

So that was all about... I thought to myself. I realized that subconsciously I was following this motto in my life, and that everything happened for a reason.

"Liberty: the condition of being free from restriction or control, the right and power to act, believe, or express oneself in a manner of one's own choosing. Freedom! Something everyone on the earth deserves no matter what race, religion, sex, or country!" These are only a few of many definitions of the word *liberty* according to various dictionaries. "If everything but *liberty* is lost, you are still rich." Wow...

So, my friend, that particular event is the quintessence of my *why*. Why it is so important to know your *why*? Because when you don't know your *why*, you are acting choosing or moving in one direction or another, there is no passion, reason, or purpose in your life! You often feel stuck, you procrastinate, and you get cluttered in your mind. You are running away from what you don't want... and you get more of it. On the contrary, when you do know your *why*, you are being pulled towards your goals by inspiration. You are in a flow. ("Where your thoughts go, your energy flows!") You are taking action because it feels right.

How has it all started, you may ask? Let me elaborate on it.

As I mentioned, I was almost killed by a falling scaffolding pole in front of the Liberty department store in central London on 29 August 2006. I was walking down Great Marlborough Street on a pavement and just passing by the three-story arched bridge over Kingly Street when it happened, just like that. I still don't understand how I survived, as it really felt like I was already on the other side. I turned my head up and I saw this huge metal pole right next to my left temple. I remember I thought to myself: *This is it.* The next thing I felt was someone pulling my head rapidly away. I felt the coldness of the metal pole falling down and scratching my back. I recall the sound of it hitting against the pavement. Everything was in slow motion, like watching a movie frame by frame. I will never forget the man who saved my life. He was a tourist from America. "Are you all right? Are you all right?" he kept asking with his American accent whilst touching my head and arms. I replied by nodding my head. I was in a state of shock and standing still. He made sure that I was OK and disappeared in exactly the same way as he appeared – unexpectedly.

I was upset for some time after experiencing firsthand "that you never know what's around the corner". Not much happened to me on a physical level, but this event had a major impact on my entire life. *Was I really supposed to die just like that without 'singing my song'? What is 'my song'? What is really life all about? What have I achieved in my life so far? Who I am and what is my purpose in life? Where I am heading and what I want to experience in my life? What kind of legacy I would like to leave?* I kept asking myself all these existential questions.

It made me realize how precious life is. I've thrown myself into a vortex of life. I've tried all these amazing and scary things, which I always wanted to experience but kept procrastinating in the past. I have travelled the world. For quite few years I was on holidays or short breaks literally once a month. I have followed my passions and interests. I have learnt how to follow my heart, how to 'plug in' to the universe, how to fulfil my dreams. I have been speaking out on what I feel strongly about according to the rule: "Feel the fear but do it anyway". I have paid lots of consequences and had to overcome many obstacles but got stronger and stronger and just kept going. I have challenged myself in all possible aspects of my life. You name it. I have done it all!

Life is just a sequence of events, one leading to another. *Everything happens for a reason.*

If not for the accident, I would have *never* applied for a job in a bank or any corporation. I was a successful entrepreneur in my own right for a long time before it happened, and I thought I had adventure in the corporate world behind me.

Digging deeper, if I hadn't worked inside of a bank for over seven years I wouldn't have had opportunity to see and experience in person what has been going on. I wouldn't be able to do my absolute best to improve it by speaking openly and writing about it. Without such knowledge I would never in a million years understand how to change the financial industry for the better. Also, I wouldn't have such strong purpose to grow as a human being.

My experiences remind me of the conversation between Agent Smith and Neo from *The Matrix* movie.

"Why, Mr Anderson? Why do you do it? Why get up? Why keep fighting? Do you believe you're fighting for something? For more than your survival? Can you tell me what it is? Do you even know? Is it freedom? Or truth? Perhaps peace? Yes? No? Could it be for love? Illusions, Mr Anderson. Vagaries of perception. The temporary constructs of a feeble human intellect trying desperately to justify an existence that is without meaning or purpose. And all of them as artificial as the Matrix itself, although only a human mind could invent something as insipid as love. You must be able to see it, Mr Anderson. You must know it by now. You can't win. It's pointless to keep fighting. Why, Mr Anderson? Why? Why do you persist?" Agent Smith kept asking Neo.

"Because I choose to." Neo replied.

I have been asked similar questions and told similar statements so many times: "Why do you keep doing it, Kasia? *Why?* You are in trouble all the time. Who do you think you are? You are not important, just an ordinary member of staff. You cannot win. We all know each other."

But I do what I do because I feel strongly about changing the financial industry for the better. *Because I choose to!* So I can finish what I have started, what I feel strongly about, and for what I have paid consequences. I am going to publish my letters and documents, but my intentions are pure. My work is *not* about naming and shaming. It is in

111

the public interest. It is about making sure that a real change in culture is achieved for the better, (and not just semantics) so situations like many customers, my colleagues, and I have gone through will never happen again. It is about me being actively involved in a transformational process and 'finishing the business' before my departure. Therefore I invite board management to participate in the closing chapter of my book, if they choose, demonstrating *real changes* and an improved applied culture for bank customers and staff.

I'm now paradoxically, grateful for all those difficult experiences as they took me well outside my 'comfort zone', resulting in tremendous personal growth. If not for the experiences I underwent, possibly, I wouldn't have spoken out so openly, most probably I wouldn't have written so much, and definitely I wouldn't have achieved as much as I have achieved in life. They prepared me for larger things, things on a much bigger scale, a worldwide scale.

If I hadn't talked to that great man Captain Lou in a corridor at one of the events in 2010, I wouldn't have decided to cruise exotic destinations with people doing all kind of business on the Internet, and I wouldn't have subsequently met the most amazing bunch of entrepreneurs from around the world, many of whom I am proud to call my friends.

Captain Lou lured me by saying: "Life is a vacation." Well, this is what I started to unknowingly implement in November 2006, by travelling a lot and fulfilling my dreams. But I was hesitating. Nobody I knew from the corporate world or any other world seemed to live this kind of lifestyle, so I thought I was just a dreamer and that it wouldn't work long-term. And then that man from America came out of the blue and told me that *this is possible*. Just like that.

If I hadn't followed my heart's call to open spaces with a red rucksack, I wouldn't have changed my plans and travelled across the States in November 2011, on the Amtrak trains. I wouldn't have seen the most beautiful scenery, which is otherwise skipped by tourists. I wouldn't have met amazing people who lead me from one destination to another and helped me to experience so many miracles. I wouldn't have personally witnessed the 'Occupy Wall Street' movement and observed violent confrontation between two opposite sides at Liberty Square in New York City. Furthermore, I wouldn't have understood that some serious ethical, spiritual, and moral 'rebirth' has to happen to people before it's too late, and I mean to everyone all over the world, without judging on what side of the 'barricade' they are on. But for my having witnessed the violent confrontation, my path most probably wouldn't have taken me to the United Nations headquarters. It's obvious I wouldn't have been thinking that I have to get myself involved in this 'rebirth' on some kind of decision-making level.

If I wasn't challenged so much, I wouldn't search for unconventional solutions. I wouldn't have read *Zero Limits* by Joe Vitale and I wouldn't practice ho'oponopono. I wouldn't study hypnotherapy and other complementary therapies or try holistic retreats. I wouldn't realize that I want to experience the best of both worlds, physical and spiritual, and that this does not contradict my relationship with God. Probably I wouldn't be interested in Sidra Jafri's eye- and soul-opening event *The Awakening* and the amazing journey, which helped me a lot in times of struggle. Most probably my path wouldn't have led me to many other great personal development experiences. I wouldn't swim so much and I wouldn't have listened to the *Pretender* by Foo Fighters hundreds of times, that's for sure.

Everything happens for a reason...

If it weren't for my beloved, amazing Mum, who has always encouraged me to follow my heart; and all the wonderful people who have touched my heart and my soul. Also the people that have challenged me; and those who have encouraged me in my endeavours to transform the system. I salute you all!

I have only one chapter in this incredible book. I am here to introduce myself to the world. Many of my letters are much longer. There are so many books within me.

I'm a proud Polish patriot, also a happy British national and a citizen of the world.

My friend, I became a certified hypnotherapist and energy healing practitioner in 2013. On 8 January 2014, I decided that I am ready to write a book about things that I feel strongly about. That's why I didn't hesitate when I got an email on the January 16 with an invitation to write this chapter, just a week from deciding to write a book until the email appeared. I write every day, but a published author is being born right in a front of your eyes. If I hadn't followed another heart's call to buy new surfing shoes in the middle of Winter, a chain of events leading me to Bali wouldn't have started. As a result 'I moved mountains' and experienced in September 2014, a month of incredible personal growth, in paradise on earth. This is how a transformational leader, coach and speaker was born. I follow my inspiration, I don't question it and true miracles happen in my life. Speaking on the stages around the world and holistic retreat on the ocean side – these pursuits are just a matter of time… a short time.

I'm a great believer in staying strong, fearless, and positive in life, especially because we live in challenging times. "Don't feel pressure, for pressure is what turns rough stones into diamonds", Mr Gerry, my diamond mentor told me on several occasions.

I've been reading and researching a lot in order to get answers and clarity in life. Bad things happen to us to make us realize our true potential, strength, will power, and heart, and to help us appreciate some amazing things that are otherwise taken for granted. Life is a true gift. Nothing in life is to be feared; it is only to be understood. Now is the time to understand more so that we may fear less. We are powerful beyond belief. If we only realized it...

The whole month of February 2014 I spent creating my mission statement and focusing on my purpose in life. Why it is so important to do that? Because without a *mission* for your *life*, you will probably just wander through *life* like Alice wandered through Wonderland, uncertain of your *purpose*. After you have your mission, decisions become much clearer. Your mission is an internal process and needs to come from the core of who you are. A *personal mission statement* is a written-down reason for being and the key to finding your path in life.

I adjusted and personalized this amazing formula of Edgar Cayce as follows:

Step 1: What is your spiritual ideal? In your peak spiritual moments, what have you recognised to be the highest truth about yourself and about life? This ideal is not strictly your mission in life, but rather describes a place within yourself – a state of consciousness – from which that mission may be directed.

Explanation to Step 1

The highest truth about myself is: *truth-seeker*.

I have been, by nature, a truth-*seeker* and a truth-*speaker*. I have sought to find a truth (my truth) for myself, my entire life. My desire has always been to scratch the surface and dig deeper. I define a truth-seeker as one who approaches life with fascination, curiosity, and awe; one who refuses to accept any pre-packaged information without thoroughly and personally investigating it. The easiest explanation of a truth I can possibly give you is this: Truth feels light. Untruth feels heavy. As simple as that. The most beautiful description I have found is: "The truest mark of a seeker is the ability to approach life with the open-mindedness of a child."

My highest truth about life is: *freedom* in its broadest sense, choice, speech, and ultimate lifestyle.

I literally see the word *freedom* everywhere. "'Cause I'm as free as a bird now, and this bird you never change, and the bird you cannot change, and this bird you cannot change. (…) Won't you fly, free bird, yeah." These words are taken from *Free Bird* by Lynyrd Skynyrd. I love this song so much; it touches my soul. The lyrics are just incredible and the solo simply sends chills down the spine. It's just a song that takes you from being sad to happy to dancing wild. It tells you that no matter what, life goes on. If you face any challenges, just listen to it and they will go away, at least for a while.

Step 2: What are your key talents, abilities, skills, and strengths? By taking a quick inventory of your aptitudes and past successes, you can probably come up with a list that is perfectly adequate for this step. Remember, we are our own severest critics. Why, for a change, shouldn't we focus on the positives only? The ingredients of both 'darkness' and 'light' are equally present in all of us, and then it is up to each individual to decide what will be brought forth – the virtues or the malevolence. Nobody's perfect, but when you focus on your bright side, there is no much room for the 'darkness'.

Explanation to Step 2

You can also ask people to help you establish your strongest points. I did this myself, and this is what my friends and loved ones came up with: compassion, intuition, integrity, determination, ability to raise spirits and increase morale, courageous, influential, motivational, teacher, intelligent and can apply, energetic, proactive, excellent communicator, positive-minded, funny.

Margaret's description of me: "Kasia has presence, style, is unique (does not follow the crowd), has elegance, speaks eloquently, and stands out. Kasia has courage and compassion with inner determination. Once she sets her goal, she will pull out all stops to achieve it. She is precise and will always follow the rules, works hard, and sets high standards. Can be formidable when necessary and is not put off by any kind of pressure when it is not appropriate. She always sticks to her guns. Kasia's inner determination and compassion also bring out empathy. She is quick to understand another person's feelings, particularly if they are anxious about something, and she will do all she can to help. She has natural instincts and demonstrates her empathy from her heart. If Kasia helps, it is always genuine. In essence, Kasia is a forthright and determined person and aims to lead by example. Her compassion and empathy make her loyal. Always practical and uses her own instincts re other people's emotions and pain."

Ambia's description of me: "Your no s**t, no b**s**t approach is highly commendable. Great respect for your focus in adhering to your moral and ethical principles as it's a portrayal of the soundness of your character which, needless to say, is beyond skin deep. I love your transparency in life in general and I truly believe it is one of your main strengths, as it complements your great integrity. The ability to make one genuinely smile is a rare ability… and you do that effortlessly with your kind nature and cheerful demeanour. I love your ability to truly *listen* and not just hear. It makes others feel valued and important. Making others feel that isn't a reflection of them but is a reflection of you and your giving nature. Sometimes the best thing you can give someone is an open mind and heart and a listening ear. Multiple talents, excellent communicator, proactive approach, energetic."

Eamonn, another bank colleague, once wrote me: "Kasia, you have a sort of personality which touches people's lives and makes them better for having known you. All the best."

So many people support my actions. Some don't, and I am fine with that, at last. "He who pleased everybody died before he was born." So you, dear friend, get over the fear of being judged, the sooner the better.

Step 3: What words capture the essence of your mission? A short, thematic summary of your soul's purpose will help you implement what you were born to do.

Explanation to Step 3

My mission is: *to free imprisoned souls.*

"Most men lead lives of quiet desperation and go to the grave with the song still in them." (Henry David Thoreau)

In this context, living a life of 'quiet desperation' means the feeling people get from simply going on with life and doing what is expected of them in order to fit in and pay the bills, without even exploring what it is they truly want out of life. They know there is something wrong, but they are too polite to complain and too busy to think about it much. A silent hopelessness, a feeling of despair, but going on with life, never letting on that they are feeling it. Many people slumber through most of their lives. They live on auto-pilot. They keep busy so they don't have to think too much. They ignore who they are. They forget what their dreams were if they ever knew. Quiet desperation blends into the background. It doesn't call attention to itself, but you see it everywhere, such as when looking at the faces of commuters racing to catch the next train.

"Billions of people just living out their lives, oblivious." (Agent Smith, *The Matrix*)

Why do people lead lives of quiet desperation? Because as bleak as it is, it's still easier than the alternative: a life of noisy hope! A life where you dare to go after your dreams even if you fail. Even when you fail again and again and again. A life where you don't quite 'fit in' to society's norms. A life that people will call eccentric or bizarre. A life filled with successes and failures, joys and despairs. A life fully lived.

What can you do about it? Wake up! Who are you? What do you really want? What does your life mean? Are you doing the things you do because it's what you chose, or did your life choose you and you just let it happen? Are you just conforming to a society that tells you, you must have and do these things? Are you living or just existing?

"Death isn't sad. The sad thing is that most people don't live at all." (*Peaceful Warrior*)

Remember, dear friend: "You must be the change you want to see in the World", as Ghandi used to say.

Does it really matter for little me to change the world when so many people do not?, you may ask yourself. The answer is: *yes, absolutely!*

When you follow your path, the sky is the limit. In such a context does it really matter that you may struggle during the process? Recently I came to this incredible conclusion that it really doesn't matter to me in the long run. Hallelujah! Does it really matter in the eyes of eternity? No! This is just a learning curve. I will continue until I have done what I came to do because I am in control of my life, not anybody else!

Furthermore, I realised that I used to struggle or pay consequences, and it affected me because that was my limited belief. Because I was conditioned this way, I was told by everyone I know that this is the only way it has to be when you choose to follow your path. "Be careful. They will make your life difficult. They may destroy you", my friends and loved ones kept repeating to me worryingly.

One of the biggest realisations of 2014 was: "Life is a choice. You can choose to be a victim or anything else you would like to be." (*Peaceful Warrior*) How refreshing!

On a beautiful sunny Sunday, March 9, 2014, I sat on a bench in Hyde Park in London, randomly opened the book *The Awakening Course* by Joe Vitale, and this is what caught my attention: "If you ever struggled in life, I have a good news for you. Your fight has come to an end."

"Oh my God, thank you!" I looked at the sky with gratitude. For many years I acted from the position of feeling the fear but doing it anyway. Now I can genuinely say that I have tamed the fear. My intentions are pure and when they stay this way I have *nothing* to worry about. Such a blissful realization!

I have also learnt that although I am passionate, feel strongly about certain things, and have pure intentions, I still need to keep improving my methods of action. To quote Albert Einstein, one of the most inspiring people in history: "Insanity is doing the same things over and over again but expecting different results."

There is no *me*, there is no *them*. We are all the same. Teaching with love, respect, and compassion, creates a win-win *outcome* where everyone comes away satisfied. This is what I want to focus on. What unites all of us is greater than what divides us; this is the way I choose to think. I would love to see others learning this lesson thought by Einstein as well.

Taking the experiences I have gone through into consideration, I really struggled with the idea of forgiving and letting go for a long time. After reading and being reminded quite few times of *The Little Soul and the Sun* story from the book *Conversation with God* by Neale Donald Walsh with its motto "Always remember, I have sent you nothing but angels", I struggled with accepting the idea even more. However, what if it was all true? What if...

"Follow your heart and look to your deepest instincts. Act with generosity; remember not all men are fools, and that only God knows the perfect truth. Be steadfast in your beliefs, but temper them with wise counsel", my friend Nicholas advised me when I encountered him for the first time that I am going to write books.

So here I am. I offer to shake hands in reconciliation and friendship.

Just to finish on this subject: "Many people, especially ignorant people, want to punish you for speaking the truth. For being correct. For being you. Never apologize for being correct or for being ahead of your time. If you are right and you know it, speak your mind. Speak your mind.

Even if you are a minority of one, the truth is still the truth." This is what Ghandi, another of the most inspiring persons of all times said.

So if you really feel from the very depth of your heart that you are right, speak your mind. Speak your mind! This may have unpleasant consequences, but when you keep your mind open, your heart open, and you do what you know to be a right thing, all these mental and emotional states such as stress, fear, and worry will not affect you long-term.

Is it going to happen immediately? The answer is: *No*. I have been there. I have done it all. It is a struggle and hard work.

Ghandi also said: "*First they* ignore you, then they *laugh at you*, then they fight you, then you win." You have to practice day in and day out. What you create now will materialize in the future. You are a summary of past experiences and decisions you have made. However I can promise you with a hand on my heart; when you are truly aligned with your destiny, with your purpose in life, with your *why*, everything will come together and you will know you are on the right path. I certainly know I am.

Dear friend, everything in life is a choice. Every single decision you make in life is *your* choice. "This is your chance. You take the blue pill – the story ends, you wake up in your bed and believe whatever you want to believe. You take the red pill – you stay in Wonderland and I show you how deep the rabbit-hole goes." (Morpheus, *The Matrix*)

In such context, the red pill and its opposite, the blue pill, are symbols representing the choice between embracing the sometimes painful truth of reality (red pill) and the blissful ignorance of illusion (blue pill).

Paraphrasing Morpheus: "I'm trying to free your mind. But I can only show you the door. You're the one that has to walk through it."

I'm doing my best to help you to free your soul in the best way I possibly can, the way I have successfully used for myself and for many other people, but the decision is yours. Whatever you decide to do, whether with me or without me, please do something! It's important that you take responsibility for your life; *this is your life after all!*

Have you noticed that there is always one person involved in all your life's affairs? It's *you!* You have a choice, you can do everything to change your life for the better (nobody will do it for you) or… you can choose to stay where you are. However, please remember what T. Harv Eker says: "How you do anything is how you do everything."

In early January 2014, I watched a great movie called *Peaceful Warrior*. This is a story of how a man named Dan Millman, a gymnast, became a warrior. It shows many ways that a person can change life for the better. It shows how love is the main and most important aspect of life, also, how everything happens for a reason, whether it's good or it's bad.

Dan: "There is nothing going on."

Sokrates: "There is never nothing going on. Take out the trash, Dan. The trash is anything that is keeping you from the only thing that matters. This moment. Here. Now. And when you truly are in the here and now, you will be amazed at what you can do and how well you can do it."

Where are you? Here. What time is it? Now. What are you? This moment.

I used this technique for the first time during a very important meeting on January 29, 2014, which happened to be the seventh anniversary of my employment at the bank. What happened to me was so extremely profound and powerful. I felt so calm, focused, and absolutely clear about what I am doing and where I am heading, like never before in my entire life. The only way I can possibly describe it in a few words is what I put in my diary: "The Phoenix has just risen from the ashes."

So, dear friend. Live your life to the fullest by just enjoying and being grateful for what you have, not lusting for the rich man's gold. Follow your heart and inspiration, find your *why* and purpose in life, and follow your path because it is true: all that you need is in your soul. Remember, without your soul you are only flesh and bones.

Break the rules! Find your freedom! Live your life! Live an amazing, epic, meaningful, fulfilled, and extraordinary life for your own benefit and for the benefit of others. And don't forget to have lots of fun!

With love,

Kasia Nalepa

New Country: New Life

Lourdes Katague

Lourdes has a graduate certificate in e-business from Box Hill Institute of Technology, Victoria, Australia, a graduate diploma in library and information management from Charles Sturt University, Australia, and a bachelor of education with a major in social studies from the University of the Philippines.

She is a certified master practitioner of transformational leadership, transformational coaching, next generation NLP, and Ericksonian hypnosis, and a certified professional speaker.

She has been trained by personal development and lifestyle masters including Anthony Robbins, Tom McCarthy, Zig Ziglar, Jim Rohn, and Chris Howard, as well as being, personally mentored by Chris Howard (bestselling author, entrepreneur and CEO of Rock House Global), entrepreneur Calvin Coyles, bestselling author Keith Blakemore-Noble, and financial master Leon van Kraayenburg, all of whom have helped her to build her own coaching business.

She is the founder of http://www.migrantempowrment.com, specialising in transforming lives of professional migrant women to express their greatness wherever they are living.

Lourdes's achievements include being nominated outstanding alumna of the University of the Philippines Alumni Association of Australia, New South Wales Branch, education and training category (100 years of Founding University of the Philippines).

With over thirty years experience as a librarian in Australia and overseas, Lourdes has trained and presented information literacy to thousands of university students and academic staff at the University of Western Sydney in disciplines of environment and agriculture, animal science, applied sciences, nursing, biomedical science, computing, engineering, and mathematics. She has presented to international clients from India, Lebanon, China, and the Philippines.

She is married to Efren Katague, with whom she has raised four children, and she is graced with two granddaughters.

———————

P eople migrate to another country for a variety of reasons. For some the move brings new opportunities. For others it is improved living conditions or preferred lifestyle. This chapter outlines the journeys undertaken by a number of women, predominantly from Asia. Many of the women in this story have gone the extra mile to get where they are today in their new country. Each story is unique to individuals with common themes of furthering education, training, or building a business to expand the possibilities available to them, and prove themselves and the skills they bring to their new country. I hope that the stories serve to inspire and motivate others to do the best they can, to persevere when they encounter difficulties, and to seek the help of coaches or mentors to assist them to achieve what they want in life.

Why do people immigrate?

The reasons people immigrate range from the desire to improve their financial status, personal development, marriage, family reunion, better lifestyle, or to seek other opportunities only available in the new adopted country.

Immigrating to another country is an enormous undertaking, bringing both positive and negative outcomes and challenges such as upheavals and changes in ways of living and working. Furthermore, motivating factors for emigration can be as important as making the move (Reasons for immigration, 2014).

Migration poses a big challenge to an individual and that person's family. There are feelings of estrangement, disruption, and dislocation in the new country of residence. The following are considered objective measures of settlement in the new country: outcomes in labour market, ability to match qualifications with a job, income measures, home ownership, or rate of improvement in English proficiency (Khoo and McDonald 2001).

According to the International Organization for Immigration (IOM) in the year 2011, almost half of the 214 million international migrants in today's world are women. Skilled professional migrant women experience undue challenges in obtaining appropriate jobs matching their level of education and professional experience after settling in the new country. Issues pertaining to the recognition of foreign credentials as well as labour market dynamics often result in working in low-skilled occupations. The IOM calls this "global phenomenon as downward occupational mobility, underemployment or deskilling" (IOM 2011).

The Australian Bureau of Statistics (1996) found that 65 per cent of migrants who arrived with post-school qualifications in the 1970s had better opportunities for qualifications recognized as compared to 58 per cent of those who arrived in the early 1990s. Migrants who arrived with post-school qualifications and who were born in the main English-speaking countries were more likely than those born in other countries to have their qualifications recognised (73 per cent as compared to 49 per cent). This was particularly so in the fields of teaching and education (81 per cent as compared to 32 per cent) and health and medicine (83 per cent as compared to 49 per cent). Formal recognition of overseas qualifications does not guarantee success in the labour market. Other barriers to employment may exist, such as lack of local work experience.

Periera (2011) noted that there are roadblocks to professional migrants fitting in the workplace and there are Asian Business leaders who formed together to offer solutions through their personal experiences. It was agreed that to overcome anxieties it is more important to concentrate on commonalities and find a mentor at work. It was also suggested that migrants focus on relationships, not just on the quality of their work. And that is the key to getting noticed.

There are five principles to guide migrant women to achieve their dreams in the new homeland. This chapter focuses on two as outlined below:

Career and money: find strategies to enable you to achieve your goals. Be determined to do whatever it takes to live the life you truly dream of. Take charge of your own education. Seek out mentors, and network to learn about your industry and expand the possibilities available to you. Look for ways you can sell your past experience and possibly language skills to local employers.

Mentors and coaches: get a coach or mentor, either professional or in the workplace, to help and guide you. Hire someone who will provide knowledge and tools to help achieve your goals guide and support you along the way. An effective coach helps you implement those new skills and celebrate your dream.

Here are some great stories of success from women who have faced the challenges mentioned above. They overcame adversities and challenges by taking responsibilities for their own lives, success, and outcomes; and they achieved rewarding professional and personal goals. I begin with my own story. Some stories contain fictitious names to protect their privacy.

– Lourdes Katague

Living in a third world country with teacher parents and four siblings was a matter of making both ends meet and surviving on the bare essentials of life. At five years old, I dreamed of a richer life and of marrying a rich man so that my children could live a better life in America. I had no idea of America or its location, except that Martin Jones, the Peace Corp volunteer who resided in our house, was from America. At that age, that was goal-setting in action. Since my parents often had work assignments away from home, I had many opportunities to talk to other people who were impressed with my speaking skills. One of these was Senator Ganzon, with whom I conversed in English. My teacher father was not impressed and called me very talkative.

My grandparents were very generous and gave me freedom to be a child, and at the same time provided opportunities to learn how to work. Grandfather opened Lourdes Store, and on the first day my enthusiasm was over the top, with me standing on a chair the whole day looking after the customers. At seven years of age I could hardly open the canister of cookies and bread, but I persisted and gave the correct change for the payments. I made it all happen. My grade one teacher was unimpressed with my absences on Thursdays. That was market day, when Grandpa and I replenished the stocks of bread, candies, sugar, and salt. That was my initiation to entrepreneurship.

Then I got married at an early age. We were independent from the start and had enough cash to live by as I went to college. It is important to emphasise that our drive to succeed attracted opportunities we wanted in life. My husband worked in McCangret Corporation and commenced communication with Keith Bainbridge, the managing director of Solarex Pty. Ltd. in Australia. He convinced Keith that he was the best person to represent the organization in Southeast Asia, and he did so for six years. When the Southeast Asian solar energy market depleted, he requested relocation to Australia. The company sponsored our family to migrate to Australia. Before moving to Australia in 1986, we visited in 1984 and surveyed our future homeland. It was a beautiful place to live, very clean, and their English was different from my American book-learned English. Then came realization of a looming challenge ahead in the employment sphere.

Before migrating to Australia, I was a special librarian in the Philippines at the office of the president of the Philippines. It was a good job back then. Relocation entails massive preparation and knowledge of the new environment. In grade four I had paired up with Rebecca, my blind classmate, to study Australia, and at university had opted to work on a project on Australian libraries. Therefore, ideas abound in relation to the future country of residence. Whilst at university in the 1980s, the University of the Philippines Institute of Library Science was not yet computerised, and resources were printed books. The book about Australian libraries became a very useful resource. When we arrived in

Australia, it was eye-opening to see computerised libraries, which were read only in the library science course.

Arriving in Australia was just the beginning. After finding a place to live and beginning the job search, reality set in. It was very encouraging to see numerous job advertisements relating to libraries and librarianship. Checking with the Australian Library and Information Association (ALIA), the certifying body for librarianship led to the discovery that Philippine qualification was only the equivalent of an assistant library technician in Australia. I sent out numerous applications but received no interviews. After another set of applications I got one interview. The interview process was memorable. In order to look presentable, I used Philippine-made shoes brought from home. Walking one kilometre in those led to a night of agonizing pain from blisters. Two days later, I received a phone call from the librarian informing me of my unsuccessful application. She went on to say that due to my husband's employment, the family was not desperate for the mother to have a job at the same time. The reason did not deter my determination to find a job, because in the home country, mothers work, too. After spending one year of unsuccessful job-hunting, enrolment in distance education was the next option. Continuing education, along with raising a family of four young children, was a zealous venture of total dedication to an immigrant woman without a network of family and friends for support. My husband worked at Cumberland of Health Sciences in Sydney and became a library patron. He befriended the senior librarian who then enquired about Efren's wife. Efren responded that his wife was a jobless librarian and studying at university. Stephen generously called at home and encouraged me to attend further interviews, explaining the necessity of more practice leading to skill improvement. The key lesson for a new migrant is to attend more interviews to constantly develop it and become confident in the process. Do not rely on applying for advertised positions. Network within your industry to learn about the hidden job market.

Shortly after, a position came up and I applied again. There was an interview, and Stephen headed the panel. For the first time in two years, a casual part-time employment was available in the library field. The part-time job led to full-time work in another educational institution, the New South Wales Technical and Further Education (NSW TAFE) Library Services. Full-time employment for a mother of three children under ten years old entailed enormous childcare fees. Receiving the salary at the end of a fortnight and having to pay childcare expenses meant exhaustion without any savings after all. The main reason for working was to gain local experience needed to work in Australia, and in order to purchase a house. We decided to purchase a house close to primary school, TAFE, and university to facilitate travelling when working. Following the purchase of our home, which was in close proximity to the University of Western Sydney, a local advertisement appeared for an eligibility list for casual assistant library technicians. Again this was a successful application, which resulted in four nights work for forty weeks a year.

This was a perfect combination for a working mother with four young children and studying distance education. My study times were between 10:00 p.m. and 12:00 a.m., and it was necessary to complete the course within ten years. Otherwise it lapsed and would require repeating the course. This strategy required full dedication and focus.

Challenges presented in life, and resilience was a friendly virtue when one of my children got ill. My belief in myself aided my survival and kept my sanity intact. Resourcefulness as a librarian was the number one skill that led the way to locating all the help and services available for her recovery. As the child recovered, my energy needed replenishment, leading to the shopping centre that landed at Bookworld bookshop. At the counter was a brochure about Anthony Robbins, arriving in Sydney for Unleash the Power Within, which was very compelling. I took the brochure home and called the agent, Mel. His friendliness opened curiosity about the seminar. And in 1998 I had my first exposure to personal development. It was the beginning of learning from personalities like Anthony Robbins, Brian Tracy, Jim Rohn, Zig Ziglar, Tom Hopkins, Deepak Chopra, Robert Kiyosaki, Tom McCarthy, Joseph McClendon III, and Christopher Howard, to name a few.

In 2001 I was successful in gaining a professional library position at the University of Western Sydney Library as a liaison librarian. The job is great. Moving forward in my career validated the fact that there is no future and career advancement as evidenced by the number of unsuccessful applications through twelve years. Working your way up the ladder is no longer an effective strategy to success.

As I developed new talents and skills and discovered individual gifts, the time came to put these new resources into practice. My self-discovery allowed me to start doing something that I love and am passionate about, which is helping other women achieve their dreams, create better outcomes in their lives and families, and make a difference in the world.

To make the dream a reality, I enrolled in a course, Million Dollar Mastermind, with Rock House Global, where Christopher Howard and his team assisted in building http://www.migrantempowerment.com. The vision of http://www.migrantempowerment.com is to empower migrant professional women to lead happy and fulfilled lives in their new country through education and coaching. Its mission is to provide migrant women with the tools, knowledge, skills, and strategies to pursue leadership in mind, body, and spirit, and to assist them to follow the life of abundance they have always dreamed of in their adopted homeland. This also led to my contribution to this book. My story is one of the stories of how migrant women turn adversities into opportunities in their adopted homeland. My battles for many years to recreate myself are gifts to all of you. Reinventing the wheel is a waste of time, energy, and resources from women and their families. Save time, energy, and all your resources by learning the lessons here from all of us. Learn lessons from the stories and apply them to your success blueprint to play a much better game without the pain. Some storytellers used pseudonyms to protect their privacy.

Accountants and Engineers Working in
a Male-Dominated Profession

Carla Velez (accountant)

In the Philippines, Carla was a university professor at the University of the Philippines, Baguio, with PhD in accountancy. As an accountant, numbers are her specialty and she is always on the lookout for profitability in both life and work. Comparing future income between the Philippines and New Zealand, she decided the latter would be the better option.

She decided that the best way to determine the suitability of the country to migrate to was to go and visit. Carla travelled to New Zealand and stayed with the a friend's sister and then proceeded to find a job in a place where she knew no one except for a Catholic priest, who assisted her in finding local accommodation. For her, it was logical to apply for an accounting job, which was similar to her current experience. Accounting principles were not the main problem, as they are similar to her country of origin. The main issue was the taxation laws of New Zealand, which she needed to learn quickly before the interview in three days. She purchased taxation books to update her knowledge within a short span of time. During the interview there was a test on solving cases under the scrutiny of the panel. She performed well and landed the job. The work entailed talking directly to clients while her conversations were monitored, with clients ranging from farmers to musicians. It was a distressing six months experience adjusting to the new environment. She was allocated clients other staff would not attend to, but did it so well that clients sought her out for service.

Learning slang and local accents of clients was imperative for effective communication. It was vitally important to understand clients to gain acceptance, confidence, and trust. Adapting to the new culture entailed observing people's behaviour. Carla made adjustments to facilitate assimilation to the office's way of life. She noted the importance of adhering to office culture. She was not stopping for breaks, but office mates didn't welcome this gesture. A break is a break. It was a lesson learned that to be accepted in the workplace, abiding to breaks in the workplace was imperative.

Together with another migrant woman, they shared an unfurnished apartment and acquired a television set as first property while sitting on the floor without furniture.

To move up in the profession and qualify as a CPA in New Zealand, further knowledge was a requirement. Carla studied New Zealand taxation to equip herself for local practice.

As years passed, it was time to change job. Carla worked with the Electricity Corporation of New Zealand as a training management accountant with main responsibility of providing training to non-accountants who are engineers in the field. It was testing time again to determine her English language competency and proficiency to find out whether trainees understand the trainer. This job called for travel all over New Zealand in a small six-seater plane amongst men. Additionally, she had to drive rental cars and navigate unknown territories. It also required working with engineers in both the thermal and hydroelectric industries throughout the country. Now, Carla was an Asian female teaching male engineers, and produced the *Big Book on Training*. Because of her impressive performance, she was offered a job in the role of management accountant.

After nine years in New Zealand, Carla spent holidays in Australia and remained there. She works as a management accountant in local councils. While there she was offered scholarship to study towards a postgraduate diploma in management of local government.

At present, she enjoys travelling the world and going home to the Philippines to visit relatives every year.

Edith Ardiente (engineer)

Edith Ardiente was born in the Iloilo, Philippines to farmer parents. There were eight children in the family with four girls and four boys. She graduated as a chemical engineer, magna cum laude from the University of San Agustin in 1966.

As a young graduate in 1970, she ventured to migrate to the United States as professional immigrant, third preference. Arriving in the US with the few dollars in the pocket, she was hopeful to get a job, although disappointment sank in after she sent job applications to big corporations and failed to get interviews. Looking back, Edith realized she was a victim of intense discrimination as a short Asian woman and an engineer in a man's world. Her spoken English was such that when people heard her for the first time they didn't understand it. She encountered lots of barriers in seeking employment, such as the employer unwilling to send her to clients due to concerns that she was an Asian woman who didn't know about engineering like Americans did. Edith argued that the curriculum at the University of San Agustin was similar to that of the Massachusetts Institute of Technology (MIT) and used similar books. The employers did not believe it (Ardiente 2009).

Her frustration led her to complete a masters degree in environmental engineering to convince employers of her ability to deal with local businesses. To start employment, she accepted work as a secretary, even though the salary was a quarter of an engineer's pay. After receiving American citizenship, she worked with the Environmental Protection Agency (EPA).

Edith passed all the challenges and hurdles of proving herself to employers and began achieving her dreams in the new country.

Edith became one of the 100 most influential Filipino women in America as vice-president of environmental and energy affairs at Navistar International Corporation, also well-known as International Harvester (Ardiente, 2010).

Edith Ardiente, staff vice-president of environmental affairs, became president-elect of the Air and Waste Management Association (AWMA) in 2004 and in 2005 served as president of AWMA, which is a non-profit, non-partisan professional organization that provides training, information, and networking opportunities to 9,000 environmental professionals in sixty-five countries (Zoom 2014).

Edith received other honours such as the Milestone Makers Award for excellence in a chosen field and excellence in leadership by the Asian American Institute Awards on 10 June 2004, at the Mid-America Club.

She is now retired from Navistar after twenty-three years of service and loves travelling the world with her husband, Nestor.

Marie Barretto (engineer)

Marie relates her story:

When I left the Philippines to migrate to Australia thirty-three years ago, I thought I would be able to continue my career as a project cost control engineer in construction. Before leaving Philippines, I was an appraiser for Development Bank of the Philippines (DBP), responsible for mass housing projects and development for land subdivision.

Within four or five weeks of my arrival in Sydney on 31 December 1980, I found my first job relating to my qualification. However, before that I had an interview with a project manager of John Holland Construction Company that constructed the Sydney Entertainment Centre at the time. I applied for a project cost control engineering job because this site was qualified for the position, but they advised me that unfortunately there were no female toilet facilities at the site. I felt discriminated against because regardless whether they have a female employee, they should have provided a female toilet facility within the site.

Thereafter, I was lucky to have an interview with Standards Australia, which is responsible for selling and preparing Australian standards for different products and services. The group manager who hired me investigated my professional qualification and experiences through my referees from companies that I worked for in the Philippines, namely Development Bank of the Philippines (DBP) and Construction and Development Corporation of the Philippines (CDCP). I worked for Standards Australia as an executive officer, a civil engineer for seven and a half years, and was responsible for several Australian standards and guidelines for civil engineering and construction materials. While I was working with Standards Australia, I applied for corporate membership with Engineers Australia. Currently I am a member of the Civil College and registered as a chartered professional engineer (CPEng) and with National Professional Engineers Register (NPER).

Following my employment with Standards Australia, I thought of moving my career in local government mainly for family reasons. I used to travel a lot within Australia for meetings regarding my projects with Standards Australia. I decided to move into government jobs and started my local government career with Sydney City Council in 1988 as a professional engineer in the traffic engineering section. Since then, I worked for two other local government agencies (Fairfield City Council for six and a half years and Penrith City Council for almost eleven years). Currently I have been with Parramatta City Council for seven and a half years. Although my job is quite stressful, I enjoy working in local government and meeting developers and consultants, especially in my line of expertise, traffic and transport engineering. In the near future, upon my retirement, God willing, I intend to do some consultancy work in traffic engineering.

Lifestyle Moves

Julie Williamson (IT specialist)

Julie hailed from the English-speaking country of New Zealand and demonstrated a good understanding of what was involved in emigrating to another country and adjusting to a new environment. She speaks English and had a degree and experience in the IT industry.

Julie relates her story:

Everyone has their own reasons for migrating to another country, and for me it was something I always wanted to do, but it took me a long time to get the courage to move to the other side of the world, and I left my life at home waiting for me as though I would return. I moved from New Zealand to the UK because I wanted to be closer to everywhere, to see the world (especially Europe), and to experience greater career opportunities.

When I first arrived in the UK, it wasn't difficult to find work, and I easily made friends, as I was living in a hostel, where it was easy to meet people. Others like me had left their lives behind. One friend of mine even had a return ticket to Germany, which, incidentally, she never used. She is still here to this day. Every year in February we celebrate another year in London and another year of friendship. This is significant to me because London is one of those cities where people come to work for a few years then leave when they want to settle down. So making and keeping friends is an ongoing challenge. Though I am not alone in facing that, I go along to plenty of social groups full of people trying to do the same thing.

After I had been here about three years, I found myself in the situation where my social circle had all but disappeared, and my friends had gone home or had left for another part of Europe in search of work. I had been working long hours and just found that my life wasn't working, my relationship with my boyfriend was ending, I was terribly unhappy at work, and unknown to me I was eating nowhere near enough to sustain the eighty miles a week I was cycling. I found myself not knowing who to turn to for help, as I didn't have any close friends that I could talk to. At that point, I did feel alone and isolated, and I admit I did think about the possibility of returning home, where I would have my family and also networks of old school friends to fall back on. However, this was partly a situation of my own making. I'm a very independent person, and even if the idea of asking for help does occur to me I find it extremely difficult to do. I always feel as though I am bothering someone or getting in the way.

It's true that over the last seven years I've had all kinds of experiences I could never have dreamed of. If I were to go home, I would need to start over. My friends and even my family have moved away from the city where I grew up. So any time I ever wonder about going back I have to think through the results I want to create in my life and the actions I will need to take to achieve them. Nine times out of ten I realize I am better off here. I find Christmas difficult because I miss my family, but I always make the best of it, often by taking my bike for a spin round my favourite park, which I am lucky enough to be able to live near. I wonder if I were to go home whether I would fit in now, as it appears to me everyone I know who has stayed back home has had a different focus. They are more settled, with a house and partner. I have no regrets about making the move. The only thing I regret is not making the decision sooner. The decision is the first step. Once you start the journey, you never know exactly where it will take you. I have travelled all over the world, experienced so many of the places I dreamed of seeing as a teenager, and worked for companies I could never have dreamed of working for back home. I can't say that I "found myself" in the course of my travels like I had hoped I would, but I still feel travelling changed my perspective in a positive way. I have been very fortunate, as I was able to integrate and find work easily.

Egle Raulickyte

Egle was raised in Lithuania, a country that is located in the southernmost Baltic states. Lithuania was occupied by the Soviet Union when she was born, and until she was 8 years old. It was an environment of suppression, war, and fighting. Her family moved to the countryside to live in natural and more peaceful surroundings. She considered herself a nature lover. Her father and mentor loved nature, too, for its peace and harmony. She lived there throughout her high school years, in balance with nature. For Egle, there were many valuable pursuits in life, such as meditation and self-discovery. She is a physiotherapist by profession and an intuitive healer. Her love for freedom, creativity, integrity, developing her intuitive skills, and learning led to a new adventure, travelling to England and working there in 2009.

To be able to work in England, she had to learn English and other languages that would provide service of value to her clients. The long hours of work prompted her to build her own business and organise events. She possesses a personality that never gives up when faced with challenges, and she knows her strength and inner power, coupled with high intentions to serve and help others.

She has worked as event manager at Rock House Global, founded by Christopher Howard, in Bali, Indonesia. She organized self and business development training in Asia and Europe while working in that company.

Currently, Egle spends time in her own business as a healer and enjoys her new pursuit of diving in beautiful Bali, Indonesia.

Education

Professor Cecilia Manrique

Professor Cecilia G. Manrique had a great life and job in the Philippines before relocating to the US to take further studies over thirty years ago. She presently chairs the political science and public administration departments at the University of Wisconsin in La Crosse. Comparative politics and international relations are her areas of interest. In addition, she specializes in developing countries, women in politics, technology, and politics (University of Wisconsin, La Crosse 2014).

She obtained her doctorate in political science from the University of Notre Dame and subsequently obtained a bachelor of science degree in computer science from Quincy University, Illinois.

She authored two editions of *The Houghton Mifflin Guide to the Internet for Political Science* as well as the *Test Banks* (2005, 2007) and *Instructor's Manual* (2007) for *The New American Democracy* published by Pearson Longman. Her other publication was a co-authored book with Dr Gabriel Manrique of Winona State University entitled *The Multicultural or Immigrant Faculty in American Higher Education*, published by the Mellen Press of New York in 1999 (University of Wisconsin-La Crosse 2010).

In addition to her publications is a chapter entitled "A Foreign Woman Faculty's Multiple Whammies" in the book *Women Faculty of Color in the White Classroom*, edited by Lucila Vargas and published by Peter Lang of New York. "This study sheds light on the background issues, challenges and concerns of immigrant faculty members of color in the United States. It accounts faculty members' decisions to immigrate, reasons for coming to America, and reasons for staying. It chronicles their current situation in academia, including the struggles associated with relating to their students, peers and administrators" (Manrique, 2002).

In 1996, Dr Manrique was named University of Wisconsin System Woman of Color. This is a recognition and award initiated by the University of Wisconsin System in 1994. (University of Wisconsin, Madison 2011).

She works with the University of Wisconsin at La Crosse chapter of the Golden Key international honour society, in which she currently serves as president of the international leadership council and member of its board of directors after serving two terms as council secretary (Golden Key Honour 2012).

Professor Manrique is an example who was willing to trade off a higher social standing in her country of origin for a higher standard of living, more academic freedom, and better access to library facilities in the United States (Manrique 1993).

Entrepreneurship

Imelda Argel

Attorney Imelda Argel migrated to Australia in 1988. As a migrant professional woman she faced many challenges, and her overseas qualifications were not readily recognised for admission to practice as a solicitor in the state of New South Wales, Australia. While working at McKenzie, Sydney, she undertook bridging courses in the evening and worked as paralegal during the day. In addition, while working at the New South Wales Department of Lands, she completed her practical legal training and master of laws degree from University of Sydney. At present, Imelda Argel is a practising migration solicitor and a registered migration agent in Sydney, Australia. She is a solicitor of the Supreme Court of New South Wales, the high court of Australia, and a legal attorney in the Philippines and in the state of New York, USA. Her registered migration agent number is 9682957 (LinkedIn, 2014).

Ms Argel's business offers a variety of services, with focus on conveyance, commercial contracts, wills and probate, and immigration for multicultural communities. She has been running a successful sole legal practice in Sydney since 1994. The Migration Agents Registration Authority (MARA), Australia, appointed her as an evaluator of the continuing professional development (CPD) seminars for migration agents. (Imelda Argel and Associates N.D.)

Ms Argel is a gifted person with many accomplishments. She is the author of Time-Saving Immigration Practice Solutions (TIPS) on General Skilled Migration (GSM), and "Visas" (a publication for migration agents published online at http://www.smokeball.com.au). She is the recipient of the inaugural NSW FAWAA (Filipino-Australian Women's Achievement Award) for her outstanding achievements in corporate practice and entrepreneurship (FAWAA 2006). Likewise, she is an awardee of the University of the Philippines Alumni Association (NSW Chapter) Achievement Award for law and community service. She is a model of perseverance and determination who excels in her profession.

She is well known for advocating the review of the Philippines Country Education Profile. This was an initiative that led to the Philippine licensure examination becoming comparable to an Australian bachelor degree.

Ms. Argel received the presidential award Banaag category from President Aquino in 2012, a presidential awards for Filipino individuals and organizations overseas, held at the Malacanang Palace, Manila, in recognition of her commitment to advocating the mutual recognition of skills and qualifications for Filipino migrants in Australia, in her legal and migration practice (Zaragosa, 2013).

Maria Pau

Maria arrived in Australia at the very young age of eleven in 1988 (http://amazon.com 2014). She is a model of lifelong learning, completing a master's degree at the University of Queensland and currently working on her PhD. Maria is a bestselling author and recovery coach, also the founder and CEO of Coaching with Substance, based in Brisbane, Queensland. Her goal is to grow Coaching with Substance Inc. as a well-known and reputable public benevolent institution that offers coaching to people suffering from substance use and abuse issues (LinkedIn 2014).

Notwithstanding academic achievements, she has been mentored and coached at ActionCoach, and her organisation, Coaching with

Substance, was recently named the best not-for-profit organisation in 2014. The 2014 Business Excellence Awards sponsored by ActionCoach: Business Coaching hosted over 520 nominations in seventeen categories from all parts of Australia and Asia. She is a passionate high achiever and lives true to her vision while living a life of purpose (Facebook, 2014).

Maria's bestselling book is entitled Kill Your Addiction Before It Kills You: How I Transformed My Life of Addictions, Bipolar, and Suicide.

Raised a Family As a Single Parent

Dolly Job

Life experiences are unique to an individual who made choices and decisions between career and motherhood. Dolly is Filipino, an auditor from the Yupangco group of companies who arrived in Australia with her husband and four children under 15 years of age in 1988. As a mother, her first priority was raising the children. A job was not even considered due to the fact that the income would go directly to childcare payment. She was a stay-at-home mum. This is an example of gender disparity in migration: women lagging behind in pursuing career opportunities due to family commitments.

As the children grew into young adulthood, the parents parted ways, leaving the mother to look after the four children with two in high school and two just commencing university. Raising four children as a single parent in a new country is the biggest challenge a mother can ever experience. However, with persistence, perseverance, and prayers, she emerged a winner. She is a model mother who raised the children very well. All of them are now professionals with university degrees and working in their areas of interest.

The mother's qualifications as accountant and auditor were still in high demand, so as the children became independent, she returned to work, securing a government job. For a mother to return to work is an achievement in its own right, by which she was able to re-establish her own identity in the new country.

Conclusion

The stories provided confirmation that many non-English-speaking professional migrant women studied again to further their education in the new country in order to gain local experience before regaining entry into their professions. There are occupations such as engineering and accountancy that they can become employed in without returning to further studies as long as these are backed by intensive overseas experience. There are women that set up their own businesses and prospered in the process. It is also evident that English-speaking migrants enjoy flexibility and advantage in moving to another country. The challenges initially encountered paid off in the end when migrant women sought out available help, particularly from coaches and mentors who provided support and guidance toward finding out who they really are and what they can do to contribute to the world. See http://hear-ourstory.com.

References

Amazon.com 2014. Maria Pau biography. [15 May 2014] http://www.amazon.com/Maria-Pau/e/B00HI4B5BE

Ardiente, E. M. Climate Change and Sustainability at Navistar, Fifteenth IUAPPA World Clean Air Congress, 2014. [18 May 2014] http://events.awma.org/IUAPPA/presentations/7B/Ardiente10-09-16Climate per cent20Change per cent20and per cent20Sustainability per cent20IUAPPA per cent20- per cent20Final.pdf

Australian Bureau of Statistics. Australian Social Trends, Australia. Catalogue number 4102.0. November 1996. [27 March 2014] AusStats database.

Edith M. Ardiente. 2014. [19 May 2014] http://www.zoominfo.com/p/Edith-Ardiente/1066427

Filipina Women's Network 2009. Edith Ardiente: 100 Most Influential Filipina Women in the US 2007. [30 March 2014] http://www.youtube.com/watch?v=rNuyfXnwXCE

Filipino-Australian Women's Achievement Awards NSW, 2006. Imelda Argel, FAWAA.

Golden Key International Honour Society 2012. Cecilia Manrique: Member Story. [18 May 2014] https://www.goldenkey.org/members-chapters/member-stories/cecilia-manrique/

Imelda Argel, Imelda Argel and Associates. [27 March 2014] http://www.iargel.com.au/content/tabID__4083/Contact_Us.aspx

International Organization for Migration (IOM) 2011. "Deskilling of Qualified Migrant Women: Implications and Solutions," "When education does not lead to decent work and full employment: the plight of underemployed and deskilled migrant women." United Nations. [27 March 2014]

Khoo, S., and P. McDonald. "Settlement indicators and benchmarks: report for the Department of Immigration and Multicultural Affairs" in A. Philipp and E. Ho "Migration, home and belonging: South African migrant women in Hamilton, New Zealand." 2010, New Zealand Population Review, vol. 36, 81–101.

LinkedIn Corporation 2014. Imelda Argel and Associates, Migration Lawyers. [19 May 2014] http://au.linkedin.com/pub/imelda-argel-associates-migration-lawyers/3b/6a3/3ba

LinkedIn Corporation 2014. Maria Pau. [27 March 2014] http://au.linkedin.com/in/coachingwithsubstance

Manrique, G. G., and C. G. Manrique. Non-European immigrants among political science faculty, 1993. [20 May 2014] Eric Database. http://files.eric.ed.gov/fulltext/ED365614.pdf

Manrique, C. "A foreign woman faculty's multiple whammies" in L. Vargas (ed), Women Faculty of Color in the White Classroom: Narratives on the Pedagogical Implications of Teacher Diversity, 2002. [20 May 2014] Eric Database. http://web.a.ebscohost.com.ezproxy.uws.edu.au/ehost/detail?vid=3&sid=5db293ef-915b-467b-bbc1-85a57977c083percent40sessionmgr4004&hid=4101&bdata=JnNpdGU9ZWhvc3QtbGl2ZSZzY29wZT1zaXRl#db=eric&AN=ED471160

Manrique, C and G. Manrique. "The Multicultural or Immigrant Faculty in American Society," 1999. [30 March 2014] http://www.uwlax.edu/murphy/authors/2010/Manrique1.html

Pau, M. "Bradley J Sugars," Facebook update, 2014. [17 March 2014] https://www.facebook.com/CoachMariaPau?fref=ts

Reasons for immigration, The Civil Society Info. [27 March 2014] http://www.thecivilsociety.info/reasons-for-immigration.php

Pereira, E. "Asians in America: Excelling in Academics, Failing To Get Ahead in Leadership," Forbes, 2011. [27 March 2014] http://www.forbes.com/sites/evapereira/2011/07/27/asians-in-america-excelling-in-academics-failing-to-get-ahead-in-leadership/

Marinque, Cecilia, PhD. University of Wisconsin, La Crosse, 2014. [18 May 2014] http://www.uwlax.edu/polisci/faculty_staff/cecilia_manrique.html

University of Wisconsin, Madison. Outstanding women of color in education awards, 2011. [18 May 2014] http://www.womenstudies.wisc.edu/WSC/events/woc/woc.htm

Zaragosa, E. Argel receives 2012 Presidential Award, NSW, 2013. [27 March 2014] http://www.pcherald.com.au/national-news/item/513-argel-receives-2012-presidential-award

Closure and New Beginnings

Duda Prestes

Duda Prestes, a certified master neurolinguistics practitioner, a member of the Brazilian Bar Association and an accredited panel member of LEADR, originally trained as a corporate lawyer in Brazil. Her twenty years of legal experience inspired her to train as a mediator in New Zealand, where she lived for over eight years. She has experience in training people to run franchise businesses, including legal and commercial protocols, as well as motivational behaviour. She also studied commercial law at the University of Auckland.

Duda has a spirit for travel. She loves to see new places, meet new people, and experience new cultures. Duda also enjoys studying and is constantly engaged in personal and professional development. Whenever possible, she likes to combine these passions by attending conferences and courses in other countries.

She strongly believes that we all have the power to start again, in a better way; to move forward happily when there is love, forgiveness, and gratitude in our hearts. A good closure gives you a clean new beginning.

started a company at the end of 2013 to spread the word of self-development and well-being in my mother tongue, Portuguese, here in Brazil, where I live. My partner at the company was a lady that worked with me in Brazil in the early 2000s.

Everything seemed going well, until one night she came to my home office for our weekly meeting and said as soon as she arrived: "I don't want to do it anymore; I don't want to invest! Let me know if you want to buy my half. I will send you the information you need, and I am not spending any more time on the project." And she left.

Buy my half of what? I thought. There was just hard work done, nothing else. A lot of effort still had to be made to make it happen. It was a Monday, and we were three weekends away from our first workshop. I was responsible for the presentation, and she was responsible for admin and finance. In the following week she came with a pen drive and said: "That's it! When you find someone to help you, they can email me with their questions." And she left again.

It took me almost three weeks to understand what had happened. Today I got closure. I ended the project and decided to start afresh and rescheduled the first presentation for three months' time.

This is my most recent and unexpected new beginning. At first I felt angry. Then I changed shoes and understood she was probably afraid of success; and now I feel grateful. It's another new beginning. I'll spread the word, focusing not just on finances but on results, on the assistance we provide for people to live a better life. That's why I now understand the universe, and the law of the universe or God, however you feel in naming this force. In my understanding you cannot have a company to help people feel stronger and better where the focus is first on how much money you will make. The main idea should be to help people, and this was not happening. And again, for this new beginning, I thank the universe for stopping the *old* new company before it started.

It will be a new beginning in the direction I feel right. And guess what: It happened less than a week before the opportunity to write on new beginnings knocked on my door. What a coincidence!

Another coincidence is that I couldn't start writing until today, after I got closure, after understanding. That's the best way to start over; that's how you really have a new beginning.

My point is we cannot talk about new beginnings, without mentioning closure.

I believe we can start over every morning, as every day gives us the opportunity for a new beginning. There are the simple new beginnings, like changing the alarm to wake you up an hour earlier than usual, so you can exercise and give your body a better chance. Or meditate every night to give your mind and soul good food.

I will share two stories with you to show how small things make great changes.

Twelve years ago, I was in a wine store and I saw a good friend from high school. We had lost contact; we had not seen each other for over fifteen years. I had – and still have – deep feelings of friendship and love for her and her family. As the feeling was mutual, she opened up to me that she was having problems with one of her brothers. They had not been talking to each other for over four years. I felt sad. She was angry at him. She thought he should apologize to her for something he did, and until he did, she would not talk to him again.

I asked her what good these feelings were doing to her, to her sister, and to her mother. She looked at me and said none. So I said that I think that no matter who says sorry to whom, that probably her brother felt the same way, and that they were missing time together, good family moments, that she could try to think as he was thinking, understand his feelings, and reach out to him with peace.

She didn't seem convinced. We left the place promising to keep in touch, but that never happened – until three months ago, thanks to Facebook, she looked for me, sent a message, and we met for lunch. It was an eight-hour lunch, believe me! Imagine my surprise when at our lunch, she mentioned our conversation that happened twelve years earlier, and thanked me for telling her that forgiveness was the best way to go. A few days after that conversation, she called her brother, asked him to meet her, and they did. She said she understood him, and he had the opportunity to understand her as well. And after that day, their relationship went back to where it was, with love, friendship, and understanding.

Returning to 2014, there is this guy who lives in Brazil, but very far away from me. He reached me through my old company's website, asking for help. So I asked him if he wouldn't mind telling me the problems he was facing, so I could try to help. And then I received a very, very big list: low self-esteem, the habit of being a drama queen, sadness, insecurity, relationship problems, work issues – they were all there. Sounded like everything in his life was out of place. I said to myself: *This is a very big job!* and started thinking on how I could help him from a distance. Then I remembered a book – actually I consider it more a manual – *As a Man Thinketh*, by James Allen. Next day I suggested he started to write, every night, just before bed time, at least one good thing that happened during the day, even if it is just a very nice, well-brewed coffee, and to also read the book and write me the good points he discovered.

Next day, I opened the email and there was: "Thank you so much! I want to be the author of my story." So he started. Every day since then I have received a message via email, saying that today was better than yesterday. I cannot be more grateful for the opportunity.

This is a simple example of how everyone of us can start over and have a better life. It is in our hands. I feel so pleased to have suggested this simple technique of writing a good thing every day, and to have shared the lessons from James Allen. Every morning when I get his messages I feel grateful for the experience.

If you are not doing this, buy a notebook and just before bedtime write by hand, with a pen, one good experience of the day. Your life will improve in a way you cannot imagine.

This is an example of a new beginning started by the conscious mind.

There are also new beginnings that our unconscious mind create. Sometimes we feel like they just "happen" to us, like when you miss a job interview, revaluate your concepts, and find a new career or opportunity in the same company you are already in and love working for. Or you get involved in an accident that shows you how important it is not to drink before driving. Or having a partnership end suddenly, just as I had.

A true new beginning can start only when we have moved on, when we get closure and are at peace with the past.

Closure is an important moment in everyone's life. When you get closure, you become stronger. Closure gives you confidence, it makes you feel safe and secure, because when you get it, you understand and accept, and clear the way to have more in life.

I have a friend that divorced his first wife over thirty years ago, and when we talk, he is always mentioning things that happened in the past, comparing current life events with similar situations that occurred over thirty years ago.

I am sorry for him. Though he has married twice since the first marriage, but without closure on what happened, he does not accept that things have changed. So in many other aspects of his life, he is stuck. When he is close to his first wife – as in the same room – you can feel the tension and his frustration. Did he have a new beginning with his next two marriages? Did he actually start over?

Closure is important. Thirty years is a lifetime. You do not want to live being stuck in the replay like this gentleman.

Have you started a new relationship? Or you are between partners? Do you have the past still present and stopping you from moving forward, being stuck? I have an easy approach to new beginnings on relationships. I am divorced twice and have no regret about the relationships or the separations.

This is not the same for everyone. My mother suffered over a decade when she and my father divorced. And I have to say it was very hard on me, too. I met a lady in a training program who, following a transformation weekend she participated in with her husband, he decided he wanted a new beginning. She did not want him to leave. It took her five years to move on. She is good now. She moved on and she has closure.

For us to be in control of a new situation, we have to let the previous situation go.

Some people can do it by themselves. They look for answers, they accept facts created mostly by someone else, they *understand* them, and move on.

Others require support to do the same thing. Closure is required in all aspects of life where there is a need to move forward, including relationships, careers, and change in financial status. The most important thing is first you have closure.

One of my own new beginnings (I have had plenty) was related to my career. I changed my professions from being a lawyer to being a mediator.

And what mediators do? We help people deal with issues, and find closure.

One mediation case involved a man who had worked for over twelve years in an IT company. He spent months developing a new product for the company, and he felt he was part of the company. At some stage the director of his department was replaced and the new person fired him. They came to mediation and I was the mediator.

It took them over two hours to realize the problem was not about the man being fired, or the amount of money the company was offering him to settle the legal procedures. The issue behind the legal action he took was claiming ownership of the product he developed. His work was not acknowledged; he was not thanked for his efforts during the time he was worked for them.

The new person had no idea what that man did for the company and the amount of work the man had been involved with developing the new product. And how could he? All he had were reports from human resources and charges showing that he should cut expenses, reduce the personnel, and relocate people.

Once the new director understood what happened, and how the former employee felt about it, he acknowledged the importance of the work done. He apologized for being so involved in the big picture that he had not fully understood the complete story. After understanding and appreciating the situation, the director adjusted the money being offered by the company. The legal procedures ended, and the former employee was able to move on; he had closure. This is so important to enable people to move forward and start over.

Another case I dealt with was a pro bono case. Two long-time neighbours were fighting over a tree. One wanted to keep it, the other one wanted it removed. This was one of the shortest mediations I have had to work with to date. In less than forty minutes the ladies realized what the real issue was and why they were having a problem. The tree was in neighbour X's property for over nine years, and it had grown a lot. She loved it; she had planted the tree when her daughter left home to study overseas. The tree has an attached value. On the other hand, neighbour Y was losing the sunshine inside her house, and wanted the tree removed. Neighbour Y was about to hire a lawyer via the community centre when they suggested the mediation process. That's when I stepped in.

I first received their pre-mediation information via email. At this stage I could not see what was behind the issue.

Mediation was scheduled. I organized tea and cookies for them. After all, they were neighbours! After a few minutes listening to neighbour Y and then to neighbour X, I realized – and so did they – that they could have resolved it over a pot of tea, in their homes, just as they used to do in the past. The problem was that, when neighbour X's daughter left to go to university, she felt lonely, and tried to reach neighbour Y a couple of times for a catch-up. At that same time, neighbour Y's life was changing, as she had her mother moving in for home care. Neighbour Y's mother had had a stroke, and was in need of support.

Neither of them told the other what they were going through. They were just feeling sad and lonely, and did not share or know how to share what they were going through. Without noticing, neighbour X felt left alone, and neighbour Y felt overwhelmed.

During the mediation, they found closure over the issue, and reached a wonderful solution for the tree problem: Neighbour Y agreed to hire a gardener to keep the treetop trimmed at a height that she could still have sunshine, and neighbour X was going to allow him onto her property and pay for the monthly trimming, and keep the tree.

The last email I received from them was to thank me for the result. They also mentioned they meet regularly as they used to.

They both got *closure*.

Pretending it is not happening won't give you closure. Neither would apathy.

Like everything in life, taking action will gain closure.

I also believe life has cycles. I understand how having cycles in life works: it helps us achieve closure when things change.

Babies get fed every day by other people. At some stage they grow up enough to feed themselves. The grown-ups still love them and wouldn't mind feeding them, but the feeding-them time is over. It's a new cycle. As we age, we look after ourselves and maybe even after our parents. As we grow old and some of us may need to be fed again, if circumstances require it, we may need a nanny (caretaker) to look after us. It's a cycle, and every step through the cycle requires closure.

Some kids may feel they are not loved as much anymore when they need to eat by themselves. Others may feel great, as now they are responsible enough to eat by themselves. The reaction depends on their self-esteem, on how the situation was shown to them, and how they saw it happening. They need closure at each step.

When we get old and some of us will require help to eat and drink and shower, we may feel loved or we may feel we are being treated unfairly. Again, it all depends on how the situation is presented and how we see and relate to it.

But no matter how it goes, when people have closure, they move on.

Sometimes the changes happen all of a sudden. We may lose someone we love to someone else, to death, or to a new place. And closure will help us move to a new beginning.

The first loved person I lost was a 14-year-old schoolmate. She was in a car accident during school holidays. Her father was our geometry teacher. We all grieved, and she is still remembered. Her father never got closure. Around three years after her death I saw him on the street close to our school. We started talking. I was 16 and haven't forgotten yet what he said: "You have to come by our home to visit, but it will be hard for you to meet M [his daughter] as she is travelling a lot." No closure. It was especially hard to him, as the school kept her name on the student class list for a couple of weeks. It was bad. He never asked for help.

Another dear friend of mine also lost her daughter. It was to a disease. But he got closure. He understood, he accepted the facts, and we talk about her and remember her birthday with respect, as she was always brave. And she had closure; she made peace with the disease before she died.

When my granddad died, I went back to work three days later, and I still remember taking the same way to work for around a week, and being amazed because the trees were at the same place, the traffic was the same, and life was taking its course even though such a wonderful person left us. When Granma died it was easier. I knew that feeling. Closure was easier.

So what can help you to get closure? For each person it is different.

Moving houses?

Starting a new career?

Starting a new relationship?

Making new friends?

Going on a holiday?

All these possibilities will work, if you leave the bad and sad feelings behind. And doing that depends on you alone. No one else can do it for you. People can help, for sure, but you are in charge.

Think through all the possibilities. Discuss them with people you trust. Read books, go to seminars, join groups. Be in charge of your life. Have a real new beginning.

Facts by themselves are not good or bad.

Is death always a good or a bad thing? It is our only assurance in life. It is part of it. And its value depends mainly on how the person was living (if we are talking about a disease) or what damage their brain will suffer (if we are talking about a stroke or a car accident). Is the person old and has lived life in full? It's only their next step. Will we miss the person? Sure we will. But we can live with the good memories. Live every day as if it was your last; do all the good you can; think as if you were in other people's shoes. I guarantee that living this way you will hardly have something to regret.

Is living in a different part of the planet from people you love good or bad? I had the experience when I moved to New Zealand, and I still have it in a different way: I'm back in Brazil, and my son still lives in New Zealand. Good for the lifestyle, bad for that night that you are feeling sad and just want to touch people that make you feel safe and are far away from you. Thank God for Skype!

Is losing your job good or bad? Usually you feel bad at the first moment, but mainly, when you are focused, a new opportunity will come and you will be more fulfilled. Remember, it can be some help from your unconscious mind. I remember when I lost a job which would be considered great by most people: fancy title, very good money, close to home. I felt sad for a couple of days, until I realized that was exactly what I needed. I just didn't have the guts to do it. I started sleeping well again, I smiled more often, and I started a new business.

Is divorce a good or a bad thing? In my experience it is always good, because when you or your partner get to that stage that you feel unhappy, you are not sharing your daily experiences. You just want to go to work. It's done, time for a new cycle. To most people it starts as bad, but becomes good when they think about the changes in their lives, the new things learned, how that relationship made them who they are today.

I'm an optimist! I see good in everything. And I assure you, it is a habit, and I learnt it from my grandad: I don't remember hearing any complaint from him, ever. He always felt sorry for people that were doing things considered bad for the average person, because he believed – and so do I – that people who behave and act in a way that is disrespectful or inconsiderate of others are sad people, people that don't focus on their own lives, that are always feeling jealous. They don't feel loved. They may *be* loved, but they don't feel like it! They don't feel grateful.

Every day I make the choice to be happy, and you can choose it, too. The first magic step: be grateful for what you have. Gratitude is magical.

Be grateful for the big things and for the small things, too. Being grateful for the small things will fill you with happiness all day around.

What are these small things, and how can you feel grateful about them?

Maybe you have pretty good health; or you don't at the moment but you are fixing it.

You have a good friend to talk to that is available; or this friend is not available at the moment, but you can remember his or her good advice and can use it now.

Your computer is working well or if it is not. You will fix it or buy a new one, or some friend will lend you theirs so you can finish your paper.

You have a job that you enjoy doing. Or if you don't have a job you enjoy doing at this moment, you decided you want a good one, and you will take the actions to grab it.

You live in a home you like. Or if you don't like it, you will start a plan to move houses.

You are having delicious food for dinner, or you are not, but the food you are having is good for your health.

It's a *Pollyanna* lifestyle! Have you heard of this book? It's a bestselling novel by Eleanor H. Porter, written in 1913, a children's book that should be read at least once by every child and adult. You will understand what a positive outlook means after reading it. She is an orphan that plays a game that could be called the happiness game, taught by her deceased father. The game consists in finding something good about any situation.

Every moment is a moment to have a new beginning. The new beginning is not outside; it's inside you. That's where the change starts.

When you allow yourself to feel upset about something that someone did to you, I recommend that you change places with that someone. When you do that, you may still disagree with the attitude, *but* you will be able to see that *if* you were that person – if you lived the same life the person did, you would most likely have the same behaviour. I'm not saying you have to agree with the attitude or that the attitude is correct from your viewpoint. It is in theirs.

And remember how many times you may have said in conversation: "You know [such-and-such] is wrong!" And someone reminded you that you've done something similar yourself. And you reply: "It was totally different in my case. I meant good. In this case, the other person is wrong but I was right!" And on it went.

For example, we all see things like this happening: A friend starts flirting with someone else's boyfriend or girlfriend. You consider it is wrong (and usually it is). *But* a couple of years ago you felt you were in love with a friend's boyfriend or girlfriend and you called him or her. Maybe you even had a date and they broke up, and you were together for a while. At that stage you thought the person might be the love of your life. Then it turned out that he or she wasn't. But the feeling went both ways. You both thought it was right. It didn't last, but you thought it would. And now when you are on the other side: "It is totally different. We were in love, they aren't!"

Or when you are out driving and a car cuts in your way. You think *That was wrong and dangerous!* But maybe one day you were worried about something and even without noticing, you cut in front of another person's car. Hmm … has that happened, yes or no?

Changing places, wearing other people's shoes is the best closure you can get in your everyday life on a day to day basis.

Play Pollyanna's game: When I was 29 years old, I contracted a rare infection in my femur, and I couldn't walk by myself. I have worked since I was 19. I love to work (and still do), but I couldn't move or drive, and the pain was high and constant. (I even had to be on morphine for a while.) One day, my son, who was 11 at the time, looked at me sadly. He didn't do well at his *capoeira* (Brazilian martial art) training. I remember looking at him and saying that in life you can choose how things affect you. "Son, I could either be unhappy because I never had to use a walking stick and now I have to, or I can be happy because I was in bed for so long, not being able to walk, and now I can through the use of a walking stick!"

Almost twenty years ago, I had hip replacement surgery, and today I am doing great, walking properly on my own and in my own style.

Another important point about having closure is to be able to move on with a new beginning by the way of *forgiveness*. Forgive and forget! People that don't forgive are tied to the past. They don't forget and they remain stuck.

When we forgive, we understand the magic of the universe: that we are all one; that our actions – or the lack of them – are causing all the things that surround us, the good – and yes, we can take credit for that – but also the bad. Usually people blame other people for the bad things that occur in their lives. They blame politicians for being corrupt, friends for being apart, family members for not understanding, employees for not working as much or as hard as expected. But remember, we, too, are also blamed by someone for something. Have you done something hurtful or wrong on purpose? Did you mean for someone else to feel hurt, sad, or abandoned? I believe not.

I believe most people do what they do believing they are doing a good thing, the right thing, and their intention is to help another.

Neale Donald Walsch wrote the trilogy *Conversations with God*, and the amazing children's parable: "The Little Soul and the Sun." I highly recommend that both adults and children read these books. They are truly uplifting and inspirational, and more importantly: they are simple to read and yield a huge amount of understanding.

There are a few points that took my attention in the books. I'll discuss two of them:

In "The Little Soul and the Sun," it is shown that we are all part of the same thing, little candles that make the sun. And that there is nothing to forgive. Yes, I know, I just suggested that we all should forgive. This is why. There is nothing to forgive. We are not better or worse than anyone. Here is the ending:

> And at all the moments in that new lifetime, whenever a new soul brought joy or sadness – and especially if it brought sadness – the Little Soul thought of what God says: "Always remember – God smiled – I have sent you nothing but angels."

In *Conversations with God – Book 1*, the author is talking to God, asking lots of questions, and he asks God:

> "How can I know this communication is from God? How do I know this is not my own imagination?"
>
> And God replies: "What would be the difference? Do you not see that I could just as easily work through your imagination as anything else? I will bring you the exact right thoughts, words or feelings, at any given moment, suited precisely to the purpose at hand, using one device, or several. You will know these words are from Me because you, of your own accord, have never spoken so clearly. Had you already spoken so clearly on these questions, you would not be asking them."

So trust yourself, your gut, your feelings. They will guide you in the right direction. When you don't, you may regret it.

Right before moving back to Brazil from New Zealand, I told one of my best and dearest friends from childhood that we should meet for lunch as soon as I arrived. I missed all the years we had not been in contact, but thanks to Facebook we were in touch. I arrived, and I deeply wish I had contacted her and booked the lunch when the thought came to me. But I had just arrived and reckoned on there being plenty of time and that I could contact her any time in the following week. I was with my Mom and my sister, having lunch. It was a Saturday. My sister's phone rang and she had a conversation with my father-in-law. We continued with lunch. On return home my Mom and sister asked me to sit down and advised me that my father-in-law saw on the TV news that my dear friend had a stroke the night before and died. I was devastated. Why didn't I listen to my intuition and at the very least call her to say hi?

This is one of the very few regrets I have. From that day on, any person that comes to my mind I contact almost immediately – a lesson that I learnt in a painful way.

In applying the rules, I believe we make our own destiny. Six months later I was walking on a street I have not walked on for over thirty years and I saw and recognized a person I had not seen in almost twenty-five years. It was my dear friend's aunty, and I got to hug her and tell her how much I loved her niece. It felt like I was hugging and talking to my dear friend. I am so grateful to the universe for that opportunity! I could now move on. It felt like a hundred kilos was lifted off my shoulders and back. That was my closure.

Do to others what you wish they would do to you. I know it is easier said than done. A couple of months ago, on my way to the office, I stopped at the gas station to buy a sandwich. When I left the car, a man, a very poor man (unfortunately, there are plenty of people in need here in Brazil, and we are told by the media and authorities that they are dangerous) spoke to me. "Lady, would you buy me something to eat?" In my fear, I pretended that I didn't hear him, and stepped into the store. Three steps in and I could hear my inner voice: *You are doing wrong.*

So I went outside and said, "Excuse me, sir, did you talk to me?" And he said that he did, that he asked me to buy him something to eat. I responded OK, and went back to the store.

And again I heard my inner voice saying, *Are you treating him well? You are still doing wrong.* So I realized that I shouldn't allow fear to control me. I went outside and invited him to join me inside, so he could choose what he wanted. We took a table together. People were staring at us. We had a small conversation about the weather, about what he was doing for a living (he shines men's shoes), and then we left the store together. I know there is still more to do, but I'm glad that I faced the fear of the unknown and gave him a good feeling of being respected, as he should be always! After all, as was very well said by Donald Walsch in "The Little Soul and the Sun":

> "Think of it this way," said God. You are like a candle
> in the Sun. Oh, you are there all right. Along with a million
> Ka-gillion other candles who make up the Sun. And the
> Sun would not be the sun without you. Nay, it would not

be the Sun without one of his candles… and that would not be the Sun at all; for it would not shine as brightly.

And further on the Little Soul asks God:

> "You mean it is okay to let other people know how special I am?"
>
> "Of course," chuckled God. "It is very okay. But remember, Special doesn't mean Better. Everybody is special, each in their own way! Yet many others have forgotten that. They will see that it is okay to be special only when you see that it is okay for you to be special."

This is a lesson that our daily responsibilities make easy to forget. But when we do remember this lesson, we feel better. We feel strong and able to do our part, which is to be happy.

I believe that to be happy is our birthright and our duty. It is an obligation. And the more other people are happy around us, the happier we are. I am talking about the happiness of acknowledging the greater good, the happiness of doing your best to people, the happiness of going to bed and being thankful for your day, the happiness of waking up in the morning ready to be better than the day before.

Compare yourself to you only. How much better is your life today than a year ago? If it is not, how can you make it be better? Live your own life. Don't be jealous of what you imagine other people have that is better than what you have. Be a better you every day. That's how you evolve; that's how your journey becomes a great journey.

Use the ability we have to understand other people, to live without judging them – or ourselves. Believe it, even when you consider you have done something wrong, believe you did the best that you could with the life experience you had in the moment. Why? Because forgiving (in the meaning of understanding) frees us of all bad feelings we may have. It enables closure!

I have no religion, though I respect all of them, as they all teach us to be good. Amongst other sayings I like, I will close this chapter and share with you a part of a prayer that is known to be written by Saint Francis:

> Where there is hatred, let me sow love;
> where there is injury, pardon;
> where there is doubt, faith;
> where there is despair, hope;
> where there is darkness, light;
> and where there is sadness, joy.

Let's shine together as the bright candles we are! And be grateful for all the new beginnings we have experienced, and the more yet to come!

The WoW Factor

David Jackson

David Jackson is an entrepreneur and business owner with a wide range of experience and qualifications that inform his coaching practices. David is the founder and owner of Chrysalis Evolution Ltd., established in 2009. Chrysalis Evolution Ltd. Is dedicated to providing training solutions. He is a qualified and certified learning and development specialist, trainer, and career, life and business coach. He is also psychometric assessment certified by the British Psychology Society. David works with individuals and organisations to provide soft skills training and employee training services at all levels.

Chrysalis Evolution Ltd. uses the latest technologies in assisting people to advance in the fields of continuous professional and personal development. David is available for individual and group coaching sessions or training events.

How to Discover Your Passion and Develop Your Long-Term Strategy in the World of Work

In This Chapter

- We will discuss the positives and negatives in the world of work.
- We will discuss the importance of having a continuous professional development plan.
- We will look at the benefits of having a continuous "personal" development plan.

- We will look at and discuss the benefits of having a strategy that includes continuous personal and professional goals.
- You will be provided the opportunity to learn more about how you can develop your CPPD Strategy and how Chrysalis Evolution can assist you with this.
- We will outline who the CPPD Strategy will benefit
- We will outline the seven phases in the CPPD Strategy.
- You will be provided with recommendations for further reading.

Introduction

Don't ask what the world needs. Ask what makes you come alive and then go and do that. Because what the world needs are people who have come alive
– Howard Martin

The WoW Factor is the World of Work Factor. Throughout this chapter are references to the term *world of work*, for good reason. Many people get their lives mixed up with what they do, but work makes up a fraction of who they are as a person. Many find themselves drifting form job to job, and if they're lucky get some match with their core strengths and unique talents. To be successful in the world of work a strategy is of vital importance. We will explore this in more detail throughout this chapter.

The work you do can mould your character and enhance your personality, but ultimately it does not define you as a human being. Many people are misaligned in the world of work and therefore end up unfulfilled, dissatisfied, and unhappy. The CPPD Strategy we will be discussing will assist you in becoming clear and focused, moving you in the right direction towards being happy, fulfilled, and satisfied in your career.

The world of work is made up of many components, and the purpose of this chapter is to explore and discuss some of these components in some detail.

The CPPD Strategy plan provides you with a career assessment, a workbook, and a system to apply in your journey throughout the world of work. This system applies to anyone interested or engaged in the world of work, whether you are currently employed, stuck in a rut, hoping to progress up the ranks, undecided about your career, looking for a change in your profession, unsure of what to do next, looking for a challenge in your career, or if you are ready to move from a short-term vision to a long-term strategy in your career development plans.

You may be familiar with the term *personal development*, which is just another way of describing soft skills training. Soft skills training is highly valued in corporate environments, and because the corporate sectors are the great leaders in the world of work, it makes sense to follow and develop in their example. When we closely examine the corporate sectors and how they value soft skills training, this presents a strong case for adding the personal development aspect to Continuous Professional Development, or CPD.

Strategy is the key to being well prepared and flexible in your professional development goals. By being clear about your strategy, you will be aligned and prepared for all inevitabilities and on track for success. This is what Chrysalis Evolution can assist you with.

Positives and negatives in the World of Work

People are always blaming circumstances for what they are. I don't believe in circumstances. The people who get ahead in this world are the people who get up and look for the circumstances they want and if they can't find them, make them.
– George Bernard Shaw

The greatest negative in the world of work is the EX Factor. Do you know what your EX factor is? I know – you might say, "Don't you mean X factor?" It is our EXposed factor in the world of work. We are exposed to economic changes globally and nationally, which in turn affects industries and companies and their production output or demand, which in turn drives business and supports employment. The focus of this discussion is not to list all of the negativities that can occur in the world of work. The aim is to be forward thinking and optimistic in our approach and provide solutions. So we will omit the long list of negative possibilities, but I am sure on reflection that you could generate a long list. The important thing to note when facing negativities and the stress they cause is to understand that the antidote to this is to have a long-term strategy to limit your exposure. This is where we can become exposed, through limited or short-term fixes and possibly going it alone without professional assistance.

To some extent we are all exposed in the world of work. Having a Continuous Professional and Personal Development (CPPD) strategy is the key to reducing your exposure and having a robust system for moving forward in a successful and positive way.

How we prepare and plan for this change should be a part of our professional development strategies and plans. It is essential that we are trained to deal with and handle these facts of our working careers. How? you might ask. With a well-defined set of skills to assist us in reorienting ourselves, reviewing our situation, and reengaging our talents towards gaining employment. We then emerge with full confidence in our abilities and in our resourcefulness. This is as essential as all of the basic career development stages, such as acquiring job-seeking skills, resume preparation, interview preparation, and so forth.

A more robust approach in dealing with negative setbacks in the world of work is to be well trained and prepared for all inevitabilities. Now, I know that there are practitioners in the fields of personal and professional development, that would say to focus on the positive and not to be spending time thinking of negatives. But a mind well prepared and based in reality will be thoroughly prepared for all eventualities. A great coaching programme will equip you for setbacks. A solid strategy backed up with a training system that fully prepares and equips you for all possibilities. "Champions are made in training." (Christopher Howard)

The following story illustrates how we can get stuck in beliefs that no longer serve the purpose they were initially designed for. The experiment:

"Why do we continue to do what we are doing, if there is a different way?" A group of scientists placed five monkeys in a cage and in the middle a ladder with bananas on top. Every time a monkey went up the ladder, the scientists soaked the rest of the monkeys with cold water. After a while, every time a monkey went up the ladder the other ones beat up the one on the ladder. After some time, no monkey dared to go up the ladder regardless of the temptation. Scientists then decided to substitute one of the monkeys. The first thing this new monkey did was to go up the ladder. Immediately the other monkeys beat him up.

After several beatings, the new member learned not to climb the ladder even though they never knew why. The second monkey was substituted and the same occurred. The first monkey participated in the beating for the second monkey. A third monkey was changed and the same was repeated. The fourth was substituted and the beating was repeated, and finally the fifth monkey was replaced. What was left was a group of five monkeys that, even though none had ever received a cold shower, continued to beat up any monkey who attempted to climb the ladder.

If it was possible to ask the monkeys why they would beat up all those who attempted to go up the ladder, their answer would be: "I don't know. That's how things are done around here." Does this sound familiar? Don't miss the opportunity to share this with others, as they might be asking themselves why we continue to do what we are doing if there is a different way.

Doing things a better way can make the difference when dealing with difficult circumstances possibly outside of your control, such as redundancy or being laid off. You may also be experiencing uncertainty about the direction that you should go, or what profession you should pursue. What may be required is to do things differently.

A different mindset is required, a comprehensive strategy with a short-term, medium-term, and long-term approach. This can be achieved through education and training to discover your purpose and unique contribution that you have to offer to the world of work.

Continuous Professional Development

The illiterate of the twenty-first century will not be those who cannot read and write, but those who cannot learn, unlearn, and relearn.
– Alvin Toffler

Education provides the basic skills to navigate our way through the world of work and to function within our respective societies. Education opens the doors, it provides us with the necessary qualifications to begin the career of our choice, after which we embark on crafting our skills in our chosen profession.

The buzz word in career development strategies in the corporate world is *CPD* (continuous professional development). You may ask why it's such a big deal. Well, as consumers of services and products, we require new, better, and faster improvements in what we invest in or buy. It is in the interest of organisations to invest in their people so they can produce improved services and products and perform to higher standards. Globally we are continuously striving for improvements. CPD is a core part of making these changes and improvements a reality.

The primary component that needs to be factored in is the person's development. The holistic approach is to integrate personal development into CPD. This translates into *CPPD* (continuous professional and personal development). This makes sense and should be part of everyone's career development strategy.

The most common approach that people employ is to have a limited short- or medium-term approach to their career development. This type of approach is limiting and can leave you exposed to changing economic environments. A long-term strategy will include room for continuous professional and personal development and upskilling. This is essential and needs to be factored into any of your career development plans.

Three components make up your overall strategy, namely your vision, your mission, and your strategy, which you may or may not have figured out. This is not critically important and most probably will change over time. The important point to note is that through your participation in the CPPD Strategy system you will uncover your authentic and unique vision. From this you can develop your mission and strategy and increase your clarity and focus on realising your goals.

To explore this a little further, your vision is about knowing who you are becoming. Your mission is about knowing how you are going to get there and how it will contribute to others' lives. Your strategy is all about applying action and having a clear plan to get you to your goals. It is also important to note the word *continuous* in CPPD. It is through the continuous efforts we consistently apply that we get the greatest results. Just observe any leader in their respective fields, whether in the world of sport, business, or something else. The people who stand out are the ones who consistently and continuously get great results in proportion to their efforts. You will get the kind of results you want in proportion to the effort you put into your CPPD Strategy.

In the field of career development, technology is playing a greater part in providing complex computational calculations, and we can employ these technologies to accurately assess our vocation (our natural ability or profession). Chrysalis Evolution provides access to world class technologies that will assist you in understanding your unique personality, strengths, values, interests, and skills. All of this combined will provide you with a holistic view of your true self, which is vital in assisting you to arrive at a well-informed decision in selecting your career. It will ensure that you focus on the career path that is suited to your unique talents.

Some key stages or levels exist in career development. There is a total of seven levels (see the section on CPPD Strategy for more details) that focus in a more strategic approach than the traditional approach to career coaching. Traditional coaching looks at the generic areas such as interview techniques, resume, job search, and so forth. This is the current system and approach. More advances and developments deliver more precise and structured systems that both make use of and go beyond the traditional approach. These advances and developments equip you with the appropriate knowledge to call upon at each stage of development in your journey through the world of work.

The importance of this is illustrated by the story of the very expensive cruise ship engine that failed. The billionaire owner was organising a trip for family and friends. One day, when the captain called to say he was having a mechanical problem with the engine, the owner enquired if it could be fixed. The captain replied that he had contacted a number of repair companies and told them of the problem but they kept drawing blanks. The cruise ship owner tried one expert after another, but none of them could figure out how to fix the engine. Then they brought in an old man who had been fixing ships since he was a youngster. He carried a large bag of tools with him, and when he arrived, he immediately went to work. He inspected the engine carefully, top to bottom. The ship's owner and captain were both there, watching this man and hoping he would know what to do.

After looking things over, the old man reached into his bag and pulled out a small hammer. He gently tapped some pipes and components. Instantly, the engine lurched into life. He carefully put his hammer away. The engine was fixed! A week later, the owner received a bill from the old man for ten thousand euros. "What!" the owner exclaimed. "He hardly did anything!" So they wrote the old man a note asking him to send an itemized bill. The man sent a bill that read:

Tapping with a hammer €1

Knowing where to tap €9,999

Your self-image can be compared to the ship engine that failed, and unless you are trained and know how to measure and calibrate this, it can be hard to adjust this technology. A qualified technician tests and runs diagnostics to identify the operation and running issues and determine the improvements or repairs. Think of the CPPD Strategy plan as fulfilling this for you, but it won't cost you as much as what the owner of the cruise ship had to pay.

Once you have uncovered your purpose in the world of work, you will commence the journey of becoming fulfilled. You may be familiar with the term "in giving we receive." To discover your vocation and work towards realising your full expression is an amazing experience. "Life's most persistent and urgent question: What are you doing for others?" (Martin Luther King)

A good approach would be to view your contribution to the world of work as service to mankind. This is not about changing your value system, but if you see this as a requirement, everything is possible. Neuro linguistic programming (NLP) can assist you to model the values of the people that inspire you. NLP also provides excellent life transformational tools, see the recommended reading section for more on this.

Continuous Personal Development

Attitude is more important than facts. It is more important
than the past, than education, money, circumstances, than
failures and success, than what other people think, say, or do.
It is more important than appearance, ability, or skill.
– Charles R. Swindoll

Personal development boils down to empowerment. If you think about that when we look at the world of work and the shifts and upheavals that can occur, such as layoffs, redundancies, and closures, you will likely agree that these experiences are disempowering for employees, their families, and the communities that experience them. The CPPD Strategy is all about empowering you and equipping you to overcome challenges that can occur in the world of work.

Personal development, or soft skills coaching, can assist in reshaping your future. Personal development can increase your self-worth and your self-confidence and can assist you to re-evaluate and reinvent your life. Personal development is all about empowerment.

Empowerment is about thinking long term, having goals and plans, thinking about new ideas, being open to and embracing change, being focused, expanding and revealing new choices, seeing things in a different way, seeing new opportunities, taking calculated risks through well-informed decisions, continuing your development and growth, and gaining new knowledge.

Empowerment is about having clarity. Successful people know what they want and where they are going, and they have a strategy to get there. Fundamentally, all of these elements are a part of a strategy. It makes sense to make personal development part of your continuous professional development plans.

I have observed that across the spectrum of life coaching, which includes career development goals, there is a common link or connectedness towards career in the world of work.

Many areas of focus exist for the client and the coach from a life coaching or personal development perspective. Life coaching concentrates on personal development, and career coaching on professional development. There is a saying that in life "we get more of what we focus on." We also get more of what we pay little attention to. You could receive coaching sessions on areas such as career or work, finances, personal development, status, contribution to others, spirituality, health and fitness, appearance, relationships or romance, family, possessions, and travel. This is not a comprehensive list, but certainly covers the main areas that life coaching explores. There are a number of factors that need to be considered when reviewing each one. You should explore them based on the context of your own circumstances.

There is a distinct link between career and work and all the other elements of life coaching just mentioned. For example, finance: most of us work mainly to get money. Health and well-being can be improved by your work or career, and inversely, health and well-being or finances can be negatively affected by a lack of career or work. Other areas such as personal and professional development can be impacted by career or work. If we consider that our work is providing service or making a contribution to our communities, this in essence is a key value of spirituality.

We can also see that many companies require staff to show up at work looking their best or having paid attention to appearance. Many relationships are formed in the world of work; many marriages and friendships are result of career or work. From work we earn money, which enables us to buy possessions such as homes, cars, and clothes. Travel can be a direct result of work or career assignments, or may be a key part of our role. But we can also fund our travel plans and holidays from finances generated from our work or careers.

Your hierarchical values system may not have career on the top tier of importance. Or simply put, career may not be a priority to you; it could be a means to an end. I have often heard people use the expression "Oh, it's just a job" or "It's a means to an end" or "I'm just in it for the money." This simply means that the role or job itself is not a main priority, it is low on your values list, or you have not yet connected with your passion and purpose.

So again, when we review the different areas of life, we see a direct link rooted back to work or career. And it is also worth repeating the fact that we get more of what we focus on or more of what we don't focus on. Much is to be gained from reviewing both the areas of life that you are getting good results in and those where you are not getting the results you aspire to. Narrow it down to a few areas and see if in some way you can link improvement to work or career as a solution to getting the types of results you want. We explore this in greater detail through the CPPD Strategy system.

CPPD Strategy

I've come to believe that each of us has a personal calling that's as unique as a fingerprint and that the best way to succeed is discover what you love and then find a way to offer it to others in the form of service, working hard, and also allowing the energy of the universe to lead you.
– Oprah Winfrey

So far we have presented to you some thoughts about professional and personal development and the links across the key areas of work and career. In this section I am going to expand upon career development in more detail and share some findings from research that I hope you will find interesting, logical, and beneficial to your career development plans.

The primary component that needs to be factored in is the *personal*, meaning the person's development. The more holistic approach is to integrate personal development into your CPD plans as CPPD (continuous professional and personal development). Professional development can be likened to hard skills development. The main objective of personal development is soft skills development. This makes sense and should be part of everyone's career development strategy.

Precision is the key to the CPPD Strategy. To illustrate this point, consider this story of a master carpet cutter. He was known nationally and globally among corporate hospitality businesses, and he was in high demand because of his reputation and the consistent quality of the work he performed and the service that he delivered. Compared to others in his industry he stood far above the crowd. The accuracy, the precision, and extremely high standards he provided in his service were second to none. He was booked out for months and months in advance, and his customers did not mind the wait because they knew he would deliver a quality service that would last well into the future. He travelled the world providing the same level of service and professionalism wherever he went.

His rivals envied him and respected him, and often they would seek his advice, which he gladly provided because he had evolved from the realm of competiveness to a mature helpful place of cooperation and collaboration. His motto was "do unto others as you would like them to do unto you," so he treated everyone fairly and professionally, whether in life or work. This is what people admired and loved about him.

One day while on an international project for a large hotel chain he was busy directing his team and installing carpets in a sizable area. The owner of the hotel chain complimented the master carpet cutter on the excellent work he was doing and consulted with him on other projects in the pipeline.

The owner of the hotel was just about to leave and he turned and said, "We have employed your services for many years now, and I have never found fault with your work compared to others we have used down through the years. Could you tell me what is your secret?"

It seemed as if the master carpet cutter was transported to another time and place. After some thought, a sage-like smile appeared upon his face. He turned to the owner and said, "It is very simple. I measure twice and cut once." They both laughed heartily and smiled and went their respective ways.

The CPPD Strategy is in many respects like the master carpet cutter story. It will assist you in measuring your best career fit so that you will also be able to precisely decide on what direction you want to go.

The CPPD Strategy works in the following areas:

- This system is useful if you feel stuck in your present role.
- It works if you feel unsure of what to do next.
- It can be a very powerful tool for professional development goals.
- It can assist you to make progress up the company ladder.
- It will benefit you with a solid assessment of your core strengths and areas for development.
- It will assist you if you are considering self-employment.
- If you are a business owner, this system is great for reorientation of your goals and designing your strategies.
- It will increase your vision and enable you to develop new strategies towards business development and growth.
- This system is great for developing your teams and setting new directions for your company.
- The CPPD Strategy plan can be delivered individually or through group coaching sessions.

At the core of the strategy is the assessment that measures your personality, skills, interests and values. From this your top career options are identified. The personality section will help you to identify the type of work that suits your natural talents and your authentic nature. It will help you to understand how you interact with others in the world of work. It will assist you in understanding your style of learning and thinking. It will help you understand how you like to work and the environments that will suit your personality best. You will gain clarity around your strengths and areas for development. This is helpful in preparing for interviews and also in developing your resume.

The section covering your skills helps you to focus on maximising your skills and to increase your fulfilment and enjoyment in your work. You will learn about skills you are naturally good at. You will understand the skills that have development potential and potential burnout areas to be aware of. You will learn what naturally motivates you and what will demotivate you in your work.

The section covering your interests helps you to learn how to target the type of work you are most interested in devoting your time and energy towards. You will learn about the types of work that you are most interested in, the activities that you prefer to avoid, and the types of work environments that are best suited to your interests.

The values section helps you to review what is important to you in the context of the world of work. You will identify the beliefs, principles, and standards that are important to you. You will learn and identify your core values. You will understand the sources of satisfaction and dissatisfaction in the world of work as they relate to your core values. You will be able to use this information and evaluate opportunities with your core values in mind.

In addition, if you are a student or interested in learning about your aptitudes, a further assessment can be tailored to help you understand your abilities in terms of verbal reasoning, checking ability, mechanical reasoning, abstract reasoning, spatial reasoning, and numerical reasoning.

Look at things not as they are, but as they can be. Visualisation adds value to everything. A big thinker always visualises what can be done in the future. He isn't stuck with the present.
– David J. Schwartz

The CPPD Strategy is a system that will give you a thorough plan to get your career and personal development goals fully aligned. In the fields of career development, technology is playing a greater part in providing complex computational calculations, and we can employ this technology to accurately assess our vocation (our natural ability or profession) in life. It is designed in several stages as follows:

Stage One, Identity: This level is the foundation stage. It helps you to review and assess six areas such as your confidence levels, self-esteem, and self-worth and to provide you with tools for development: To develop deeper belief in yourself and your abilities, generate motivation and increase productivity. To develop your personality, work ethic, values, attitudes, and a healthy approach to work and life. To generate and foster a positive outlook and develop resilience, perseverance, courage, flexibility and realism.

Stage Two, Alignments: This level assists you to review seven specific areas such as your experiences, mindset, and core values. It will help you to assess your areas for development and understand your core strengths.

Stage Three, Levels: This level reviews nine specific areas, assesses you for education, qualifications, what routes you have come, and what routes are open to you in your development plans.

Stage Four, Pathways: From this level we assess eleven areas and do a comprehensive assessment that will form the basis and core of your strategy. You will engage in a world class online assessment that will generate a thirty-two-page comprehensive report that will assist you in understanding your unique personality, strengths, values, interests, and skills. Combined it will provide you with a holistic view of your true self, which is vital in assisting you to arrive at a well-informed decision in selecting your career. Five scientifically matched career categories with several career options in each category will be identified based on your unique profile. This will guide you towards a career that will ultimately increase your satisfaction and your performance in your role, and will sustain your motivation. You will have discovered your purpose and passion in life and get on track towards living a happy, fulfilled career. We also help you to assess your life from a life coaching perspective.

In addition to your personalised career report, you will receive the CPPD Strategy workbook that will guide you in the complete process of your career and personal development. All the core areas of career development will be addressed here such as:

- *Job-seeking skills.* You will learn key skills to assist you to stay focused in your job-seeking activities.
- *Cover letters and application forms.* You will learn the key points in writing your cover letter and how to write a cover letter to get your resume noticed.
- *Resume.* You will be provided a template for developing a resume that will help you to stand apart from your competitors.
- *Portfolio.* This is helpful for attending interviews and demonstrating your achievements and certifications.
- *Interviews.* Learn how to prepare for the interview and how to perform to your best on the day. Gain insights into the interview process and ensure that you are confident to get noticed and land that job.

Stage Five, Environments: In this level, thirty areas are explored to assist you in understanding the types of environment that work for you and what role you see yourself having.

Stage Six, Formats: There are eight areas to explore here to assist you to define what your ideal career will look like in terms of the conditions that will work for you.

Stage Seven, Benefits: there are twenty areas to review here to help you understand and design the types of benefits you wish to be rewarded for your efforts.

The CPPD Strategy is a comprehensive and long-term strategic approach that is designed to give you a more robust and structured system for your personal and professional development. The industry requires change, and we increasingly require systems that can aid us to be prepared and focused for all stages in the evolution of the world of work.

For testimonials and more information, please check the "Further Reading" section at the end of this book, where you will find information on projects we have worked on and more on the CPPD Strategy. If you know others that you think would benefit from this information and the

CPPD Strategy package, please inform them of this service. See also the "Contact" section if you would like to get in touch.

Become who you were meant to be.
– The Lord of the Rings, Return of The King.

Summary

Certain things catch your eye, but pursue only
those that capture your heart.
– Native American Indian saying

In summary, we have discussed the WoW Factor and how you can benefit from developing a long-term strategy that includes personal development in addition to your professional development goals and plans. We have discussed how we can be exposed in the world of work to setbacks and negativities and how working a CPPD Strategy can ensure you are prepared to stay on course to succeed. We have outlined the benefits of personal development or soft skills training. We have discussed and explored continuous professional development. We have linked the benefits of adding personal development to your continuous professional development plans. We have explored the connectedness between career or work and many areas of life coaching or personal development areas of focus. We have explored and discussed what the CPPD Strategy system is and how it can benefit you in your professional and personal development goals. We have outlined who the CPPD Strategy will benefit and who can use it. We have provided recommendations for further reading and details on how you can contact Chrysalis Evolution for more information on how you can start the CPPD Strategy.

4QI – A Questionable Intelligence for Change

Patrick White

Patrick White is a consultant, executive coach, and trainer specializing in business strategy, business finance, marketing management, and organizational behaviour.

After a successful international corporate career in a variety of industries across thirteen countries, with responsibilities for up to 14,000 staff, he went on to become a serial entrepreneur. He has owned fourteen businesses in the hospitality, retail, IT, and food and beverage industries. His most recent business covers fuel and oil distribution and had a turnover of $US 2.6 billion, with 600 full-time and numerous part-time staff.

For the last twenty-three years, while owning these businesses, he has also worked as a high-level management consultant and executive coach in various business and not-for-profit sectors as well as an international public speaker and trainer on a variety of business and people management topics.

He continues to deliver regular public and in-house training seminars and to speak at international conferences. In the last twelve months he has worked in Switzerland, United Kingdom, Italy, Czech Republic, Ukraine, Russia, Malaysia, Singapore, Australia, Sudan, Oman, Kuwait, Saudi Arabia, Libya, Iran, Qatar, United Arab Emirates, and Bahrain.

Patrick has also published various articles and papers on business strategy, negotiation skills, influencing and persuading, emotional intelligence in the workplace, sales and marketing, and issues around training. He is author of the book Business Cookery – Tried and Tested Recipes for Business Success.

After many years studying at various institutions, a successful corporate career, time as a serial entrepreneur, and of late, a consultant, executive coach, and trainer, at the age of 62, I realised that the important decisions in business and life revolve around four simple questions. Constantly asking them, however, leads to a much greater success at what we are doing, whether it be in business or personal development.

I will get to what the four questions are later as I need to paint the picture about how this all came about.

I came to this realisation as the result of bringing together two important events that had occurred years apart in my business life. The first event occurred when I was visiting Japan in the early 1980s, during the corporate phase of my life. I was a senior executive for a large Australian conglomerate. The company I was working for had numerous divisions, one of which was the distributor of a well-known brand of Japanese car and another division that was the distributor for another well-known brand of Japanese electronics. This job necessitated visiting Japan on numerous occasions. These visits were made both more enjoyable and instructive because we also had a Japan-based director who used to guide me around the intricacies of dealing with the Japanese. It was during one of these visits that I was introduced to the *Kaizen* philosophy. I was told that roughly translated, this refers to a philosophy of continuous improvement, particularly as applied to manufacturing. It was one of the cornerstones to the success of Japanese industry after World War II, and helped them become dominant as manufacturers prior the growth of other countries like Korea and China. In simple terms, it focused on how to reduce the costs of inputs in production and how to fine tune the processes used to ensure that products were manufactured in the most efficient and cost effective way. This meant looking at even the smallest details to see if they could be improved. It helped transfer views on Japanese products from being cheap and nasty to their revered status later, as being the epitome of high quality.

This concept resonated with me immediately, and I could see how it could be applied in many other areas of business not involving manufacturing. It could be applied to logistics, accounting processes, organisational structures, and numerous other everyday activities. It therefore became part of the mindset I had to managing the various entities that came under my control, to the point that I tried to make it an important part of the culture in any organisations I was managing. In my non-manufacturing businesses it meant asking the question "What can we do better tomorrow than we are doing today?" My view was that this question should be an agenda item on every team meeting. It would help engender a culture of positive change.

The second event occurred in 1999, when doing a 360 appraisal type personal assessment during my time as a major distributor for an oil company in Australia. This was as part of a leadership course the fuel company had organised for its distributors to attend. Unfortunately, because I did not have much business respect for the person who was delivering the results of my assessment, I tended to miss the significance of what he was telling me. In fact, it was not the results that were the most important, but the type of personal SWOT (strengths, weaknesses, opportunities and threats) analysis I had to do to improve my leadership skills. The self-critique required me to examine what I was doing well and what could I do better.

Having sold off the businesses that I had owned, my wife and I decided to move to London, United Kingdom, and spend some of our retirement time there. We had meet in London thirty odd years earlier as poor travellers and decided it would be nice to return to the scene of the crime, but this time with some spending money. As I needed to have something to do, I set up a business consultancy in the hope that I could share some of the wisdom I had learnt during my career. As a result of requests from clients, this also morphed in to a training business as well. Subsequently I met someone who then became my business partner, and she brought her coaching skills on board. Now we were into executive coaching as well.

It was during a training session, when I was giving a public course in Saudi Arabia on leadership, that I found myself repeating some of what I had learnt all those years earlier. My passion for introducing the Kaizen philosophy to anyone who would listen was always there, but for the first time I now combined it with the 360 degree self-critique methodology I had later learnt but had not heeded as well as I should of. Initially it was only two questions, and then in later courses three questions, and finally now four questions. So now we had Kaizen plus, or as I later come to call it, 4Q. This seemed to be understood better and avoided the use of Japanese words, particularly as many of the audiences I addressed were people speaking English as a second language. Why complicate matters by using yet another language? This was Kaizen in action.

It did not matter what course I was teaching, whether it was a Mini MBA, marketing, leadership, teamwork, emotional intelligence, or numerous other courses. I could always quote the four questions as a way of approaching a problem, bringing about a change or for personal development. Interestingly enough, when the attendees at the various courses, both public and in-house, gave their answers to the group work or case study they often quoted the four questions as a way of rationalizing their arguments. They seemed to get it, and the four question approach had meaning for them.

Based on the fact that we talk of IQ (intelligence level), EQ (emotional intelligence), FQ (financial Intelligence) and SQ (social intelligence), it seemed logical to call my four questions 4QI (four questions Intelligence).

It now strikes me that if one of my previous managers or leaders had introduced me to these questions it could have saved me energy and anguish. It may have stopped me spending a lot of time trying to apply many complicated management theories and solutions to issues I faced on a day-to-day basis. Suggested management theories or solutions come and go, but the four questions are always the same whatever the problem or circumstances are. They provide the framework in which you apply the learned knowledge. They help us turn knowledge into wisdom. They help deal with change.

Knowledge can be obtained by reading a book. However, it is the application of that knowledge that is the most important thing for success, not the knowledge itself. So what are these questions, and how do they apply to business and to life?

The four questions are very simple to state. The challenge is to find the correct answers to them. The questions are:

1. What am I [are we] doing well?
2. What am I [are we] doing that could be done better?
3. What am I [are we] doing that I [we] should stop?
4. What am I [are we] not doing that I [we] should be doing?

Use the *I* form the question when referring to yourself and the *we* form when referring to a group, team, or organisation. Below, when I talk about applying the four questions to leadership by way of example, I use the *I* form. However, if we were talking about our company's marketing strategy, you would substitute *we* in the question.

For example, when I am giving the Mini MBA course, the topics normally are:

Leadership
Teamwork
Change Management
Strategy
Business Economics
Accounting and Finance
Negotiation Skills
Project Management
Marketing
Quality Management
Presentation Skills
Personal Development

In every one of these topics, asking the four questions is applicable about the competencies and attributes needed to do each well. This helps lead to the right choices for improved or corrective action to be made and to ensure success in each topic when applying them. It also applies to other courses I have given such as emotional intelligence, motivating staff, employee relations and retention, and many others. Again, while I can teach the knowledge, as I said before, the four questions provide the transition to wisdom. Getting knowledge is easy – just buy a book. The hard part is learning the wisdom to apply the knowledge. As the old saying goes, we all know that a tomato is a fruit. That's knowledge. Wisdom is knowing not to put it in a fruit salad.

So how do you apply 4QI in practice?

The methodology is simple. First, find out what the required skill sets, competencies, behaviours, attributes or whatever else is required are. Having ascertained them, then ask yourself the four questions to establish what level of intelligence you have regarding them. In other words, find your 4Q quotient. Let's now look at applying 4QI to four different areas: leadership, team building, emotional intelligence, and running a business.

To illustrate, first I'm going to apply it to being a great leader. Here I'm talking about leaders who lead because people want to follow them, not leaders who get their power purely because of their position.

The process is simple.

1. Identify what you need to ask the questions about – in this case, the factors that make for great leadership. This will obviously involve some research or observation on your part to establish what they are.
2. Ask yourself the four questions in relation to these factors and the components of these factors. As you will see below, this involves twenty-nine characteristics broken down into three categories. (The words in italics)

Many great things are written on the topic of leadership, and a lot of money is spent on leadership training. With a few notable exceptions, very little of it is applied, based on my experience as a consultant and the feedback I get from the many attendees who come to my courses. Other factors like quarterly results, the bottom line, managers' egos, poor leadership, and attitudes to staff seem to get in the way. As my mother used to say, "The road to hell is paved with great intentions."

Obviously, the first thing to be done is work out what am I going to ask the four questions about. To do this you must work out what are the key factors for success and how I am doing. Based on my experience dealing with and observing many great and successful leaders, the requirements for pronounced leadership can be broken down into three key factors:

1. The leader's personal characteristics and makeup;
2. That leader's having a novel outlook;
3. That leader's "turn on" capability.

These apply whether they are business leaders, family leaders, club leaders, or whatever type of leaders they are. So let's look at these one by one.

There are many *characteristics* a great leader needs. The following list is not exhaustive or in any way, nor is it in any order of priority.

-   *Commitment* – Am I [are we] totally committed to what I am [we are] are trying to achieve? Do I lead by example? Am I a role model?
-   *Focus* – Do I concentrate on the main game or get sidetracked easily?
-   *Confidence* – Do I exhibit confidence in what I am doing? People like to follow a confident leader.
-   *Demanding* – Do I expect high standards of all those involved?
-   *Courageous* – Am I making the hard decisions that need to be made?

- *Humility* – What is my order of importance? Is it myself first, then the group or organisation second, and finally the individuals third? Or is it the individuals first, the group or organisation second and myself last? I am sure you can figure out which is the correct order. Am I about making others shine before myself?
- *Open* – Am I prepared to be available and talk to everyone I impact and all the stakeholders involved in a friendly and helpful way?
- *Respectful* – Do I treat every person or group with respect and without prejudice or stereotyping?
- *Honest* – Am I a role model? Do I [we] walk the talk with regard to our values and behaviour?
- *Reflective* – Do I continually re-examine what we are doing and how we are behaving, and do I look for more effective ways of doing and behaving? This is like having a personal Kaizen look at ourselves.
- *Energised* – Followers do not want a tired leader. Do I exhibit a high level of energy to those around us, even if I don't feel like it sometimes?
- *Relentless* – Can I carry on even when the going gets tough to ensure I achieve the goals?
- *Non-jargony* – Do I ensure that when I speak to people I do so in a way they can understand?
- *Vulnerable* – Am I trying to come across as Superman or just a normal human being doing the best job I can do?
- *Curious* – Do I question things continuously or just accept the status quo? Am I happy to embrace change whether it is easy or hard?
- *Passionate* – An absolute necessity for a leader. Do I show passion and make others around me feel passionate about what we are doing?

Now let's turn our attention to having a *novel outlook*, the second factor required for great leadership. What are the key ingredients to ensure you as a leader have the right outlook? The following eight may be of use:

- The ability to *look laterally* at things and not just with a narrow focus. Am I lifting my head and seeing the big picture? Am I a *human doing* or a *human being*?
- Do I understand that the rules and norms can be questioned and, if need be, ignored? Am I prepared to *bend the rules*? All progress is made by people bending the rules. Are we being ruled by the policy police? Do I slavishly adhere to accepted behaviour?
- Great leaders *like pressure*. They want challenge. This is not to be confused with stress.
- Leaders perform best when they surround themselves with people who have the right attitude. They *rate attitude*. That attitude is to be successful and enjoy a challenge.
- *Risk taking* is an integral part of leadership. Decisions have to be made; otherwise there is no progress. All decisions have some element of risk. Great leaders don't shy away from this.
- To lead one needs followers. We need to *be accessible* to those followers, whoever they are – our children, our team members, and so on. If we are not accessible it will make it hard for them to know what we want them to do, why we want them to do it, and when we want them to do it.
- Great leaders are *strongly visionary*. They are concerned about what is to be achieved, how it is to be achieved, and when it is to be achieved. This requires a strong future orientation.
- If you are a leader in an organisation that has customers you need to be *customer obsessed*. You need to realise it is satisfying the customer that is the key to our success. Anything that compromises that success cannot be tolerated. In other situations, it may be the success of the group members that we have to be obsessed about, e.g. family members, team members, or other followers.

The third and final factor that makes for great leaders is their *turn-on capability*. There are several components to this, and if the leader has these then he will build followers.

- Great leaders are *good listeners*. Two ears, one mouth is often applicable in the ratio they use them. *Listening* here means *active* listening, that is, being fully present for the speaker.
- Being a leader is not being a one-man band. It requires *involving people*, talking and listening to a range of opinions before making a decision. An authentic leader allows other opinions to be expressed.
- *Trust* is a vital component to ensure successful leadership. People want to be trusted, and they want to see that trust in action. Without trust between people you can achieve very little. We all rely on each other.
- As we are all well aware, people like to be appreciated, whether it is our child who makes his bed well, a sports team member who makes a good play, or a staff member who does his job well. Leaders *appreciate* people regularly.
- Making things we want to do or even things we have to do *fun* makes for a more enjoyable life experience. This is not too hard to do if you put your mind to it.
- Finally, we need to show that we *care* about the people that are important to us. They are not just numbers or tools we will use for our own selfish motives.

Now that we have the knowledge of what is required, we apply the three questions. The answers guide us for the way forward.

The example above of leadership is an *I* application of the process.

Let's now look at a *we* application of the process. In this case, we might want to look at how a team is performing. It could be a business team, a sports team, or even a family, or any other group that needs to function as a team to be successful. Like leadership, there are various key traits a group needs, to ensure that it will function effectively as a team.

Again from my experience, there seem to be thirteen characteristics a team needs to have any chance of functioning as an effective unit. The key traits in no particular order are:

Trust – The members of the team must trust each other. When one person says he will do something, it gets done.

Empowerment – The leader has genuinely shared his power around the team members, and they feel they have responsibility and ownership of the tasks allocated.

Proper authentication – To ensure true empowerment, all team members' opinions should be listened to.

Ability to manage conflict – Amongst any group of people there will be differences of perspectives and opinions. This is desirable, but it needs to be managed to ensure the group will perform in the end as a team and abide by the decisions made.

Good communication skills – Team members need to be able to communicate with each other in the form that is appropriate for the messages to be passed. This communication should allow for feedback and not just be a monologue.

Delegation as a necessity – Delegation should be real. That is, the task should be performed by the lowest-paid person who has the capability to perform it.

Ability to be creative, innovate, and take risks – The team cannot stand still. As the saying goes: "If we always do what we have always done, we will always get what we have always got."

Excellent leadership – The team needs a good leader who not only has to make decisions but also guide, mentor, and counsel the team members.

Integration of different personalities – There are often as many personalities in a team as there are people. This is desirable, as the person who appears negative is just as important as the members who want to "have a go." It provides balance. There will always people who want to be dominant, others who are consensus driven, and some that just deal in facts and figures and seem somewhat emotionless. It is the leader's job to make it work.

Success in encouraging and handling change – A team must be continually looking do things better, having a Kaizen mentality.

Setting goals and objectives – These are the glue that binds the team together. Without clear goals and objectives which are known and clearly understood by the team members, we will never make a group into a team.

Development and training of team members – You need to meet the personal aspirations of each team member. Nobody wants to stand still. They want to feel that they are learning and developing as a result of being part of the team.

Having researched the information above, we can now apply the four questions to see what we need to do to improve team performance. The answers should help us progress to a development plan to improve the functioning and success of the team.

Now let us look at a topic that is much more personal.

The topic of *emotional intelligence* is one that seems to be on everyone's minds as of late, and for good reason: It's one of the best ways for a person to seize control of life, not just in business, but in personal affairs as well. This chapter is not meant to be a dissertation on emotional intelligence, Better-stated treatises on the topic may be found elsewhere. Suffice to say that in general, having control over your emotions is always a positive thing. You will be able to retain control of your responses in meetings or negotiations; you will be able to ask the right questions and judge reactions in your personal relationships; and perhaps most importantly, you will naturally become more in tune with your own emotional state.

Having a strong emotional intelligence isn't all about you, though. Of course, you'll benefit from this aspect of it as well, but not *only* you. One of the key strengths of having a high emotional intelligence lies in how it increases your ability to foster relationships with others.

Whether it's establishing rapport quickly with a client who you're trying to negotiate a deal with, or even just talking to an old friend, having a high emotional intelligence is going to help you out. Because you're more in tune with your emotional states, you'll also be more receptive to the emotional states of others. You'll become more empathic, and people will naturally grow to trust you and confide important matters in you.

Emotional intelligence is not just for the workplace, but for all of life. Because it improves the way you connect to the rest of the world in a direct fashion, it's no exaggeration to say that it's one of the most important undertakings you'll ever embark upon. Given its importance, it would seem a good place to use the four questions. Yet again we need to find out about what to we need to do to apply them.

In 1995, Daniel Goleman published a book called *Emotional Intelligence: Why It Matters More Than IQ*. This book was an immediate success. In it Goleman stated that there are five traits that research has shown to help predict both business and personal success. These traits became the foundation for understanding which people had high EQs. The traits are:

Self-Awareness – People with high emotional intelligence are usually very self-aware. They understand their emotions, and because of this they don't let their feelings rule them. They're confident – because they trust their intuition and don't let their emotions get out of control.

Self-Regulation – This is the ability to control emotions and impulses. People who self-regulate typically don't allow themselves to become too angry or jealous, and they don't make impulsive, careless decisions. They think before they act. Characteristics of self-regulation are thoughtfulness, comfort with change, integrity, and the ability to say no.

Motivation – People with a high degree of emotional intelligence are usually motivated. They're willing to defer immediate results for long-term success. They're highly productive, love a challenge, and are very effective in whatever they do.

Empathy – This is perhaps the second most important element of emotional intelligence. Empathy is the ability to identify with and understand the wants, needs, and viewpoints of those around you. People with empathy are good at recognizing the feelings of others, even when those feelings may not be obvious. As a result, empathetic people are usually excellent at managing relationships, listening, and relating to others. They avoid stereotyping and judging too quickly and they live their lives in an open, honest way.

Social Skills – It's usually easy to talk to and like people with good social skills, another sign of high emotional intelligence. Those with strong social skills are typically team players. Rather than focus on their own success first, they help others develop and shine. They can manage disputes, are excellent communicators, and are masters at building and maintaining relationships.

There are also four other dimensions that have to considered. In 1990 Peter Salovey and John Mayer published an article called "Emotional Intelligence." In it they talked about a four-branch model of EI that included the ability to:

- *Identify Emotions:* Can you figure why people act the way they do?
- *Use Emotions:* Can you use your feelings to help you gain insight into others or to enhance the way you decide and think?
- *Understand Emotions:* What is the depth of your emotional knowledge?
- *Manage Emotions:* To what extent do you allow your feelings to positively affect your decision making?

Being able to also handle the four branches above, along with the five Goleman traits, is all part of being emotionally intelligent. Now again, having established what we need to do to have a high EQ score, we can ask ourselves the four questions. Those areas in which we are not strong form part of our personal development plan.

Let us now look at an entirely different use of 4QI.

Up to now we have been focusing on soft skills. Let's next look at an area which also requires attention to hard skills.

Every business owner faces a daily challenge to succeed, whether it's managing inventory, increasing sales, resolving customer concerns, or simply making sure the shop door is unlocked on time in the morning. Not a day goes by without some issue presenting itself and needing to be addressed. Unfortunately, a large number of business owners become so focused on the daily problems like these that they lose sight of other broad issues of equal or greater importance. Losing sight of these things might be easy to do, but it is also a dangerous way to do business because it sabotages the long-term success and profitability of the business itself. It's like focusing all of your time and effort on putting out fires but paying no attention at all to preventing those fires in the first place.

As an entrepreneur who has owned and operated multiple businesses, I am often asked by attendees at various workshops that I deliver, "What are the key things that you need to do to be successful?" Being an entrepreneur can be exciting and challenging, but without controlling certain aspects of the business, we will not survive in the long term. To answer this question, I usually talk about ten specific areas. This list is not definitive but certainly covers areas that I would be asking the four questions about.

1. *Do I [we] know the customer's needs?* Don't assume that you know what your customers want just because you knew what they wanted two years ago when you launched your business. Their needs have undoubtedly changed in some way as time has passed, but since you have been so involved in running the business, you have likely not paid attention to these changes. One of the biggest mistakes we see is when business owners are so confident their clients need what is being offered that they don't realize their clients simply don't want to buy what is being offered. To avoid letting this happen to you, it's critical that you engage with your customers to really listen to what they say (and sometimes to note what they don't say). Set aside other distractions, and focus in on the voice of your customers; turn up the volume on those voices so they are easier to hear and understand.

2. *Am I [are we] focusing on profit, not cash flow?* It is very easy to become overly focused on profit; after all, it's the profit that makes your business successful, right? To a certain extent the answer to this question is yes, but to an equal extent the answer

to this question is certainly no. Profit is important, but cash flow is just as important if not more important. A great number of very profitable companies end up failing and going under because they pay too much attention to profit and not enough attention to cash flow. They simply run out of money.

3. *Have I [we] set the goals big enough?* When you were growing up, perhaps your parents told you to dream big, set your goals high, and reach for the stars. Somewhere along the way, though, it became much simpler (at least in the short term) to set smaller goals that could be reached more quickly and easily. The problem is that when you spend your time and energy setting small goals, it's much like setting off on a long journey without making a plan for where you're going to go. Instead of mapping out your route in advance, you wait and choose which road to travel on whenever you happen to reach a junction or intersection. While this may be exciting, fun, and adventurous, you are much more likely to end up driving round in circles so that you never reach a worthwhile destination. Just as a leisurely Sunday drive may take you meandering through the countryside without purpose or direction, setting goals that are too small sends your business meandering through its operation without purpose or direction. You will never achieve long-term business success if you don't plan ahead, set meaningful goals, and put your time and effort into meeting those larger goals.

4. *Do I [we] treat marketing as an important activity?* Only by taking the marketing approach can your business grow, prosper, and build up a lasting base of loyal customers. When you follow this path, you establish and reinforce a distinct brand for your company. Most people think a brand is a logo, a colour, or a trademark phrase, but these are just a few of the tools a business uses to communicate visually. Branding is a much broader and deeper concept, focused on developing an intense understanding of what your organisation is all about. This in turns gives your

employees and your customers a strong appreciation of your values and the way you do business.

Effective marketing takes a bit longer to generate results than sales do, but the results you get are much stronger and longer-lasting because they lead to more loyal customers who come back to buy from you repeatedly. What's more, this is a much less expensive way to run your business; the cost of acquiring a new customer is much, much higher than the cost of keeping an existing customer. This is why the most profitable customers are those who are repeat buyers.

5. *Do I [we] have a Kaizen philosophy throughout the business?* When your business has a Kaizen approach, you and your team pay a great deal of attention to fixing problems and learning from them when things go wrong. However, you and your team pay even more attention to looking at things that are going very well and asking yourselves, "How can we do this even better?"

6. *Do you know your competitors inside out?* Unless your business is a pure monopoly, your customers have the option of making choices about where and from whom they buy. They can just as easily decide to buy from your competitors as from you. How, then, can you influence their decision-making process and get them to buy from you instead of from someone else? What can you do to help them make an informed choice and turn to you for fulfilling their needs?

The most important thing is to identify your competitors and know as much about them as possible. Look at the situation from the customer's perspective, taking into consideration which businesses offer which products or services and how those products or services compare with each other. Only when you know your competitors inside out can you determine how to differentiate your business from theirs and convince customers to spend their money with you.

7. *Are you a too-tough negotiator, a.k.a. screwing your suppliers?* When you negotiate too harshly and focus too much on getting

a lower price, your suppliers will very likely make adjustments to meet that price. These adjustments quite often mean a dramatic reduction in the quality or effectiveness of what you buy from them. For instance, a supplier might need to use inferior products or equipment in order to reduce the price you pay. Or they might be forced to outsource work to overseas contractors who don't understand your needs or simply are not capable of doing the job properly.

Remember, working with your suppliers is a partnership rather than a competition or an adversarial activity. Treat them with respect, honesty, and integrity, and they will return the favour. Your suppliers are stakeholders in your business, so treat them as you would any other stakeholder.

8. *Do you understand the critical drivers in your marketplace?* Your business operates in a marketplace where an array of factors influence and entice customers to make certain decisions about what and from whom to buy. These factors are known as the *drivers* in the marketplace; in other words, they drive customers to make certain decisions. Drivers influence different individuals in different ways, so part of successfully navigating your business through the marketplace is having a solid understanding of which drivers are most critical to your target audience of customers and potential customers.

9. *EI, EQ, NLP – What are they?* It used to be that the only qualification you needed to successfully manage people and interact with customers was seniority. The more years you had under your belt doing a particular job, the thinking went, the better able you were to handle the extra responsibilities and challenges of being in charge. The world of business has changed dramatically since those days, and so have the qualifications you need to be successful.

Research shows that entrepreneurs tend to have a high level of technical skills in whatever field their business operates. This is a real advantage when getting a business off the ground, but as the business grows and matures, an entirely different and new set of skills is required to create long-term success. These are sometimes called the *soft skills*, and they are much more focused on non-technical things that may seem unimportant at first but are actually critical to the survival and prosperity of your business. If you are not actively developing your soft skills, you are operating at a distinct disadvantage in today's business environment.

10. *Do I [we] have timely data to make decisions?* It's a nice fantasy to think that you can go into a business situation and have enough knowledge and skill to just wing it along the way. You may have even tried this approach at some point during your life and experienced one of those rare occasions where it actually worked. But no matter how smart, creative, charismatic, or engaging you may be, if you allow yourself to get into the habit of winging it in relation to your business, then your business is bound to fail.

You might not fully agree with this, especially if you have read one of the many business biographies (such as Richard Branson's *Screw It, Let's Do It!*), where the world's most successful entrepreneurs relate stories of how they have relied on gut instinct or intuition to build their successful businesses. As tempting as it might be to rely on this approach yourself, remember that these biographies also contain strong warnings about the limitations of guts and instinct. They emphasise just how important it is to pay attention also to details such as cash flow, market position, and what market data reveals.

Having listed ten key factors that need to be managed when running a business, we can ask the four questions about each of them.

This chapter has discussed four simple questions about important matters that impact your success. In each of the topics discussed, establishing the key factors and then answering each of the four questions will help to foster continuous improvement and ensure that you are building in positive change in your undertaking.

Power Choices at Pivotal Points

Ian Crawford

Ian's early life was all about sport. As a physical education teacher, he taught and coached in the United Kingdom, France, Spain, and Canada in sports ranging from soccer to shooting, archery, and abseiling. During time with mountain rescue in Wales and as a personal trainer in London, Ian worked closely with Elite Sporting and the Olympic team.

Ian returned home and became an organisational consultant, which saw him work throughout Australia, Botswana, Lesotho, Malaysia, and India.

As the owner and principal trainer of Candor Training and Consultancy, he now trains and coaches managers and leaders in Australia and internationally, including India, Denmark, Mongolia, China, and Vietnam. Ian specialises in assisting leadership groups to develop sustainable high-performing teams.

In addition to his leadership work, he continues to be a highly regarded performance coach for business owners and members of professional sporting teams throughout Australia. Clients include Rio Tinto, BHP Billiton, Mearsk Oil and Gas, Barrick Gold, Vietnam Oil, Downer EDI, Woodside, Orica, the federal government, state governments, local governments, Xstrata, and the Australian Sports Commission.

Recently, Candor Training and Consultancy received a 100 Most Influential Businesses award. Ian is a contributing author for Australia's leading leadership magazine, CEO.

Ian is also contracted as Rio Tinto Global Master Facilitator, where he is solely responsible for training and accrediting trainers worldwide.

Ian is a sought-after coach and facilitator around the world for his unique, inspiring, and challenging style of delivery that moves participants and organisations to achieve more success than they ever thought possible.

Eight steps to eradicate behaviours that are holding you back from living the life you deserve

A young athlete catches a pass from his basketball team mate. It wasn't a great pass. It was off target, sloppy, and not quite strong enough, but the athlete receiving it took possession with an air of grace and ease, as if the ball was meant to be in his hands, like something special was about to happen. That was no surprise, as this basketballer was special – so special that coaches from six different countries had flown in to watch someone who was touted as the next great international star. For now, the gifted athlete lived up to their expectations as he glided gracefully down the court, making all before him look slow and clumsy.

The athlete called a number representing a set play, one that had been practised until it was ingrained into the subconscious of the entire team. Something special was about to happen. The first pass was superb, as was the second. Then the player holding the ball decided to shoot instead of making a third pass. The shot fell short.

The athlete, with experts from all over the world watching, changed – and when I say changed, I mean he exploded. His face turned red and his hands clenched into fists as his temper rose. Almost out of control, the athlete raced over to the player who had made the failed shot, grabbed him, and unravelled a verbal tirade never heard before in the local stadium.

His opportunity to become the "next great thing" crumbled right there. The coaches who had travelled so far to see this star stood up and left. In doing so, leaving the young athlete's dreams in tatters.

Across town, a new manager arrived at work. Everything seemed the same as any other day, except that today this manager had to make a presentation to the senior leadership group. It was a twenty-minute review of the last six months' business performance. The manager despised public speaking. However, he felt ready to make what was surely going to be at the very least a passable presentation. The manager had put a massive amount of time and effort into developing and practising the speech. This held him in good stead, until twenty minutes from presentation time. The first signs started subtly, with a slight tightness in his stomach, which continued to grow. Also increasing were his temperature and shakes. Then the beads of sweat started. By the time the manager arrived in the presentation room, not only was he barely able to string words together, the words were out of order and inaudible.

Have you ever experienced a behaviour or action that, once it happens, you know immediately that you could have handled it better?

It may not be as severe as those described here, but do you get nervous in certain situations, have negative thoughts when you don't want to, overeat, often get angry at the kids or with that person who pulls out in front of you while driving home?

Or perhaps it's the self-talk that convinces you, when you wake up in the morning ready to exercise, that "rest is an important part of any exercise program." You're right, but not on day one!

We have all been there – a time when our thoughts, words, and ultimately our actions have not been the most appropriate to assist us in reaching the goal we were hoping to achieve. In fact, they took us in the opposite direction.

If you have ever experienced anything like this, then you are exactly where you need to be.

These two stories are real life examples of people who have come to me for coaching to help get rid of those "unhelpful" behaviours. The strategies I outline here are what I use when personally coaching clients.

Keep in mind that these strategies are useable anywhere and any time you want to change a non-productive thought or action or to enhance a productive thought or action.

So what are you waiting for? Let's get started!

Choose...

Every New Year's Eve millions of people decide to make changes to live a better and more enjoyable life. Some people call them goals, others changes, and some of us call them New Year's resolutions. You know... the lose weight, stop smoking, spend more time with family, eat better type of resolutions.

I'm sure you will not be surprised to know that 92 per cent of people (75 per cent in the first week) do not achieve their New Year's resolutions. Why is that? Their goals seem to be important. Why don't people stick to them?

Well, it's quite simple really. They don't choose to. Yes, you heard me correctly! I have no doubt that people believe it's a *good idea* to change. What is missing is a truly deep desire to effect change in their lives.

So when I say choose, I mean really choose. That deep down, foot-stomping, no more EVER feeling, where you know that the line in the sand has been drawn type of choosing. The real choice, that if made right now and held on to, will change your life forever. You need to be ready to close the door on that old behaviour and know that you will never, ever open it again.

That may seem a little dramatic if you are trying to stop eating so much chocolate. But... it is the *only* starting point that will give you the very best chance of *successfully* changing.

Recently, a man approached me to assist him to stop smoking. When asked for what reason he wanted to stop smoking, he replied, "Because my wife told me to!" I knew that this was going to be a struggle. He finally decided that he wasn't ready to stop smoking, and we parted ways. Why? There was no desire *from him* to quit smoking. When I asked him if smoking was a problem and if he really wanted to stop smoking, he said no. Seven months later he returned with his own reasons. I was then able to then assist him to stop smoking.

So, are you ready to change? Are you ready to leave that unhelpful behaviour behind forever? Excellent! Time for action! Here is the next part of choosing.

It's important for you to understand that the outcomes you experience in your life, both good and bad, are simply outcomes of your thoughts. Did you notice that I used the word *experience?* I understand that people have unfortunate things happen in their lives and that our experience in these events varies between individuals.

For example, we have all been in a situation where someone has pulled out in front of us whilst driving. One driver will shrug their shoulders and let it go, whereas another will get angry, cursing at the other driver for the next ten kilometres. Both people experienced the same situation, yet it is how they *perceived* the situation that caused the mild response or emotional outburst.

One person focused on, *What an idiot that driver was to cut me off! I'm going to follow him and give him a piece of my mind.*

Meanwhile, the other person thought, *That person may have cut me off to get their sick child to the hospital.*

It was the same situation, same evidence, although a *very* different experience for each person.

What you and everyone around you are experiencing right now is filtered through your own thoughts and emotions. And the way you filter a situation can change your experience – which is *really* exciting! You don't have to wait for anything external to change around you. You can make the changes right here, right now.

To coach you through these strategies I have put together an *Action Book*. This will assist you to complete the upcoming activities, record your thoughts, and establish clear action plans to move you forward. You can find it at http://www.candortraining.com/pivotal-points. Go and get that now. It's critical to taking action and using these strategies successfully.

Unravel the Unwanted Problem

Let's start with some action.

In the *Action Book* there is a section entitled "Describing the Problem." In that section your task is to write down the problem you would like to get rid of in as much detail as possible. This is a time to let it flow, no holding back, just write until you can write no more.

When I am coaching people and I ask them to describe the problem they no longer want, I'm continually surprised at how nondescript and wandering the information tends to be. Detail is fine, but when it rambles and has no direction, it tells me that this is the first time they have actually given conscious thought to the issue they are facing.

This may sound strange, but people tend to allow their problems to simply impact on them rather than to clearly define them. To put it another way, it appears that people tend to *allow* it to happen to them rather than give some real thought as to why and how it happens.

So before we move on to the next step, go back to your writing and make sure it's a description of your issue that answers these questions:

1. What are the triggers for the problem?
2. What feelings do you have once this trigger occurs?
3. What do these feelings cause you to do?

While completing the activities in this chapter, you may start to feel sad, angry, or a range of emotions you know aren't going to help you. If this occurs, stand up, walk away from the task and go do something else, *anything* else, until that emotion fades away. Then return to finish the task. You will have to trust me when I tell you that simply moving away when you get negative emotions actually assists in breaking the problem down. Even if it requires you to move away a hundred times, it's essential that you don't just stay there and be sad or overwhelmed (or any other emotion that presents itself to you).

Remember: A problem well-described is a problem half-solved.

Exciting End Point

One of my favourite sayings comes from the late, great leadership guru Stephen Covey, who discovered that highly effective people always "start with the end in mind." (Covey, S. 1989)

Before we can start to build a better behaviour in your world, we need to have a clear definition on what the end point – your new and more empowering behaviour – will be like. First you need to complete an activity.

Describe the way you would like to act or what you would be like, when you have your new behaviour. What's the end point'? How will you know that you have achieved what you want to achieve? Spend a few minutes thinking and recording your thoughts and feelings down in the *Action Book* under the section "End Point 1."

Welcome back. If you have just kept reading this section without doing the activity, then put the book down and do the activity! Remember: *real change* only occurs with action.

Earlier on, you were asked to describe the problems you are facing. My guess is that the description of your positive outcome, your new behaviours, was described with a lot fewer words, physical movement, and emotion than when you described the problem you are leaving behind. Right?

Without exception, when I am coaching people and ask them about their end point, I get one of two responses. The first is a weak description of what they want to achieve, which in a lot of cases is made up on the spot. The second is a blank stare.

Consider this: your brain is an incredible piece of machinery that is able to take in, process, modify, store, and respond to a vast amount of information, incomparable to anything mankind has been able to build.

Unfortunately, in most people, their unhelpful behaviour is often experienced as a highly vivid picture with stereo sound, strong words, and powerful emotions. On the other hand, the desired state is a photo representing the behaviours, with little colour, no sound, weak words, and limited positive emotions.

Our powerful supercomputer of a brain loves brightly painted and vibrant pictures and will automatically go to that place with joy and ease. Presently, the attractive picture we have in our head isn't the place we want it to go.

We need to flip things around. We have to make the behaviours we want appealing to the brain. Stephen Covey further commented:

It is based on the principle that all things are created twice. There is a mental (first) creation, and a physical (second) creation. The physical creation follows the mental, just as a building follows a blueprint. If you don't make a conscious effort to visualize who you are and what you want in life, then you empower other people and circumstances to shape you and your life by default. (Covey, S. 1989)

Recently I was working with an elite athlete who had just competed unsuccessfully at the Olympic Games and was starting her long journey to the next Games. She had found getting up for training a struggle, which was unusual for her. When I asked her to describe her end point, it was simply, "To win a gold medal." I am sure you will agree that is a great goal, even if it isn't that imaginative. So after talking to her about end points and how to use them, we revisited her end point and she came up with:

"It is the now the final day at the Olympics, and as I look down I see and feel proud of the Australian Olympic uniform that I am wearing. I know that all the hard work and training has led me to this very moment. As my eyes rise to the crowd, I hear the glorious hum made by the collective cheering of over 90,000 people. My eyes search for my parents in the crowd. I feel the ribbon from my gold medal gently rubbing my neck. I hold the gold medal in my hand and look down at it, feeling its clean edges of. The national anthem starts to play and I stand tall, very tall, knowing that this is my time – my time to celebrate."

The question is, what is going to provide the on going motivation to get up early, train, deal with injuries and all the other challenges? The first version, "to win a gold medal," or the second version? Of course it is the second one that paints a picture and creates strong emotional links for the Olympian.

Your action in this section is to go back to your *Action Book* and rewrite your end point under "End Point 2." This time, make it vivid and exciting and include what you want to see, hear, and feel when you have reached the destination you are looking for.

Pain Pleasure Paradox

Nature has placed mankind under the governance of two sovereign masters, pain and pleasure. It is for them alone to point out what we ought to do, as well as to determine what we shall do.
– Jeremy Bentham (1779)

Have you ever considered why people continue to do things to themselves that they know are unhealthy and harmful, but do it anyway?

Our brains are incredible things. They have the ability to input, store, and use information within milliseconds when needed. This function allows us to live our lives and while we are busy doing what we do, it protects us from harm and lets us experience pleasure.

Ultimately, our brain is attempting to move us from pain towards pleasure. We see this all the time: when we get hungry, we seek out food; or if we have physical pain, we seek out ways to relieve us from this pain. Everything we do, say, and think is always moving us away from what we perceive as painful and towards what we perceive as pleasurable. Things can sometimes get a little mixed up. What our brain sometimes *thinks* is pleasurable, is what is actually holding us back.

For example, a young woman came to see me about assisting her with issues she had around eating and obesity. Somewhere in her subconscious brain, the idea of eating a large amount of food and not exercising was pleasurable. Think about it – why *else* would we choose to overeat (or smoke, etc.) when we consciously know it is bad for us? By understanding the pain and pleasure model, I know that for some reason this woman continues to eat this way to move away from her definition of pain and towards pleasure. So for me to assist and for her to move forward, we needed to understand what that pleasure was and, in doing so, turn it into something that empowers her rather than repeating unhealthy and undesirable behaviours over and over again.

During our first coaching session we started to talk about some of the reasons she would consume so much high calorie food knowing it was impacting her health. After a lengthy discussion, she admitted the reason she remained this weight was because "at least people noticed me when I am fat." That is, when she walked into a room, people would look at her because of her size. As a coach, I don't have to understand reasons, I just accept that it is real for them.

Understanding the pain and pleasure concept can be a *life changer. So how do I use it to make decisions?* I hear you ask. Good question! Stay tuned.

As the self-help guru Anthony Robbins once said, "The secret of success is learning how to use pain and pleasure instead of having pain and pleasure use you. If you do that, you are in control of your life. If you don't, life controls you."

Basically, the more pain we place on something, the harder and faster our brain is going to move away from it towards pleasure.

So the reason you still have the behaviour you want to change is that there is still not enough pain associated with it to stop it. When we look at some highly destructive habits like smoking, drug taking, or overeating, people *know* they aren't good for them, consciously, that is. But while they still continue to undertake the habit, we know the pleasure it brings on for the individual, whatever that is, is greater than the pain they are experiencing.

Case in point: I have a friend who works in the transplant unit of a hospital. His job is to rehabilitate patients who have had lung transplants. He regularly tells me that after people have been given a new set of lungs and in turn, a second chance at life, they can still be found smoking again, even though smoking is the habit that almost killed them! So even though they know consciously that smoking will give them ultimate pain (meaning that it will eventually kill them), deep in their subconscious brain there is the perception that *not* smoking is more painful.

You can quite easily see how powerful this pain and pleasure concept is, can't you?

So let's use your newfound knowledge. Grab your *Action Book* and go to the page entitled "Pain Pleasure Paradox," thinking about the issue that you want to change. Write in the left hand "pain" column all the painful things that will occur if you do *not* change the behaviour you have now. The key to success for this activity is detail. Write as many things as you can *in detail*. The more, the better. If you feel upset or uncomfortable while compiling this list… *good*! Get stuck into it!

Once you have completed the "Pain" column, it's time for the fun bit – to *dream* about what you will achieve once you have changed the behaviour. So move to the "Pleasure" column.

This time get your end point in mind and write down all the positive and exciting things that will occur as soon as this issue goes away forever.

Remember, it is specifics we are looking for. So if one of your responses is, "To spend more time with the kids," keep going. *What* are you going to *do* with the kids in that time? Where will you take them? How will you *feel* about spending more time with your children? Even name the specific park you will start taking them to and the activities you will do together.

Or if it is to stop road rage, the outcome might be "To feel very calm on the drive home from work." What will you be doing (or feeling) on the way home? How will you feel about that? How will you feel when you arrive home from work without any anger?

If you don't want to write words, draw pictures. If you don't want to draw pictures, cut out photos from magazines to represent what will happen when this issue is no longer with you.

Detail… detail… detail!

Final tip: If I said to you, "Don't think of a yellow taxi," what would you do? Same as everyone – you would think of a yellow taxi before trying to quickly get the images from your brain and not think about it!

The reason we do this is because we cannot process negatives. So when I ask someone, "Don't…" their first thought is to do exactly what I have asked them not to do. If you are a parent, you know exactly what I am talking about. You might have asked your child countless times "Don't put the glass there" or "Don't forget to put the dirty laundry out." You then get incredibly frustrated when they do the opposite of what you have asked. So when you are creating your list of positives, list what you *do* want rather than what you *don't* want. For example, if you wrote down, "Don't get angry at people who pull out in front of me," flip it around and list the things you would rather do: Listen to favourite music; feel calm and relaxed on the inside; take a deep breath and let it go.

Spend some time right now starting the exercise. Keep going until you have nothing to write. Leave it for a while and return to it later. Once again, this is all about detail and making it all compelling for you. Remember, there are no right or wrong answers, just *your* answers.

Time to get into it… Time to dream… Time to write down all the positives that will occur when this problem disappears forever.

Sometimes you will find that this process evokes some interesting emotions, and you need to be aware of how you respond to that.

Make sure you don't drop down into a blame mentality. If you find yourself saying, "How stupid am I to act like this?" or something similar, stop and step into a *responsibility* mindset. This is a mindset where you can get excited. You now understand that *you* are in control of your thoughts and have strategies that can change the old habits and install bigger, better, more empowering strategies.

Position Pivotal Point

I mentioned earlier that people tend to move into the "no longer wanted" issues without even realising it. What we also know is that there is always a trigger – a point in which we move from just walking along the street feeling happy into the pathway that takes us to where we don't want to be.

When we identify this point and become aware, it allows us to control which path we go down. This is the reason I wanted to make the end point so vivid and strong. If we don't have an array of paths to go down then we will always go down the same one.

Here is your action point for this section. Picture yourself just going through your daily life, enjoying the things you should be enjoying, where the issue you no longer want is not there. Keep doing this until you find you are reliving the old habit you no long want.

Stop! Now rewind the pictures or movie in your mind until you find the point that you moved into the poor habit. What did you see? What did you hear? What did you feel? Keep moving the movie backwards and forwards until you find what it is. Importantly, do not judge what you find. There is no right and wrong. During my time as a coach I seen had trigger points that were white toy rabbits, a doorknob, a husband's certain look, and the smell of coffee.

Spend some time thinking about this and make sure you find it. If you don't find it the first time, that's OK. It will be there and it will come to you.

Once you have got it, write it down in your *Action Book* under Position Pivotal Point.

Well done!

We are now going to take that trigger and make it more obvious in your mind, so that you never again move past it without seeing it. What we want is to make it so obvious that you cannot step over it and into the problem. We want to you walk into it and notice it and in doing so, have choices about what you do next.

So place the trigger back in your mind and:

1. Notice what you see around you. What do you see when you have identified the trigger? Once you notice it, turn up the colours so they are most appealing to you. If pictures are black and white turn them into brightly coloured ones that grab your attention. If it is just a picture, turn it into a blockbuster movie. Finally, make the trigger huge. If it's a small white rabbit, turn it into a Godzilla-sized white rabbit. Make it so big that you will never walk past it again without noticing it.

2. Notice what you can hear around you. Are there any sounds associated with the trigger? If there are, turn them up so they are noticeable for you. If the sounds are in mono then up it to stereo.

You are in control of the volume button, so go ahead and make the sound perfect for you.

3. Notice the feelings around you. What about the feelings that you have associated with the trigger? Is there a small feeling in the middle of your chest? Then make it bigger so you notice it every time.

Remember, there is a place in your *Action Book* for you to write down all the sites, sounds and feelings associated with the trigger point.

Recall our manager at the start of this chapter who had a presentation to deliver at work. You would have noticed that he was progressing through the day without a hitch until it suddenly took a turn for the worse. When I worked with him, we found that the trigger was seeing the personal assistant setting up the room for the presentation. Once he identified this and completed the strategies we have just gone through, the issue simply disappeared. Being aware of something allows you to control it. If you do not identify it then you are just a passenger.

Make It Small... Make It Insignificant

A complex web of emotions and feelings drives our behaviours. If they are positive and empowering, it is great; and if they are not, we feel the need to reduce them and get rid of them.

Next, go back in time to when this problem was occurring and step into it like you are there again. When you are there, follow these steps:

1. Notice the pictures used to represent the problem. If these are coloured pictures, turn them into black and white. If they are in a movie format, then slow the movie right down and maybe even put it in reverse. If the pictures have clarity, then change the focus to make them fuzzy and blurred. Continue to adjust the pictures and to make them less appealing to you.

2. Notice the sounds used to represent the problem. Listen to the sounds that are around you and turn them down low, so low

that you have to strain to hear them. You may also want to add some music that gets inside your head and stays there forever, annoying you over and over again. I find clown music is a great choice!

3. Notice the feelings that you have while standing in the problem. Go ahead and turn those feelings down and move them somewhere else. Maybe you have pressure in your chest the size of a basketball. Turn that feeling into a ping-pong ball and move the feeling to your big toe. Make all things that represent this problem less appealing.

4. Finally, take the picture in your mind and step out of it. Make it so that it looks like you have taken a photo of yourself inside the problem. Now move that photo away from you... further and further ... and as you do, notice that it is getting smaller and smaller until you can hardly see it anymore. As it moves away, notice your attachment to it getting less and less.

Disarming Distraction

If you go forward into your future and visualise a time when the problem you once had would have occurred, what do you find? If you have completed all the steps and activities above, you will find that the problem has reduced in its complexity and strength.

You're nearly there! We have just a couple more steps to really cement the changes in place.

If you find that you are starting to have the feelings or thoughts that you once had, then take action as fast as you possibly can. Remove yourself from that situation and do something... *anything* that removes the negative thoughts and emotions from your mind. So drop what you are doing, go outside, watch a YouTube video, go for a coffee, do five-star jumps, or sing the national anthem. It doesn't matter what it is, just do something until the negativity has gone. Return to what you were doing and implement the strategy outlined in the next section. If you did the Pivotal Point activity, you will find this easy to identify, although the key is to take action straight away. Not in ten seconds or in a minute… *straight away*. Also, no matter how many times it happens… repeat. It may happen a lot to start with, but it will reduce quickly.

Quality Questions Quickly

Our brains do not like gaps at all. Actually, they hate them. So when you do the distraction strategy above, your brain now has a new direction you are allowing it to go in. So we need to ask ourselves these quality questions to assist the development of some new pathways in our brains – *new empowering* pathways.

The questions to ask yourself are:

1. Are the thoughts I am having right now leading me towards the end point?

    Yes – Celebrate and congratulate yourself.
    No – Ask yourself the next question.

2. What thoughts and emotions do I need to be having to lead me to the end point I deserve right now?
3. What other thoughts and emotions do I need to be having?
4. Repeat until you cannot think of any other thoughts and emotions you need to be having.

This process provides you with options about your thinking patterns rather than automatically diverting to the ones that haven't helped you in the past.

For example, if you are about to do a presentation to the senior leadership group and you begin to feel incredibly nervous, ask yourself:

*   Is the way that I am feeling right now going to lead me to a good presentation? If the answer is yes, well done. If the answer is no, go to the next question.

- What specific things should I be thinking, feeling or hearing that will take me to a good presentation?

Each time you return to the thoughts that lead you away from the good presentation, repeat the questions above. They are simple but powerful.

It may seem a lot of work, but you will be incredibly surprised at how quickly the brain adapts and the changes will start to occur automatically.

Let's try it… write down in the *Action Book* some of the thoughts and feelings you need that will lead you to the end point you deserve in section titled "Quality Questions Quickly".

Wrap Up

The strategies outlined in the previous chapter may seem a tad overwhelming to take in on first read. But what I have found when coaching clients is that after they have had a chance to practice a few times, it becomes second nature, and they start using the strategies in many different situations without thought. Also, once you get the hang of the process, you can assist friends and family to move through their issues and problems as well.

So the next time you are faced with a behaviour you no longer want, follow these steps:

1. *Choose* – It's time for you to draw the line in the sand and say, "These behaviours and actions are no longer going to restrict the life I deserve."
2. *Unravel the unwanted problem* – Get *very* clear about what the problem actually is.
3. *Exciting end point* – define a strong, vivid and powerful description of how the end point will look, sound, and feel when you have reached your goal.
4. *Pain pleasure paradox* – Your brain will always move to what it defines as pleasurable, although sometimes that is not what is going to create your compelling life. Take responsibility

(not blame) and redefine what really needs to be painful and pleasurable in your life.

5. *Position pivotal point* – Every thought, behaviour, and action has a trigger point. Once we know what it is, we have to make sure we do not walk past it again into the unwanted behaviour, but use it as a crossroad for better decisions.

6. *Make it small…*– If you change the way a problem represents itself in your brain, you will get a different outcome.

7. *Disarming distraction* – Never *ever* allow those old thoughts and behaviours to creep back into your world. Once you notice them, get up and distract yourself until they go away. Then fill the gap.

8. *Quality questions quickly* – Change the way you see the world, and set down new thought patterns instantly by asking just a couple of simple quality questions.

For most of you, this will be the only process you need to get you back on track. If you require more assistance please, contact me at candorperformance@gmail.com or contact your local counsellor, psychologist, coach, or a close friend. Whatever you do, just take action. And I would love to hear how you go with these steps, so feel free to contact me at the email above which is specifically for readers of this book only.

I'm sure you agree that people seek to live the most powerful, thrilling, and empowering life they can. Grabbing hold of the strategies outlined in this chapter and then taking massive action with them is how you can get past the barriers holding you back in reaching the life you richly deserve.

So what are you waiting for?

Singing – Antidote to Modern Life

Colin Bennett

Colin is a leading international health and safety consultant, having worked in North America, China, India, and throughout Europe over the past twenty years. He has worked in many industries including chemical, construction, motor manufacturing, railroad, steel, and aluminium smelting. He has accredited contractors annually for a global petroleum company and runs management training courses. Prior to this he worked in the electricity and nuclear industry for thirty-one years.

He is principal of the companies Managing Safely Tuition and Safety Partnership, amongst others. He is licensed by the Institute of Occupational Safety and Health (IOSH) to run their Managing Safely and Managing Safely Refresher courses.

Apart from singing, his other pastimes include painting – he is a prolific producer of oil on canvas works in portrait, landscape, wildlife and flowers; gardening; he maintains a large garden of vegetables, fruit, and flowers; and he also provides the award-winning hanging baskets for his daughter's ice cream parlour. He plays numerous musical instruments (piano, organ, guitar, ukulele, piano, accordion, flute, and three saxophones). He engages in photography, and has won awards for his photographs. He does website design, including the website for his daughter's ice cream parlour, TasTe of Sidmouth and for one of his quartets, 4getmenots. Colin applies magic to all his interests. (He is an accomplished magician). Colin maintains an active interest in property investment, including a holiday apartment in Sidmouth.

With Anne, he can often be found making ice cream at their daughters Hazel and Laura's TasTe of Sidmouth or spending time with their beloved grandchildren Steph and Josh.

Introduction

A single note sounded on the pipe organ and echoed around the walls of the eleventh-century church. A little choirboy was nudged forward and began to sing the first verse of "Once in Royal David's City," solo and unaccompanied. As the sung final word "Child" gradually stopped reverberating off the acoustically friendly stone, there was a collective gasp from the congregation and apparently not a dry eye in the building, such was the exquisiteness of the treble voice.

The church was St Clements, West Thurrock (now famous for the filming of the funeral in the film *Four Weddings and a Funeral*), and yes, the little four-year-old chorister was me.

I stayed in the church choir until I was about 16 years old, but my sweet treble voice had long disappeared and been replaced at puberty by a raspy, unreliable bass voice. Apart from a one-time performance at the school-leaving party of an Elvis Presley song (singing the wrong words) and backed on guitar by Gary Boatman, I didn't sing in public again for nearly thirty years. What a terrible waste!

At the time of writing, I am chairman of the British Association of Barbershop Singers (BABS), a registered company and national charity in the UK. BABS has nearly 2,500 singing members in sixty choruses and over a hundred quartets. The association is affiliated with the Barbershop Harmony Society in the USA and connected via the World Harmony Council with fourteen other national barbershop associations around the world.

I would like to tell you how singing has influenced my life and what I have discovered about the many health benefits that singing can bring to ordinary people affected by the stress of living in this modern world.

Singing Again

The next time I was tempted to sing in public came following a move to the East Sussex village of Etchingham. I was coerced into becoming a church warden of the beautiful fourteenth-century Norman village church, and although I don't think the two events were connected, the rector left soon after. Taking advantage of the interregnum, and somewhat inveigled by the magnificent stand-in vicar Harold Spriggs and his wife Jacquie, I started an annual Music and Flower Festival with the main intention of encouraging villagers to enter the village church. There were enormous double doors in the west wall of the church which hadn't been opened for years because of unsafe fixings. We got them fixed and were able to open the doors onto the adjacent gardens where the annual Village Summer Show was held.

The Music and Flower Festival started on the Friday evening with the church decorated lavishly by villagers, organisations with numerous floral decorations, and live music playing. Throughout the weekend, local people were asked to sign up to a rota of musicians who could play the organ or bring their own musical instrument to perform background music for those viewing the flowers or just listening. The main event of the weekend was a band concert in the church on the Saturday evening. This usually featured the East Sussex Youth Wind Orchestra and became a highlight of their calendar, mainly due to their stipend of a cream tea in the rectory gardens prior to the concert (and the interval refreshment in the De Etchingham Arms Public House opposite).

The weekend concluded with a sing-your-favourite-hymn service on Sunday evening, generally followed by more refreshment at the said De Etchingham Arms. It was on one of those occasions in the pub, whilst discussing the success of the weekend, but also bemoaning the fact that there was no church choir to help with the singing, that my singing career was about to be restarted. A suggestion was put forward that we should start a village choir. For no particular reason apart from the fact that I wasn't paying attention due to fatigue, I was elected as the musical director!

The choir had a number of notable performances, including the premiere of "Penny Black" based on the Beatles' "Penny Lane" at the Stamp Festival jointly organised by my particular friend, Brian Pitt. The church had a connection with the design on the original Penny Black Stamp. The choir later sang at society weddings and performed at country house Christmas events.

Introduction to Barbershop Singing

After an interval of a couple of years and following another house move, this time to the South West of England, I was once again sat in a pub with my wife, Anne. She was commenting on the fact that I hadn't kept our promise not to buy each other gifts for our twentieth wedding anniversary and asked me what she could buy for me. Looking around the interior of the Pony and Trap, Chew Magna, I noticed a poster advertising a choral concert at the Colston Hall in Bristol the following week and suggested she obtain tickets for that.

The concert featured a large Welsh male voice choir supported by the Great Western Chorus. The chorus were much more impressive to me than the choir even though they were much fewer in number. For a start, they had learned their music and words so were not reading from manuscripts, and second, as they sang, they also moved – even danced!

When chatting with one of their members during the interval, I discovered that they were singing barbershop music, and I was invited to their rehearsal on the following Wednesday. I was made very welcome and quickly auditioned. I initially sang bass, but when I realised I could not plumb the depths necessary to be a bass, I changed to baritone, which I sang for a number of years.

Whilst preparing for contest one year, the musical director asked for volunteers to change to tenor as there was a shortage, and that is the part I continue to sing today.

A quick explanation about barbershop harmony: It is four-part a cappella singing and unusual in that, unlike most choral genres, it is not the highest pitched voice that sings the melody. That is sung by the second highest, called the *lead*. The tenor harmonises above the lead, often in falsetto, and the bass and baritone below.

Shortly after joining the Great Western Chorus, which at the time numbered about eighty men, I got together with three other members, Ken Jewell, Jim Gough, and Nick Fox, to form a quartet called M4. Ken was the lead, Jim the bass, Nick the tenor, and I was the baritone. This created new challenges for me. As each of us was the only one in the quartet singing our part (unlike the chorus), there was nowhere to hide. Singing in a quartet is the nearest I get to singing solo as I had done at four years old. The sensation you feel when everything goes right is nothing short of exhilarating. I was hooked!

I think you remember your first quartet like you do your first love. You wonder how you stumbled into it and how you managed to learn what to do. I certainly remember having lots of fun and enjoying the companionship and mutual learning (in both situations).

When I changed to tenor I joined my second quartet, called Jack the Lads, featuring Jim again as bass, but with a new lead, Ken Godsell, and baritone Alan Gray. As the name implied, we also had lots of fun.

The opportunity arose for me to sing with another quartet made up of singers from the Coventry Chorus and GWC. Alan had asked if I would be prepared to help the chorus out by singing lead at their upcoming trip to Cork, Ireland, at the Irish Association of Barbershop Singers (IABS) convention. Whilst there we entered a quartet called Mid West consisting of Bruce Worrall and Andy Grey from Coventry with Alan and me from GWC. One rehearsal at my house sticks in the memory when the quartet and our coach, Cherry Hartshorn, managed to consume two litres of my home-made port in the afterglow.

The GWC was very successful, having won the national championship six times, and always in demand for shows as they were also renowned for being a highly entertaining chorus. Notable appearances were on prime time live national television, singing on the Michael Barrymore variety show. The highlight was undoubtedly being invited to sing on a Royal Command Performance at the London Coliseum. Spending the day in the company of numerous international stars was the icing on the cake.

These bookings led to appearances with the chorus on US nationwide TV. In 1996 the chorus visited the SPEBSQUA international convention in Salt Lake City. A UK TV producer asked the chorus if we would be involved in any record-breaking events as she was now working with the TV show *Record Breakers*. We explained that there would be a mass sing of over 10,000 singers during the convention, and she arranged for the American crew to film a sketch with members of the chorus and over 10,000 other singers! The interviewer was none other than Ron Reagan, the president's son, and he and his team were great fun to work with. Members of the chorus were shown being interviewed on CBS, and a recording of the sketch was also aired on the UK *Record Breakers* television programme.

The chorus continued on tour after the convention, visiting three choruses on the way. The first was the Garden City Chorus in San Jose, where we were made really welcome at their rehearsal night. After three wonderful days, we set off to San Francisco en route to our next chorus, based in Seattle. As we entered the arrivals hall, we were greeted by singing from the North West Sound Chorus who were bearing a huge welcome banner.

After a great time in Seattle, we set off by ferry to Victoria, Vancouver Island. As we approached Victoria harbour, we could hear the strains of "You're as Welcome as the Flowers in May" being sung by the Village Squires Chorus, who were our hosts at our final chorus.

We bid farewell to some of our chorus who were flying home whilst a party of us travelled by ferry to Vancouver to join a coach for a tour of the Canadian Rockies. The tour was memorable for not only the spectacular views but also the several unusual places for a barbershop quartet to sing. We sang on the Capilano suspension bridge, on a snowmobile, on a glacier … in fact anywhere we could. The one exception being when we stopped the coach to see close up a bear that was feeding!

Moving On

My work as a health and safety consultant and the travel it entailed made it increasingly difficult for me to attend regular weekly rehearsals. I was beginning to think I would have to give up singing when I saw an advertisement by John Wiggins. He had the idea that if he were able to assemble a group of experienced barbershop singers who were of a sufficiently high standard to pass a rigorous audition, the resulting chorus would reflect the standard.

It became possible for me to continue singing with a chorus in spite of my work commitments because the rehearsals were only once per month on a Sunday. Since they were all day, John argued that with good quality singers it would be equivalent to four weekly evening rehearsals. Somehow I passed my audition, and Gentlemen Songsters became my chorus for the next ten years. The members came from all over the UK, so a central rehearsal venue was found. The chorus competed a couple of times and placed around tenth in the national championships. It performed at a number of concerts, including the inaugural concert of a newly reconditioned theatre pipe organ.

It wasn't long before four of us got together to form a quartet. 4Star consisted of Bob Fletcher, Roy Hodge, Neville Turner, and me. We also met monthly on a Sunday, so I got to rehearse for two whole days every month and performed at a few gigs.

One notable one was in Dublin, Ireland, at the IABS Convention. I had recently been working there, and a client, Jim Minogue, insisted that when my quartet visited, we and our partners must go to his house for some Irish stew supper in return for a song. It was a memorable evening, with much alcohol consumed, lots of singing, and, with typical Irish hospitality, the Irish stew turned into a three-course gourmet dinner. When our taxi failed to arrive to take us back to Dublin, our hosts Catherine and Jim insisted on driving us in two cars back to our hotel.

This wasn't ideal preparation for our contest; we came in seventh. (There were seven entries.) The weekend got better, though, after we sang to a barman at the afterglow. The following morning we toured the Guinness Experience, culminating in a trip to the circular bar, with a magnificent city skyline view. To our surprise, the barman from the previous evening was serving. He offered to double our order of four pints of Guinness if we would sing a song. How could we refuse?

He announced on the public address system that we were now going to be entertained by the Irish national champion quartet! This was doubly embarrassing, as the two judges who had placed us last were in the audience. We had obviously impressed the barmen, though, so we gave it our best shot, and surprisingly, the audience were very appreciative. The barman insisted over the public address system that we sing a second song, which we agreed to in return for a triple order of Guinness! The rest of the day passed by in a bit of a haze.

I sang with another quartet whilst in Gentlemen Songsters. An existing quartet from the West Midlands Chorus, Accord, was missing a tenor, and Roy from 4Star asked me to fill the spot. With Henry Foster and John Brough, we sang at many venues, including the Friendship Force of Somerset annual lunch. As this was a home gig for me, I set up a pre-glow on the Friday night at a local pub where the landlord stupidly agreed to pay us in pints of beer instead of money. After an hour of singing and drinking, he was already regretting his decision.

Another regular gig with this quartet was the annual Orthopaedic Equipment Exhibition in Birmingham, UK. We were engaged by a company that made medical tools and wandered around the exhibition singing as we went. We had our photograph taken in front of a mock-up of a traditional barbershop (complete with traditional barber), and this picture has been spotted in many barbershops throughout the country.

Returning to the Great Western Chorus

On a visit to the GWC in late 2007 with the then chairman of BABS, Bill Harvey, I was encouraged to return to the chorus. My work pattern had changed somewhat from that which caused me to leave ten years earlier, and with the impending demise of Gentlemen Songsters, I rejoined.

This gave me the opportunity to join my most successful quartet so far – the 4getmenots. We got together soon after I rejoined the Great Western Chorus. The lead was Colin Barley, bass Stephen Derrick, and baritone Steve Thorn. After about a year, Colin decided to stand down and was replaced by a new lead in the chorus, James Emery.

The Gets, as we became known, rehearsed weekly, and at the time were the only chorus quartet. This meant that we were featured on chorus shows and also invited by other choruses to sing on their shows. We also represented BABS at a Making Music national conference in Cardiff, Wales, running a workshop and singing on the evening show. We were featured on a chorus Christmas show in the beautiful town hall in Wells, Somerset, the smallest city in England. One of our songs, "Mary Did You Know," so inspired the curate of St Cuthbert's church in the city that he asked the quartet to sing it, along with other appropriate music, at their Epiphany service, which we were delighted to do.

We had lots of fun gigs, including singing to a group of Japanese visitors at an exchange with the Friendship Force of Somerset. Another time we opened a concert in the ancient church in the village of Stanton Drew and then had to leave before the refreshments, as we were the after-dinner entertainment at another venue for the Rotary Club.

The Gets competed several times in the BABS national quartet contest, achieving a highest position of third in the country. We subsequently recorded a CD with the help of Pete Nugent and Nick Fox that we are very proud of. I have asked for the title track "From the First Hello to the Last Goodbye" to be played at my funeral. I thought it would be rather cool to sing at my own internment! A lot of our success is due to the expert coaching we received over the years from the likes of Cindy Hansen-Ellis, Jim Cerutti, and Paul Davies.

The quartet decided to disband when James moved to Poland to marry and live. Our last major gig was as the guest quartet at the Dutch Association of Barbershop Singers national convention.

As mentioned previously, the chorus had won six national championships in the past, but not for the preceding eighteen years. Whilst I am sure there is no connection, the chorus won their next national championship at the BABS convention in Cheltenham, UK, in my first year back with them. This meant we were eligible to represent BABS at the international in 2009, which was to be held in Anaheim, California.

The cost of getting the chorus there was considerable. The chorus was split into fund-raising foursomes, which meant the Gets had to come up with some fund-raising ideas. Our bass, Steve, was an experienced rock climber, so we decided to launch a sponsored abseil. I am not particularly good with heights and suddenly remembered the first thing I was told when I entered barbershop: "Never trust a bass!" However, with some trepidation, I led the way down the rock face. The quartet and the chorus raised sufficient money to contribute a substantial amount of the cost of the chorus going to Anaheim.

The venue was adjacent to the original Disney Theme Park, so there was an opportunity to sing with the Dapper Dans in Main Street.

The following year the chorus was eligible to re-compete in the BABS national contest, this time held at Harrogate, UK. Once again we were successful in winning the national championship, which entitled us to compete at the Barbershop Harmony Society International Convention in Kansas City.

This meant we were on the fund-raising trail again, and the Gets ran a "promise auction" and "race night." The promise auction involved collecting promises from people to perform a service or provide a resource that people could bid for, with the proceeds going to the chorus travel fund. The race night required bets to be taken on which of eight horses would win a race. People could bid to be a horse owner, the sponsor of the race, the jockey, and so forth. When all bets were placed, a DVD was chosen at random and displayed showing the race. Winners were paid according to the odds, with a portion retained for chorus funds. The quartet raised over £2,000 sterling on the night.

The flights to Kansas City were more complex to organise, as there were no direct connections. They were also considerably more expensive than those two years earlier had been.

When the chorus returned, they voted to stand down from national contests for three years. This enabled them to recover from the four years of contest pressure and fundraising and explore other avenues. This included entering the Llangollen Eisteddfod in the male voice choir category and also performing at the Royal Albert Hall in London at a charity fundraising concert.

The chorus re-entered the BABS national contest in 2014 and won runner up, the silver medal position.

BABS Board of Directors

During 2005, I was headhunted to replace the retiring administration director of BABS. Following interview and election, I took up the post in January 2006.

The post also included being the company secretary and the secretary to the trustees of the charity. Grants amounting to more that £20,000 are given out annually to provide education on singing in the barbershop style. Part of my role was to advertise the grants and to administer all the applications prior to presenting them to the trustees for consideration.

Another important part of my role was to ensure that the legal and administrative processes of the association required of a registered company and national charity were adhered to correctly. It became clear quite quickly that the governing constitution of the association, the Memorandum and Articles of Association, was significantly out of date. It then became a major task for me, involving many hours in the company of a barrister, to ensure that the association was being managed in accordance with the current legal requirements.

Another aspect of the role involved the insurance of the association. When I joined the board, protracted negotiations had been ongoing for upwards of ten years for the association to become members of Making Music, the National Federation of Music Societies in the UK. Fortunately, their Membership Manager was also newly appointed, and we were able to quickly agree to a membership deal, including insurance, that was mutually beneficial.

There then began a long and close relationship. We were invited to attend the biannual meeting of the representatives of most national singing organisations in the UK, called TONSIL. I think we were viewed a little sceptically by the traditional choral organisations at first, but this was soon to change when we were asked to teach some of their members how to sing!

At a previous BABS AGM, the Taunton Barbershop Harmony Club had demonstrated to the other clubs how they had recruited new members by running a free Learn to Sing course. The BABS board saw the potential and committed resource to rolling this out across all the clubs. Since that time, the BABS membership has continued to grow year-on-year.

I included this information in a report to TONSIL, and Making Music asked if I would make a presentation to their national conference. The tendency amongst most singing organisations at that time was for numbers to be falling, and my presentation was to show how BABS was bucking the trend and continuing to grow.

The presentation described barbershop music and how we were able to teach non-singers how to perform four-part a cappella harmony singing in a six-week course. With the help of a quartet called This Way Up, I was able to demonstrate the process to the assembled company.

We were then asked by Making Music if we could adapt our six-week course to conventional choral soprano, alto, tenor, bass (SATB) harmonies. I bravely agreed that we could, and a trial was set up with the famous Egham Choral Society.

BABS organised the marketing of the course, the provision of the teaching material, the music, the tutor, and consultancy to the host choir on managing the administration of the course. The choir arranged for an adjacent room to their rehearsal venue, with a capacity of about twenty, to be available to the recruits. When the number of applicants climbed above 300, other plans had to be made!

The course exceeded all expectations. The excitement on the faces of the learn-to-sing delegates throughout the course was a joy to behold.

One thing that struck me about the success of the course was the way most of the delegates were sat forward at the front of their seats, eager to learn. The course was a resounding success with the Egham Choral Society, adding some good singers to their number and also starting a second choir with about ninety additional singers. Both choirs are still going strong today.

This led to Making Music combining with the Choir of the Year organisers to offer courses close to regional heats. We selected the lucky participants from all those that applied and set about organising seven six-week courses in the same year, some running simultaneously. It is doubtful that another organisation would have been able to allocate sufficient resources throughout the country to provide the level of coaching this project required. Jon Conway organised a training course for selected BABS coaches to convert them from barbershop to SATB tutors.

A similar pattern to the trial at Egham was repeated at the seven locations, with the available places well oversubscribed. This was largely due to the expert marketing campaigns run by our marketing director, Laurie Whittle. Laurie adjusted each campaign to suit the local environment, which proved to be quite variable, but always with the same level of success. Each of the courses converted recruits into choir members and, more importantly, people who thought they couldn't sing into singers.

Following this very successful year of courses, we ran several more, including one in Cumbernauld in Scotland.

In 2012 we were asked to run two six-week courses simultaneously, one in the City of London and one in the south of London. Both were required to finish coinciding with the finals of the Choir of the Year to be held at the Royal Festival Hall (RFH) on the Southbank. The Choir of the Year organisers asked if we would also run a workshop at the RFH as the audience and participants arrived. With about 150 of the combined Learn to Sing delegates and host-choir members, we were able to meet the request ably co-presented by Paul Davies and Stuart Lines. During the workshop we had a guest tutor in the form of Greg Beardsell, the

National Youth Choir Director, who was one of the three Choir of the Year finals judges.

At the time of writing, we have just completed our thirteenth Learn to Sing Course for Making Music with Leicester Philharmonic Choir.

Inspired by the success of these courses, we decided to run a National Learn to Sing Day. We provided national marketing and directed interested parties to a website that allocated them to the nearest chorus of the thirty-nine that participated. We had true national coverage, from Aberdeen in Scotland to the Isle of Wight in the south of England and from Lincoln in the east to Anglesey in Wales to the west.

Paul Davies composed and arranged a song especially for the day, and the one-day training course was adapted from the six-week course by Rhiannon Owens-Hall. The one-day course attracted nearly 1,600 new people to singing.

The year 2014 is BABS's fortieth anniversary year, and one of the celebratory events planned is a National Learn to Sing Fortnight, hopefully with all sixty of our clubs participating. The idea is that the clubs will run the course on their normal rehearsal night on two consecutive weeks, splitting the one-day course material in two. The course will finish with a mini-concert in which the participants show off to their families and friends.

To date, BABS has introduced in excess of 10,000 members of the public to singing.

From Administration Director to Chairman

It was decided in 2010 that I should apply to become vice chairman of BABS. The post lasts for two years and normally leads to a two-year term as chairman.

I was duly elected, and in 2013 became chairman. Much of the first year was involved in planning for the fortieth anniversary celebrations, which are currently taking up all of my second year as chairman.

Part of my role as chairman is to represent the association at other organisations' conventions. During my first year I attended the European

Barbershop Convention in Holland, the Barbershop Harmony Society International Convention in Toronto, Canada, the Sweet Adelines' International Region 31 convention in Tyneside, UK, the Irish Association of Barbershop Singers convention in Waterford, Ireland, and the Ladies Association of British Barbershop Singers convention in Llandudno, Wales.

So far in this second year of my chairmanship, I have attended the Spanish Association of Barbershop Singers convention in Calpe, Spain, SAI Region 31 convention in Nottingham, UK, and have been invited to the BHS International Convention in Las Vegas, the IABS convention in County Down, Ireland, and the LABBS convention in Harrogate.

BABS runs many educational events and always starts the year with a Directors' Academy. The musical directors and their deputies are invited to an education and coaching event, usually led by an international coach. This lasts for two days, with the first day for everyone and the second day usually focussing on top-gun coaching.

BABS has its own guild of judges who are certified and receive update training and coaching at regular intervals to enable them to judge our contests and those of other international associations.

BABS runs a three-day Harmony College each year at a university campus that is open to both members and non-members. The college features a number of educational streams in singing, arranging, quartet, chorus, directing, and other subjects. The able faculty are usually supplemented with international guest coaches.

The main event that BABS runs each year is a four-day convention which is held at various national venues. This is where the national contests are held to find the champion chorus and quartet for the following year, both of which are invited to the international convention, usually in North America, the following year. In addition, the convention features several top-class shows with international choruses and quartets along with other events. One of the most popular barbershop events is the *afterglow*. This is held every night at the convention and after all club shows. Basically everyone is invited, including the audience, to a venue with food and drink available, and anyone who wants to gets the opportunity to sing in a convivial atmosphere. It usually ends up with everyone singing together, and if you don't know the song, you just stand alongside someone who does and copy them!

The BABS convention held in my second year as chairman was a very special one. It was the main event to celebrate the fortieth anniversary of the founding of the association.

It started a day earlier than usual with a black-tie Gala Awards Dinner for 270 invited guests held in the elegant Royal Hall at Harrogate, UK, a delightful Victorian kursaal theatre. The guest of honour was the Lord Lieutenant of North Yorkshire, who is HM the Queen's personal representative. He read a special message from HRH the Prince of Wales, congratulating the association on its anniversary. Following dinner, there was an awards ceremony led by a toastmaster in which the significant contributors to the forty years of the association were honoured. It was a grand affair similar to the Oscars ceremony, with triumphant music playing as the recipients were announced and made their way to the stage followed by a spotlight.

Following the Gala Awards Dinner, the second day of the convention included the semi-finals of the quartet contest in which eighteen entries competed for the six final places. In the evening there was a European Concert with quartets from Ireland, Spain, Sweden, and the UK, and choruses from Germany and the UK. Alison Harbord from LABBS and I were masters of ceremonies for the concert. I managed to include in my introductions some magical illusions, which is another interest of mine.

When the afterglow was in full swing, disaster struck. The electrical transformer supplying the main auditorium exploded! With over 3,000 paying delegates, the organising team led by Derek Parmenter, the special events director of BABS, and supported by Alan Bithell, Laurie Whittle, and Alan Goldsmith had to decide whether to cancel the event. Fortunately (and unusually) the Royal Hall was available all weekend. Although it was smaller than the auditorium, it could be adapted to fit contests and shows planned for the remaining three days. With a tremendous amount of support from the Harrogate International Centre staff, everything was moved to the Royal Hall, and incredibly, the chorus contest started and finished on time. A total of forty-seven choruses competed on that day, with up to ninety singers in each chorus.

230

To commemorate the anniversary, a Retro Supper was held that evening, featuring a dish typical in the UK in 1974. To accompany the food, a cabaret featuring the seven international quartet champions performed at different locations around the centre. The day that had started with a catastrophe ended in triumph. The show and contest schedule for the rest of the weekend was adjusted to suit the changed venue, ending in what reviews called the best BABS convention ever.

Health Benefits of Singing

Many studies done over a number of years have focused on the health benefits of singing, and the evidence is overwhelming.

- Singing releases endorphins into your system and makes you feel energized and uplifted. People who sing are healthier than people who don't.
- Singing gives the lungs a workout.
- Singing tones abdominal and intercostal muscles and the diaphragm, and stimulates circulation.
- Singing makes you breathe more deeply than many forms of strenuous exercise, so you take in more oxygen, improve aerobic capacity, and experience a release of muscle tension as well." (Professor Graham Welch, Director of Educational Research, University of Surrey, Roehampton, UK)

AIG, the largest insurance company in the world, had a TV ad where a middle-aged man is singing karaoke, rather poorly, but enjoying himself immensely. The voiceover interjects, "Singing can reduce stress and add fifteen years to your life." Amazing! Gardening adds one year to your life, meditation adds three, owning a pet seven, laughter eight, but singing adds fifteen! These statistics were based on actuarial assessments.

Studies have found three common characteristics in centenarians: social networking, exercising the brain, and staying physically active. With the opportunity in a barbershop chorus for socialising, camaraderie, vocal education, music learning, breathing exercise, and choreography, it's easy to make the case that staying active in a barbershop chorus gives you a much higher probability of living long, productive lives.

Singing also strengthens the immune system, according to research by scientists at the University of Frankfurt in Germany, published in the US Journal of Behavioural Medicine. The scientists tested the blood of people who sang in a professional choir in the city, before and after a sixty-minute rehearsal of Mozart's *Requiem*. They found that concentrations of immunoglobin A – proteins in the immune system which function as antibodies – and hydrocortisone, an anti-stress hormone, increased significantly during the rehearsal. A week later, when they asked members of the choir to listen to a recording of the *Requiem* without singing, they found the composition of their blood did not change significantly. The researchers, who included Hans Guenther Bastian from the Institute of Musical Education at Frankfurt University, concluded singing not only strengthens the immune system but also notably improves the performer's mood.

Gene Cohen of George Washington University tracked a senior singers choir in Arlington, Virginia. The choir singers' average age is 80. The youngest is 65 and the oldest 96. Preliminary data shows the singers suffer less depression, make fewer doctor visits a year, take fewer medications, and have increased their other activities.

There is plenty of evidence to prove the health benefits of singing, and it is not difficult to find somewhere to try it. I have included a number of references of worldwide organisations who welcome new singers. You never know – it might improve your health and lengthen your lifespan.

In Conclusion

I have plotted my singing career from a solo four-year old chorister to chairman of a national singing organisation not to boast, but to demonstrate that singing is within reach of everyone regardless of background and perceived singing ability. Go on, give it a try!

From Dry Inland Australia to the Tropical North!

Heather E. Traeger

Heather lives her passion every day by helping small business owners in the private sector and managers in the not-for-profit sector with their staff management solutions, ensuring they meet their legislative requirements to avoid fines and maintain positive reputations as preferred employers, maintain motivated and productive employees, and, most importantly, continue their own leadership development to drive their businesses to success, including winning awards.

Heather spent twenty-one years as a single parent. During that time she took risks others might not take, including building her own passive solar home. She left the close support of her parents and friends for a job promotion, to a country town 600 km away, where she and her boys knew no one. To complete her degree while working full time, she had to drive 114km each way between home and university on the road between Melbourne and Sydney against the headlights of trucks and road trains, arriving home late at night Today she uses her past experiences helping people desperate for change to find their strengths and purposes so they can create and live the lives they dream of.

Heather is serious about her contribution to society, her family, and real estate, as well as about investing precious time and money into her personal and spiritual development.

"To permit your mind to dwell upon the inferior is to become inferior and to surround yourself with inferior things. On the other hand, to fix your

233

attention on the best is to surround yourself with the best, and to become the best." (Bob Proctor)

The Long Trip North

Here we were in June 2000, Brendan and I – husband and wife. We couldn't believe how we got to here. It made us laugh! We'd been neighbours ten years before. I even dated someone else for three years. And yet, here we were, technically on our honeymoon. You would never match us in a dating agency. We were opposites, but our values aligned. Neither of us desired to live together before, and now we were married.

We decided to take a couple of weeks to drive from northeast Victoria to Darwin, 4,000 km north. Our first stop was Mildura, which sits in the top corner of Victoria, just across the Murray river from New South Wales, and only an hour to the South Australian border. We stayed overnight with my parents, as we might not see them for a while.

The next day, after a stop at the visitors' centre to see the amazing statues and stories of the brave white men who'd explored the middle of Australia looking for the non-existent inland sea and led the way from Adelaide to Darwin over 150 years ago, we headed to Port Augusta, South Australia. I was grateful to be living and driving on well-made roads, with roadhouses for fuel and a coffee, cold drink, and snack for us every few hundred kilometres.

It was all new to me. I'd never driven through this country before, and I soaked in the sights, continually amazed at the isolation. We stayed in a cave-type motel in Cooper Pedy, famous for its underground living and opal mining.

Everywhere we looked there were piles of soil, the remnants of small mining sites made by the sheer sweat of individuals keen to find the elusive colourful hydrated amorphous form of silica hidden in the brown rock. The wind was hot, and if you took a piece of bread to make a sandwich, it would soon be lightly toasted by the wind and sun.

After two nights in Alice Springs to break up the journey, we travelled on, straight up the Stuart Highway, up the middle of Australia, a continent as large as the USA, but with a tenth the number of states. Then it was time to move on again.

We made a fuel stop at Wycliffe Well, famous for its UFO sightings. People travel here from all around the world to scan the night sky in case they're lucky enough to sight an unidentified flying object.

Later on we stopped at the Devil's Marbles (eggs of the dreamtime serpent), totally enthralled by this fantastic collection of rocks in the middle of nowhere. It was hard to find any shade in the afternoon sun, but luckily someone in a van sold hot and cold drinks, mainly to the young Japanese tourists bent on adventure.

At Katherine we stayed two nights. We swam in the deliciously clear, fresh thermal springs near the town caravan park – a delightful experience. The following day we took a boat tour along the Katherine River winding its way through the magnificent Gorge.

The guide pointed out the high cliff from which Jedda had jumped to her death in Australia's first coloured feature movie, *Jedda*, directed by Charles Chauvel in 1955. The Katherine Gorge is home to freshwater crocodiles and large saltwater crocodiles – called *saltwater* crocodiles because they make their own salt. They can be found at sea and in rivers across northern Australia. Even today crocodiles remain dangerous.

Finally, we drove the last leg of our trip, a mere 300 km to Darwin, with a population of 120,000. On arrival, we were given two options by Defence Housing for accommodation. The first was an older style tropical house with small rooms and asbestos bathroom walls sited on the navy base; the other was a reinforced concrete home in a regular suburb. The latter type of house was built immediately after Cyclone Tracy (1974), which left 41,000 of the 47,000 residents homeless.

New City, New Home, New Job, New Lifestyle – Yet, Some Things Don't Change

We chose the latter, and Brendan then left for six weeks at sea. I had the joy of unpacking box after box of essential living needs. Those not essential remained unpacked. On Monday I started work as a human resources manager for a department similar to the one I'd left in Victoria. There was no one at home to share my experiences with that first day and week on job.

One of my former Victorian bosses and his wife loved travelling around Australia, and they decided to drop in and see me. They observed that although I'd married, nothing in my life had really changed. I laughed and had to agree with his insight. While I was married, Brendan spent many weeks away, so I was still on my own. The thing is, I love being on my own and am very happy that way.

New People

I used to go walking after work to exercise and get the feel of the neighbourhood. One lady who often arrived home about the same time as I did, lived with her husband and had a blue heeler dog similar to one I once had.

She invited me to have a drink, white wine. Although I'm not a white wine drinker, I make an exception when I'm with Shazza. I was glad there was someone close by who I could drop in on every now and then.

When Brendan came home a few weeks later, I told him about our neighbours and my new friend, and let him know Shazza uses words I'd never heard, probably because she'd once worked as a cook on a prawn trawler. She could match any sailor's vocabulary!

My new manager, Vicki Long, invited me to join her and her husband to a live theatre production. They picked me up and dropped me off. I've always been grateful for that invitation to get out and about.

One of Brendan's best friends, Anthony Greenwood (Greenie), lived in Darwin with his lovely wife Dawn and four children. They're always welcoming and generous, and I could drop in any time I needed to be part of a normal busy family.

I eventually joined the Rotary Club of Darwin Sunrise, as I'd been a member when I worked in Tatura, Victoria. I was also an alumnus of the Rotary Group Study Exchange program in 1995. A few years later, I was asked to be president, and that year was grateful to be supported by a board of generous, supportive people.

During my first few years in Darwin, I went along to woodwork classes, which I'd started in Victoria. I eventually made our wedding bed, a great coffee table, a mirror, and two hall tables. Few people have furniture made with their own hands.

Massive Staff Turnover in Darwin

As a human resources manager, one statistic I find shocking is the level of staff turnover across most businesses, in both non-governmental organisations (NGOs) and government departments. Managers and training staff find it hard to get to high levels of productivity because they are forever retraining the next new employee. Down south, acceptable staff turnover might be about 15 per cent, and anything up to 30 per cent gets additional attention. In Darwin, some organisations experience a turnover rate of up to 125 per cent!

My first job in Darwin was with a government department. Then I moved to an Aboriginal lands rights organisation. This work was interesting because there were lawyers and anthropologists involved in legal matters that were changing the history of some Aboriginal communities and people identified as *traditional owners*. TOs are recognised in law as the rightful owners of the land. One of the downsides of this type of organisation is that some of the policies and processes don't apply equally to all people.

Standing on Principle

The CEO often varied the principles of human resource management on a whim, making it hard to enjoy the job as fully as I had hoped. I'm the type of person who is willing to take a stand on principles I believe are important. I've learned there are situations where you highlight irregularities, but while bringing these to the attention of appropriate people, you know in your heart nothing will change. So you take a stand and resign because it's the best thing to do in the circumstances. One outsider is unlikely to make a significant difference. In nine years of working in the Northern Territory, I found myself taking a stand at least three times, but never once had to do it during my thirteen years of working in the Victorian Public Service.

Darwin is developing from a wild untamed place to one that is attracting overseas and interstate companies that are bringing their own values and expectations. This is positive change.

Values and Culture

The states in Australia have differing histories, geography, and economics, attracting companies and people with matching values to live and work in them.

Values and culture are entrenched, and if you're ever looking to make significant change in any organisation (even a family), you'll need to deliberately attract at least 15 per cent new people who demonstrate the values and culture you want for the future. Only then will others in the old group begin to adapt to the new while resisting at first. There are many in Darwin who pine for the old Darwin!

Take time to think about your answers to these questions:

What are you prepared to stand up for?

What won't you stand for?

Health Department? What Is That?

Because I always had an open relationship with the unions in any organisation I worked for, including as HR manager, I was able to secure a two-year project position with the Northern Territory Department of Health and Community Services. This was an exciting project, trying to move items listed in the Nurses Certified Agreement into action.

Certified agreements are created when the three parties in the workplace – management, workers, and their representatives – negotiate a pay rise, usually in return for some level of continuous improvement.

When enterprise agreements are negotiated, it usually takes six to nine months, requiring intensive work by all parties, agreed to by ballot. Then the agreement is taken to the Fair Work Commission to be certified, thereby becoming law for the parties during the period of the agreement, usually two to three years. Many ideas and possibilities for improvement are discussed and agreed to during negotiations, but rarely are they manifested during the agreement period.

It seems that sometimes the ideas, while agreed to by all parties, remain only as intentions until the next agreement, usually because of a lack of resources rather than a lack of will.

New Career Challenges

I had never worked in health services before, so I enjoyed the experience. I was made coordinator of the Nurses Certified Agreement Task Force, working with two nurses and reporting to principal nursing advisor, Dr Greg Rickard – a nurse with a PhD.

The job of the two nurses and me was to develop an action plan, identifying those projects which could be completed quickly and those that would be done in stages and required greater levels of research and consultation, including comparing what was happening in other jurisdictions.

This project lasted two years as originally negotiated between the Department of Health and Community Services and the Australian Nursing and Midwifery Federation (ANMF).

One of the last projects for me to manage, in consultation with the principal nursing advisor, was the annual Nursing and Midwifery Awards. This required identifying the categories, developing the documentation, advertising in the media, and regular liaison with staff from the Media Unit, promoting the awards across the department and other agencies where nurses worked, collecting nominations, hosting the selection panel, and recording outcomes. It also required typing up all the core information of nominees and presenting that to the Media Unit, so on the night, the PowerPoint presentations were all correct and in the right order.

This event was also a fun night and very important. In Darwin, most of the big events are hosted by the relevant minister in Parliament House, in the Great Hall which comfortably seats 300 guests. Greg and I always made sure we organised free entertainment as guests arrived and were seated. This was provided by the dancing or music students from various high schools, which gave them exposure to playing in public.

I enjoyed working with the nurses over the two years, and made a few new friends. That experience segued nicely onto the next experience.

A Bubbly Mood

On the evening of the annual Nursing and Midwifery Awards, we were on the lawns of Parliament House overlooking the harbour, drinking champagne and laughing, as the evening had gone off without a hitch, and we were grateful all the hard work had been worth it. Nurses across the Northern Territory who'd won awards, their families, and their colleagues were all happy too. It was an evening of catching up with old friends and colleagues, and meeting new ones.

On that note, Greg introduced me to Dr Michael Wilson, another nurse with a PhD, who'd just moved from Victoria. As I was introduced, I extended my hand, said hello, and immediately followed with, "What job do you have for me?" I meant it! This was an unusual approach to a stranger, but as the evening was a success, I was on a high and on my first or second glass of champagne.

Michael replied, "Well, I don't usually do this, but here's my card. Please give me a call." Which I did a week later.

Michael had come to the NT as the executive director of Northern Territory General Practice Education to change its culture. NTGPE operated out of rented premises on the grounds of Charles Darwin University in the same building and floor as the School of Business and Law.

Excellent HR and QA challenge

When I finally caught up with Michael, I explained that as I had been a human resources manager for some time, I wanted to add some other challenge to that title. As NTGPE was a relatively small organisation, Michael gave me the Quality Assurance responsibility too. This made an exciting change and allowed me to interact across the organisation to its stakeholders, the funding body in Canberra, and staff from the Department of Health and Ageing.

I worked at NTGPE for four and a half years, where my major achievement, besides setting up the HR aspects of the organisation, was gaining reaccreditation of NTGPE as a regional training provider. This took a lot of effort from the part-time medical educators, the full-time Aboriginal cultural educators, and other staff. That project lasted twelve to fifteen months from beginning to end.

The audit team comprised a range of medical practitioner, peers across Australia, and staff from the Department of Health and Ageing. On the day of the team's arrival, we greeted them with the dancing troupe, One Mob Different Country. This is a group of men who dress in traditional red loincloths and white ochre painted arms, faces, and chests. They proceeded to demonstrate traditional Aboriginal dancing. Their unique quality is that they are inmates, and the dancing is one of their rehabilitation exercises!

This traditional greeting was followed by a bush walk, looking for bush tucker along the way, a quick look at the coastline nearby, and then back to the Chinese gardens on the grounds of the University for original turtle stew and damper, with butter and golden syrup, washed down with bottles of cold water and hot tea. It was a unique and impressive cultural welcome to the start of a hard week of lots of travel in the heat and humidity while the audit team tried to concentrate on their review of NTGPE's medical education.

Another New Professional Experience: University Lecturing

Teaching has always been a passion of mine. My first teaching took place when I was about eight years old and pretended to take the roll and teach my (invisible) class in my bedroom, using chalk on the blue painted wall for a blackboard.

Later, I became a secretarial college teacher, then a technical and further education teacher, a vocational trainer. I loved this latter role. For four years I worked four days per week, or 0.8 full-time equivalent (0.8FTE) while I completed my undergraduate degree in human resources. I already held a graduate diploma in educational administration, but my career goal was to become a human resources manager.

While I was working for NTGPE, I was offered some casual lecturing for one term for Charles Darwin University's undergraduate students who were studying human resources. I really enjoyed the mix of students and using my practical experience along with my own studies. In the following two years, I lectured MBA students in the subject of HRM.

The opportunity to lecture came about partly because of my qualifications and because I worked on the same site as the staff of the School of Business and Law. We shared the same tables at morning tea and lunch.

A New Personal Experience

One public holiday in July 2010, I was at home trying to put my taxation paperwork onto Manage Your Own Business (MYOB). My husband had gone to complete an afternoon shift at his work. I'd been sitting for some time getting frustrated because MYOB was never my favourite accounting tool.

At about three o'clock I thought it was time I took a break. I walked from the office to the kitchen, filled the kettle with water, turned it on, and felt unwell – quite odd – and realised I wouldn't be able to make a cup of tea but needed a drink of water. I needed to lie down on the couch.

As I lay down, I realised there was a mighty pressure on the left side of my chest, and that my arm, left leg and foot, and left side of my face was sort of numb. I said out loud to myself, "Oh, I think I'm having a heart attack, or maybe it's a stroke," because of the numbness I was feeling down one side.

I took two Aspro clears, picked up my handbag, sunglasses, and a book to read, and drove myself to hospital. I had a work vehicle, a manual 4WD! I couldn't actually feel the clutch with my left foot and had a few corners and roundabouts to manoeuvre on the way to the hospital. I mentally told myself to forget how I felt, and to take extra care even if it took me a little longer to get to the hospital. I needed to get there as safely as possible. In hindsight, I shouldn't have driven at all.

On arrival in the emergency department, I was seen to fairly quickly by the triage nurse who took my blood pressure, temperature, and a short history. She told me to wait. I waited a little while with everyone else. Eventually I was called to the next area where I would be seen by a nurse who organised an ECG, but that didn't reveal anything of interest. I was then seen to by an overseas-trained doctor who had no idea.

While I read my book on the bed, his preliminary tests showed nothing of significance since my strength tests were good; I'd been lifting weights at the gym. He became a little annoyed with me and told me there was nothing wrong, but to go home and see my local general practitioner the next day. He typed up a letter for me to give to my GP.

As I walked out, I had to limp on the tiptoes of my left foot because each time I put my heel down, it was as though an electric tingle burst through my whole left side, and it was too uncomfortable. I went home to bed.

Brendan arrived home wondering what the eleven missed calls on his phone were for.

The following day, my busy GP saw me at noon. He asked what had happened and ran his hand down the left side of my body. I explained that while I could feel his hand, it was as though it was through a sponge. He asked me what I thought of the other doctor's letter. I said it seemed to say nothing. My lovely GP, Dr Michael Paroulakis, stated that the other doctor (I'm not sure he was even fully trained) thought it was all in I my head, which we laughed at because technically it was.

I returned to the hospital and was admitted to the Rapid Admission and Planning Unit for the maximum two nights so I could be observed closely by nurses. I wanted to sleep but had to be continually woken to be checked on, as did all the other patients, some of whom were in much worse condition than me. I quite happily hobbled to the toilet on my own but was continually growled at because I was supposed to call for assistance. But I didn't need it, and they were busy with others needier than me.

After a scan that revealed some damage to my brain, they put me in a regular ward for the rest of the week. I think I was allowed to be discharged a week later only because it was my birthday. I wanted to get home because nothing else had changed.

I had experienced a rare type of stroke, a pure sensory lacunar stroke which occurs in the thalamus. It sounded more like an exotic Thai massage.

So I researched online and found one of Australia's eminent stroke specialists, a man who researches, studies, and lectures around the world on strokes, in Melbourne, four and a half hours away by air. I made an appointment as early as possible and saw him four months later. He told me that this type of stroke is rare, there is no known reason for these, and they've never been known to be repeated. He'd recently seen a young man in his late twenties and a younger woman a few days before who'd experienced the same type of lacuna stroke.

So after spending a week in hospital, all the travel, and the waiting to see the stroke specialist, I was told to go home and enjoy lots of good red wine. I still felt as though I had a bag or two of wheat sitting on my left chest. Even now when I'm tired, that sensation returns.

While it may have been stupid bravado on my part, I missed only one Monday lecture at CDU, the one where I was in hospital. The second week, luckily for me, was another public holiday. So by the third Monday, I was back to lecturing and back at my full-time job with NTGPE.

Some said I shouldn't have been back at work, but my wonderful GP, Dr Andrew McDonald said that rehabilitation is getting back to your normal life as fast as possible, and was the best thing to do.

A Whole New Direction

About six months before the stroke, I'd stopped enjoying my work. All the activity around the reaccreditation had ended because NTGPE was granted reaccreditation status. There followed the inevitable physical letdown. Also, the executive team had been together for about four years. At the annual executive retreat in October, I said that I thought it was time for change. Perhaps we were all beginning to think alike, as there seemed to be no particular new direction or focus, just more of the same planned for the future.

I left at the end of the year to have a go at starting my own business in HR-IR consultancy. Then one by one, all the executives left within about six months of each other to make way for new energy, new ideas, and a new focus.

A New Tentative Move

My first foray into working for myself was tentative, and within a few months I found a new start-up organisation doing exactly what I was trying to do. So I took a role with them, thinking they'd have all the structures in place and the marketing strategy in action. But no! I found the documentation all over the place, there was no corporate look, and there was no marketing, no database of clients, not even a website. When I left six months later, there still wasn't a website.

I soon felt let down and left to work briefly for a not-for-profit organisation which had been without an HR manager for some time. A few weeks into the role, it became obvious why it was a hard role to fill. The national organisation was run centrally – and poorly – from Sydney. Everyone in regional roles around Australia was fairly new and angry. It wasn't for me. Many of us felt they did not demonstrate the values they stood for publicly.

So I'd seen and experienced enough to know I really wanted to work for myself, to take on clients I wanted, to do a variety of jobs that would use all of my skills and experience and allow me to take on some training for private training providers, and I'm much happier.

My business model is one of learning slowly, burning money on poorly designed websites, and expensive newspaper advertising. Yes, it needs development and I need development as a new business owner!

Lifelong Learning

Over the years, I've consciously invested a lot of money and time studying formal and informal courses.

To undertake my degree, I drove to Charles Sturt University in Albury, New South Wales, from Benalla, Victoria, a distance of 114 km from door to door! I drove because there's no suitable public transportation. On lecture days I left home at 7.30 a.m. to pick up a fellow student in Glenrowan (Ned Kelly country) and drive on to Albury. After lectures and tutorials, I arrived home after driving into oncoming semi-trailer headlights all the way (it was a single lane highway then), around 10.30 p.m.

My son, who was still at high school, and I would go shopping then. It was quiet and provided a break from studies for both of us. I did this for four years, while teaching 0.8FTE at TAFE.

Personal and Professional Development Opportunities

I graduated in April 1995, and in May, left Australia for a Rotary group study exchange. I was fortunate to win this competitive experience, as I was just about to turn 40 years of age, and they prefer younger people to ensure participants can contribute to their profession for many years. I've certainly done that.

We travelled to Massachusetts to spend five delightful weeks being billeted with various families, visiting significant sites, spending time on vocational visits, and making friends quickly and saying goodbye soon afterwards. I saw *Les Miserables* in Boston, also experienced the Boston Pops, and watched a Red Sox baseball game. Almost daily, we gave a presentation to Rotary clubs across Massachusetts. We had a ball.

New York, New York

I remained for another three weeks by myself, staying in New York for four days and five nights, moving to Washington, DC, for a few days, on to Chicago for a few days, and then six days and nights with a delightful family on a farm in New York State. They lived in a wooden cottage by the lake. We drove around their dairy farms and past their hundred acres of potatoes, hundred acres of corn, and so on. I loved it. I spent half a day driving around to photograph red barns and visit a covered bridge. I even attended a wedding.

This was a significant opportunity to learn about myself, about Rotary, and to do a lot of public speaking. It was a trigger for me to write specific career goals once again, which I achieved in less time than I planned once I got back to Australia.

Let me encourage you to look out for exchanges and other professional development opportunities and to apply for them believing you can achieve them!

Fairley Community Leadership Program – Based on Williamstown Leadership Model

About twelve months into my first job as a human resources manager, which was 60 km from my home in Benalla, in Tatura via Shepparton, I was selected for the twelve-month Fairley Community Leadership Program.

This is a great model for developing current and future community leaders. It requires commitment of employers to pay for their staff to participate as one of about thirty people within the region, from a range of industries and life experiences, who want to make a difference in their local area and have an interest in its future survival. Selection is competitive, and success requires commitment from every participant to do their part in organising events, chasing guest speakers to match the particular theme, and attending the twelve-hour sessions. Activities were held in various places across mid-northern Victoria, so some early risings and late homecomings were inevitable.

During this program, participants operated in syndicates of six to coordinate and chair each of the twenty-two programs. We examined a broad range of issues in regional and rural Victoria, such as youth, health (including suicide), women in leadership, water quality, regional manufacturing and food production, employment and workforce, tertiary education opportunities, Aboriginal community, media, politics, GM foods, and many others.

This program was conducted one day a fortnight, with two weekends and a graduation dinner. Exposure to the range of topics, guest speakers, and extensive networking was beneficial.

Where to from Here?

Over the next decade, my future will evolve into something completely different. Deep in my heart, my purpose and deepest interest has always been around preaching and teaching. Because I'm inspired by the works of Catherine Ponder and Ernest Holmes, I think my studies and work will be in that arena.

I've worked with Bob Proctor, met John Assaraf and Loral Langemeir, and met and attended a short course with Dr John Demartini, all from the inspirational movie *The Secret*. I've also studied with Brian Tracy. I cannot state emphatically enough, if you want to progress personally and professionally, you must keep moving forward mentally, emotionally, spiritually, and academically.

Entrepreneurial and Business Coaching

For many years, I've travelled to study with Chris Howard, and his work changed my views and my sister Lynley's life.

I'm being coached by Chris in his Million Dollar Mastermind group, conducted in Bali, Indonesia (a two-hour flight), and on the Gold Coast, Australia (a four-hour flight). I love his teaching, his material, and his knowledge.

As a result, I've engaged two part-time university students on a casual basis, which I might turn into an intern arrangement, to assist me in business. I believe this is a good business model and that it forces me to be more systematic and focused. It's also the first time I've felt like I'm really in business.

My business helps small business owners and managers in the private and not-for-profit sector to be compliant with employment-related legislation, as well as coaching in management and staff performance matters. I conduct mediations, as well as life and career coaching sessions, especially for people made redundant. And I get to deliver training for others, privately and publicly.

Who Am I?

I'm forever grateful I had loving, supportive parents who gave me a firm foundation and were good role models in getting along with other people, being emotionally resilient, taking responsibility for where you are in life, and viewing problems as everyday challenges.

Because of that, I believe I could live almost anywhere in the world and adapt and thrive happily. I'm glad to have been born into a society where women (usually) receive equal pay for the same work as men, that we have four weeks annual paid holidays and up to two weeks paid sick leave (unless, of course, you work for yourself), and that there is such a thing as a single parent pension.

My life has not been easy, and if there's a hard way to do something, I'll pretty much find it!

I'm contributing to the upbringing and thinking of my grandchildren, all of whom I adore with all my heart. I loved my grandmother, and I love my grandchildren.

This year will be my first foray into the CEO's Sleepout, an annual event arranged by St Vincent de Paul Society to raise funds and bring attention to the needs of homeless people. I'm involved because I admire the work of the Society and because I was homeless for a while when I first divorced with two small children. But that's another story.

Free Online Monthly Magazine

Please visit my website at http://www.StaffManagement.com.au and register for my free online monthly magazine. This magazine provides information for small business owners, including staff management matters.

If you offer goods or services to a small business community, please contact me, as you may be able to advertise or joint venture with me, depending on our client needs.

Key Things Learned Since 2000

1. To trust myself, to take bigger risks, to value family.
2. Be prepared to invest in self-development programs because the best investment is in yourself. You can lose a job, a partner, a house, and more, but the value of self-development gives you the edge.

3. To value my health and enjoy holidays where I want while I can.
4. To love reading, especially with highlighter pen in hand.
5. Written goals can move a lot quicker than you think.
6. You don't have to follow the normal pattern of school, university, work, marriage, children. You can do all of these in any other order or none of these. You'll be all right.
7. Love teaching and mentoring to do more of what you love.
8. Love yourself; pause and take time out!
9. Take up every opportunity for improvement, learning new skills, challenging beliefs and attitudes, and being an open system so you remain dynamic.
10. Be aware of your higher calling, and notice where your energy is naturally drawn, without effort.
11. Never tire of new beginnings because movement creates and attracts new vibrations, experiences, people, and energy.

If I Can, You Can Handle Anything!

Candice Marie

Candice Marie is a beautiful survivor and a courageous soul indeed. An inspirational leader and life coach, a cultivating graphic designer and photographer, Candice is a breathtaking talent whose creativity has transcended into this, her first book.

Candice's eyes have not always seen their best days. When she was in her twenties, Candice was told she had just five years to live, but became a cancer survivor. Anyone who has experienced the battle of cancer personally or through loved ones knows that putting a number to how long you have left to live your life can be terrifying, but this British native and Australian resident overcame her death sentence and turned it into strength and motivation, which she now shares with the world.

Her motivation was winning; she was determined not to let cancer beat her, as she had already lost loved ones to the cancer industry. So she fought and started to live a life of happiness and health whilst raising awareness to what's really going on in the world. Aided by tons of research and by crossing paths with some of the world's most inspirational people, she created an informative health guide. Through her website and public speaking she is educating and empowering people to take control of their own health. Candice learned the importance of taking responsibility of her own life and maintains a healthy mind, body, and soul by carrying less stress and ultimately doing what makes her heart sing.

Through the years, Candice Marie has made waves in television appearances and various passion projects. She now lives out her dream of running her own modelling, photography, and creative vision agency.

After settling into the fact that she can control her timeline and not letting cancer define her life, she started to score some winning points. Candice is currently working with DreamCatchers International, changing people's lives daily by empowering them to realise their full potential. She certainly works hard at making dreams come true and loves to travel the world doing so, touching people's lives every step of the way.

The human spirit is stronger than anything that can happen to it.
– C. C. Scott

After thirty years on this planet, I've experienced more than your average person – from a devastating house fire, to losing loved ones to cancer, and then being diagnosed with and curing myself of cancer. I think it's safe to say that I know a thing or two about new beginnings and winning.

At the time, life's trials seemed unjust, but now I have come to the realisation that everything has happened to enlighten me to my higher self and show me my real purpose. What I considered bad truly was a blessing in disguise. I simply needed time and thought to find out what the lesson was.

I'm going to share with you some of my struggles, from which I have come out a much stronger and wiser person in the end. How now, with every hardship I encounter, I accept it because I believe it will only lead to better things. *Positivity* is key everywhere in life, for a negative mind cannot produce positive outcomes.

Burning Lessons

In school, you're taught a lesson and then given a test. In life, you're given a test that teaches you a lesson.
– Tom Bodett

I first learned the concept of starting over and beginning new when I was seven years old and my house burned down. My parents had gone out for a romantic meal together, leaving my older sister to babysit. Much to their detriment, being a somewhat wild teenager, my sister invited some "friends" over to enjoy our empty house. (Besides my baby sister and me, that is).

I was all tucked up in bed and heard a lot of commotion downstairs. I went to investigate, and soon found that the Jaffa cake packet (popular in the UK) had somehow, amidst the teen gathering, "set itself on fire" on our kitchen bench top. This immediately alarmed me and sent me into a state of fear.

A daring young man fearlessly put out the fire, and I was at ease again. However, seeing the burn marks on the kitchen side forced me to turn to my slightly tipsy sister and say, "You're gonna be in so much trouble!" At which point I was ordered back upstairs, but not for too long before I was startled by an even louder racket consisting of loud screaming sounds. I got halfway down the stairs to see our beautiful burgundy curtains going up in flames. My older sister was trying to put the fire out with a kitchen bowl full with water. This method was useless and the fire grew.

The "funny" thing is, that week I had been taught all about fire danger, and being the take charge kind of girl I am, I immediately ran back upstairs to my baby sister's room and put my newly acquired knowledge into practice. Holding onto her for dear life, I crouched down low to avoid the thick smoke lurking its way around our home.

Making it safely downstairs and through the front door into the breathable air, I frantically banged on the neighbour's door. They didn't answer, but luckily the family who lived on the other side came out to investigate why their house was filling up with smoke. Once they saw the extent of what was going on, they all leapt into action, pulling my older sister out of the burning house, calling the fire brigade, and ensuring we were all safe.

It soon became apparent that we had a great neighbourhood watch scheme in place, when the people opposite came out to lend a hand

and even offered for us to stay with them until our parents returned home. When my parents did arrive back they were greeted by a crisp white note attached to our deep fried front door informing them of our whereabouts.

From the window, I saw my parents car pull up, then drive away again. My mum, even before she got to see the note, assumed that her children had not made it out alive. She drove off, leaving my dad to find the note and make her aware of our whereabouts.

We lost all our worldly goods, so we all had to start over again in that respect, but the thing that hurt us all the most was that our beloved family cat Gizmo didn't make it out alive. This pained us more than losing our possessions, and even more than finding out that our home insurance had run out the previous month. Every cat I owned thereafter received that same name in honour of our treasured family pet, Gizmo.

As if we hadn't been through enough, some opportunists broke into our charred garage and stole anything we had left, leaving us officially to have to start over, totally from scratch, which in hindsight was not a bad position to be in.

After hugs all around, we started to plan how we were going to recover from this. From a very young age I learned the art of being strong and resilient in times of struggle. I learned that nothing lasts forever, life is short, and much like photography, you develop from the negatives.

With such powerful and high-achieving parents, we were soon back to our former glory, if not more glorious than ever. My parents alone were a movement by themselves, but together they were a force to be reckoned with. Never to be defeated, they teamed together and came out the other side winning and smiling. But the smiles did not last.

Lost Love

It is better to have loved and lost, than never to have loved at all.
– Alfred Lord Tennyson

My mum was just 16 when she fell in love with my dad. They both described it as being love at first sight. My mum was pregnant at the time, and my dad, ever so charismatic and gentlemanly, vowed to take care of my mum and her unborn miracle. Together they produced two of their very own miracles: me, named Candice Marie, and my beautiful little sister, Holly Caroline, who throughout life has been more like my own child.

After eighteen years together, my parents grew apart. They both gravitated towards partners of similar age and interests. I was only 13, and my little sister was just 5 when they broke up. It was not the most amicable of separations, and the sad thing is that they have virtually not spoken to each other since then, seventeen years on.

Subsequently, all the relationships I had in my young adult years failed tremendously. My choice in men was not the best. This was also the case with my choices of friends (to a certain degree), and contributed to my decision to pack my bags and leave home on a journey of self-discovery.

We met for a reason; either you're a lesson or a blessing.

Nomad Traveller

The world is a book, and those who do not travel read only one page.
– St. Augustine of Hippo

I had always wanted to travel the world. Upon leaving high school, I even added it to the Ambitions section of my curriculum vitae, putting it out to the universe in print to help it become a reality. By my mid-twenties, I worked two jobs and saved the money for an around-the-world ticket.

It was the beginning of February 2009 when I embarked on the life-changing adventure to live out my dream. I had already travelled to many parts of Europe, as well as my all-time dream destination Egypt, which was a surprise birthday present from my best friend Jamie. I've always had a deep yearning to see more of what the world has to offer.

Leaving my boyfriend in bed and my friend sleeping on my couch with my cat, I grabbed my backpack and set off to catch a morning flight to America. I ventured to LA, Vegas, Fiji, New Zealand, and then on to Australia, where I had a year's working holiday visa to make use of. I landed in Sydney and travelled up the east coast until I reached Cairns.

Travelling in true backpacker style, I was on an extremely tight budget, and once I hit Cairns in the beautiful Queensland region of Australia, it was time to find myself a job.

I searched for weeks with no luck, until I finally found something. I answered an advert in the Cairns local newspaper for a duty manager of Dreamtime Travellers Rest. After an incredible interview, I moved in.

Being the tour and travel agent as well as the manager enabled me to test out all that the area had to offer. Before long I was a certified scuba diver, and I'd been on practically every tour the region had to offer. I was in my element.

The Show Must Go On

Good times become good memories and bad times become good lessons.

Whilst living the dream in Australia, my best friend Jamie (31) and my cousin Frankie (13) both passed away from the chemo treatment of cancer, but not cancer itself. I flew home to say my last goodbyes and raised money for various cancer charities by jumping out of a plane at 15,000 feet – although I never knew where the money was really going.

As Jay and Frankie would have wanted, I soldiered on and returned back to Australia to work. The Dreamtime job soon came to an end, and I moved over to NJOY Travellers Resort, also in Cairns, where I had the pleasure of meeting Jez, one of the funniest guys I have ever met. After he left Cairns, we stayed in contact.

Before long I had enough money to continue my journey. Melbourne was my next stop, and then the Southeast Asian leg of my around-the-world trip. I ventured through Singapore, Malaysia, and Thailand, where I was reunited with Jez in Bangkok. We then travelled through Thailand together and on to Cambodia, Vietnam, Laos, and back to Thailand before parting ways. Again in true backpacker fashion, I ran out of money in Singapore, and the cheapest flight was to Perth. Jez was already there, and he persuaded me to venture over to find work.

Mining Boom

You gain strength, courage, and confidence by every experience
in which you really stop to look fear in the face.
– Eleanor Roosevelt

Again Jez and I went our separate ways A year after my first Perth landing, I found myself working in Karratha after moving up there to be with a guy I'd met in Perth.

When in town, I saw a poster advertising cervical smear tests, and I hadn't been tested in years. I booked myself in, which proved to be a wise decision, as the test results came back showing abnormal cells in my cervix, which were not far off being cervical cancer.

Thankfully, the outcome was good for me. I had the cells zapped off with laser surgery, and to date the cells have been normal. I immediately raised awareness to encourage more people to get tested, as I knew that many of us didn't think about it.

The Honeymoon's Over

We shall draw from the heart of suffering itself
the means of inspiration and survival
– Winston Churchill

Soon after, my partner dropped an engagement ring into a champagne glass on Valentine's Day. We were married two months later on Easter Sunday, April 2011, on the beautiful Rottnest Island.

Just before going on our Euro-tour honeymoon in June 2011, I noticed a small lump above my right collarbone and thought nothing of it until it started to grow.

By the time we had come back from our honeymoon a couple of months after first discovering the lump, it had increased in size, and I had it checked at our local hospital. After much persuasion, they finally agreed to give my neck an ultrasound scan, which showed there to be many more lumps, all having their own blood vessels. Within a couple of days, I was going in for surgery to have a biopsy to remove the initial lump for further testing.

Much to my dismay, just five days before my twenty-eighth birthday, the results came back as papillary thyroid carcinoma, a type of thyroid cancer.

Toxic Overload

*Respect yourself enough to walk away from anything that
no longer serves you, grows you, or makes you happy.*

There I sat, in a mournful state for hours, crying at having just been told the devastating news, truly believing that my world was over, when in actual fact it was only just the beginning of a life-changing and enlightening journey. I had been given an amazing gift that would open my eyes and enable me to become the person that I was always destined to be.

Growing up, I was never taught the importance of nutrition and its connection to diseases, nor was I made aware of how to promote healing from within.

It's no wonder that my body was toxically overloaded; my whole world was cancerous at times. My teenage years were filled with partying and stressing. I also had faulty non-medical grade PIP implants inserted at the age of 23, which leaked and would also have wreaked havoc on my internal balance. And I spent half my life in and around toxic relationships.

Like many, I did not know what I was actually doing to my body by adopting such a toxic cocktail of different elements into my everyday life. Chemical-laced products from shampoos and toothpaste to cleaning products, foods, and alcohol were but some of the toxins I subjected myself to. As cliché as that may sound, I have come to learn that good health really is about nurturing your mind, body, and your soul in all aspects of life.

They Live On

Family means too much; friends are too valuable. And life is too short to put off sharing with people how much they really mean to you.

As soon as I got the initial diagnosis and surgeon's referral letter, I was constantly haunted by the fact that the majority of patients don't die from the actual cancer, they die from the barbaric and medieval treatment of cancer, which is exactly what happened to my best friend Jamie and little cousin Frankie. Their nightmares also started with the discovery of a small lump.

Jamie's lump was in his testicles. He went in for surgery and had the lump removed. Given a 90 per cent survival rate, after having surgery to remove the lump, lo and behold – the cancer had spread upward into his stomach, so he was put on the most aggressive form of chemo. Having been moved hospitals during treatment, he contracted pneumonia and shingles because his immune system had been weakened by the chemo treatment. The hospital failed to diagnose this in time, and the shingles began to take over his body until he could no longer fight it. They made the decision to put him into an induced coma, where he died from a heart attack at the age of 31.

Then there's my little cousin Frankie, just 13 years old when she, too, found a lump. The lump had initially started out the size of a pea just under her skull at the back of her neck, and increased to the size of a golf ball in just six weeks. After countless trips to the doctors and receiving varied reasons for the lump (from a blocked hair follicle to a swollen gland), her parents took matters into their own hands and persisted with the local hospitals instead, until they were finally granted scans.

Just before Christmas 2008, the scans came back showing an unidentified sarcoma tumour. She stayed in hospital over Christmas to undergo chemo treatment.

Frankie underwent chemo for months until she received the good news that the tumour had virtually vanished. However, waiting for the last set of chemo, Frankie said, "Mum, I've got another bubble-gum." The cancer had started growing again. It took over all the muscles and veins around her neck area and went into her lungs. There apparently wasn't anything that they could do apart from give her some painful radiotherapy.

Throughout her treatments, Frankie only cried once and that was when she was told that there was nothing more they could do for her. Frankie made her mum promise never to cry in front of her. Sue, Frankie's amazing mum, said that this was the hardest thing she's ever had to do, especially when watching her own child suffering and in so much pain from the treatments. Beautiful and brave Frankie passed on 29 July 2009.

Knowing all this, and however much my intelligence, logic, reasoning, and gut instinct steered me towards curing myself the natural way, all the scare tactics used by the industry made me think that I had no time to try something other than their barbaric ways, and unfortunately their methods of persuasion worked.

Fearing for my life and believing their lies, I went down the traditional medical route, allowing them to cut me open and radiate me. Needless to say, the surgery only made matters worse, and as with Jay and Frankie, it had in fact helped to spread the cancer, giving me just five years left to live, apparently.

The cancer had spread into more of the lymph nodes in my neck and also the nodes going down into my chest and into my right lung. They also removed my parathyroid glands "in error," meaning that for the rest of my life I will require calcium supplements. This just goes to show that it doesn't matter how much you research into choosing a more experienced and accredited surgeon, it all boils down to luck and what happens on the day of surgery.

You Don't Have to be Afraid of Cancer Anymore

*If children have the ability to ignore all odds and percentages,
then maybe we can all learn from them. When you think about
it, what other choice is there but to hope? We have two options,
medically and emotionally: give up, or fight like hell.*
– Lance Armstrong

Being only in my twenties, I was shocked to be told that I had only five years left on this planet. The thought of enduring more energy-draining, sickening cancer treatment lowered my spirits, and I refused to go through any more hospitalisation.

I felt that my only hope for survival was to become my own health warrior. I wanted to explore natural alternatives in order to get myself to a state of optimal health that could help keep me alive. I had absolutely no idea where this road would take me, but I felt it was the only way. If I had to die, I wanted to die feeling good, not weak and ill in a hospital bed.

The first step I took was doing Web research, which revealed a wealth of good advice. I began to eat lots of cooked tomatoes (lightly heated with a touch of cold pressed, extra virgin olive oil) each morning. I stocked up on cancer fighting foods such as bok choy, blueberries, broccoli, and teas, including Rooibos, dandelion, and green. I drink only distilled or spring water, and each morning I have some warm with fresh lemon and Himalayan salt, and I drink a glass of filtered water with a quarter teaspoon of aluminium free bicarbonate soda to alkalise my body whilst I sleep. I cannot stress enough how much lemons and bicarb should become part of your daily routine.

I talked to a naturopath who introduced me to an array of supplements and herbal tinctures, such as cat's claw, which is a very powerful immune stimulant. I was also introduced to a different type of blood test that gives you insight into what your live blood cells are actually doing in their living form and whether they are behaving normally. I strongly suggest everyone makes an appointment with a naturopath for a live blood analysis.

The naturopath also recommended that I take some supplements to help my immune system function properly and to support a healthy cardiovascular system and provide protection against oxidative cellular damage. Enzymes along with probiotics were prescribed by my naturopath to restore my digestive system.

That advice was for me specifically, but I would like to share with you the important strategies that can lower anyone's risk of cancer. I learned these with the help of Mark Simon at the Nutritional Oncology Research Institute in America (NORI).

Mark informed me that stress reduction might be the most important non-diet factor for reducing cancer risk.

Part of NORI's program required that I drink carrot, celery, and beetroot juice daily, and that I go onto a fruit-only diet. Pineapple, papaya, mango, and kiwi were all recommended for their powerful proteolytic enzymes that lower inflammation and can dissolve fibrin, which protects cancer cells. After I expressed concern, Mark reassured me that these fruits are low on the glycaemic index and will not cause blood glucose spikes if consumed whole and fresh; nor would they fuel tumour growth, although highly processed fruit juices will spike blood glucose and should be avoided. I also learned that it is protein, especially animal protein, that fuels and stimulates tumour growth more than any other macronutrient.

Mark also told me to get more oxygen to the cells through deep breathing and exercise. He also emphasised that I needed vitamin D, which is such a vital nutrient for overall well-being. Unfortunately, although the best way to get the vitamin is through sunshine, many of us lead indoor lifestyles.

I also learned that cleansing from inside out is essential to leading a healthy life, but rather than starting from a toxic state, it is best to fully detox and cleanse your system first. Call it a full system reset.

One way of doing this is by juice fasting. I absolutely swear by it, as not only does it rid the body of excess fat and toxins, it also comes with a magnitude of healing properties. We should all be giving our digestive systems a well-deserved break from processing heavy foods, thus allowing our bodies to heal.

We all fast at night. That's why our first meal is called *breakfast*. Foods that are easy on the digestive system, such as steamed vegetables, soup, or a freshly squeezed green juice are highly recommended as your last meal of the day, rather than the heavy, meaty, and starchy dinners we are used to.

Apart from food, your body absorbs chemicals from household items such as toothpaste, shampoos, cosmetics, and cleaning agents. Opting for genuinely natural or organic personal and home care products will leave you and your mind healthier.

This can be achieved by learning to control your emotions through the art of meditation, yoga, tai chi, or other martial arts. Ground yourself by reconnecting with nature, and do what makes your heart sing; live for love and not for fear.

What it all boils down to is that the ultimate answer to the growing cancer epidemic is optimal nutrition. Reduce toxic chemicals in food, products, and the environment; limit the use of antibiotics and pharmaceutical drugs; and work on reducing stress.

All of this worked for me. After my "treatment" of surgery and radiation, my tumour marker was at level 13, which indicates an extremely high level of cancer in the body. After consulting NORI and changing my lifestyle, just six months after the initial test, my tumour marker was at 0.7, which was then reduced to 0.3 in the coming months, and it is currently sitting at 0.2. This means there are no large tumours left in me. By changing my lifestyle to a more balanced, joyful, healthier way of living, I will be cancer-free and carefree for the rest of my days.

My Top Ten Tips for a Cancer-Free Life

1. Limit or avoid all animal products, including dairy and eggs.
2. Limit or avoid processed foods.
3. Eat as high a percentage as possible of raw, organically grown fruits and vegetables, especially berries.

4. Sea minerals like seaweed, blue-green algae, and sea or Himalayan salt are cellular building blocks, so include them in your diet.

5. Limit all cooked foods. Whilst you don't have to go completely raw, lightly steam veggies like carrots and tomatoes. Overcooking kills nutrients.

6. Avoid all fried foods at all costs.

7. Supplement with selenium, iodine, and vitamin D. Most people can benefit from more calcium, magnesium, and aluminium-free bicarbonate of soda in their diet.

8. Do not be overly concerned with protein intake. Protein needs of an adult are greatly overstated. The average adult needs no more than ten to twenty grams daily. Fruits and vegetables will fill the protein requirements without eating concentrated proteins such as tofu, nuts, seeds and supplements.

9. Learn to control your emotions through the art of meditation, yoga, tai chi, or other martial arts. Ground yourself by reconnecting with nature.

10. Most importantly, do what makes your heart sing. Live for love and not for fear.

The Truth Will Prevail

Three things cannot be long hidden: the sun, the moon, and the truth.

From the initial diagnosis to present day I have encountered so many aspects of the cancer industry that sicken me, but one of the worst things that I have come across is the lack of emphasis on nutrition and its undeniable importance to a cancer patient's survival and overall recovery. From the moment I stepped foot into the hospital, I was appalled by the poor food options and the extremely limited knowledge of nutrition by anyone, doctors and catering staff alike. Indeed, hospital food has a reputation for not being the most delicious or even the most nutritious, but it is high time for this to become a statement of the past and that one of the ever-failing institutions of today's world will wake up and take action. More people need to be made aware that food plays a major role in preventing and causing ill health and that every time you put something into your mouth you are either preventing or causing disease. It is that simple.

Today's cancer treatments focus on the symptoms and not the actual cause, so if you get to the root cause of the disease, which is highly likely to be due to malnutrition and deficiency, it would simply require some serious detoxing and replenishing. It is the "health" (or rather, "sickness") industry's duty of care to ensure that we have access to the right knowledge, thus becoming our own health advisors, and to "Let thy food be thy medicine," but sadly it is not in their interest for us to be in prime health, but for us to be consumers of the sickness industry.

In today's society we put our lives in the hands of others, giving doctors and surgeons a somewhat godlike status. It is troubling to know that doctors actually have only about six hours of nutritional training out of around six years of medical school, showing that pharmaceutical drugs are favoured over nutrition. So it's no surprise why this is the case when it makes the doctors' wallets fatter and keeps their bosses at the pharmaceutical companies greedily satisfied. An incentive system works amongst the medical industry professionals. You should ask yourself who actually trains a doctor, what text they follow, and why they are so quick to prescribe a pill for every ill? All the answers "lie" with the big pharmaceutical giants.

We need to ask some serious questions, like, "How many more people must suffer and lose their life to cancer due to ineffective and toxic treatments?" "Why are research dollars 99 per cent directed towards radiation, chemotherapy, and other outdated methods?" "Why is there no room for innovations that use a drug-free and natural approach to healing?" Our medical system suffers from excess control from large corporations, a revolving door policy at the FDA and NCI, misdirected and misappropriated funds from cancer foundations, and corruption within the cancer societies. Cancer is a 200-billion dollar business, with no incentive to find low-cost treatments based on diet and lifestyle.

I trusted the doctors and surgeons, but I soon realised that once you are diagnosed and in that system, you are then referred only to their way of thinking, and there's no time to think for yourself. You're not even given another option, just their chop and burn methods. Surgery, radiation and chemo, that's it. No alternative therapies. And while we're on that subject, why exactly do they called it "alternative medicine" when it's the original medicine that humans have been using for thousands of years, whereas chemical medications were discovered about a hundred years ago?

Reborn

If you do what you need, you're surviving. If you
do what you want, you're living.

There are only two ways to live your life. One is as though nothing
is a miracle. The other is as though everything is a miracle.
– Albert Einstein

My motivation now is winning in all aspects of life. I'm determined not to let anything beat me. I've already lost loved ones to the cancer industry, and I'll do everything I can to help stop this. I'll continue to fight for what's right and to live a life of happiness and healthy living, whilst raising awareness to what's really going on in the world. While compiling tons of research and crossing paths with some of the world's most inspirational people, I've created an informative health which you can find in the "Further Reading" section at the end of this book. Through my website I am educating and empowering people to take control of their own health.

Thanks to the cancer, I learned the importance of taking responsibility for my own life and to maintain a healthy mind, body, and soul through embodying less stress and ultimately doing what makes my heart sing.

Yoga makes my heart sing, as does surrounding myself with beautiful souls. In May 2011, I was at my daily yoga class when I received a call to tell me that yet another beautiful soul had been taken from the world.

Jez had left Australia to move back to the UK and was attending a stag do at a popular UK coastal town called Newquay. Being turned away from the club for being too intoxicated, Jez headed back to his hotel. En route, he tripped on a rock, fell, and hit his head. He was found on the beach and pronounced dead at 2 a.m.

This just goes to show how precious life is, and that we never really know what's around the corner. Life is so short, and I live each day like it's my last. My heart now sings at the thought of our paths crossing again on the other side.

Life BC (Before Cancer)

Only put off until tomorrow what you are willing to die having left undone.
– Pablo Picasso

Having successfully completed my GCSE exams, I left high school not entirely sure of what I wanted out of life, and so continued onto college to study A-Levels in art and design, psychology, sociology, performing arts, English language, and English literature. Upon leaving college, I continued on the educational path and enrolled in a national diploma in multimedia course, which covered several creative subjects and would help me to make a more informed decision about my future. Having always had a burning passion for all things creative, I thoroughly enjoyed this course, which led me to continue onto further education, taking on degrees in both graphic communication and multimedia technology and design at two of London's top universities. Despite having been awarded an excellence scholarship for my bachelor of science degree, I still needed an adequate source of income to see me through, and so in between college and university I applied for and was accepted to an advanced hairdressing course that would enable me to gain a trade and ultimately help to fund my way through the rest of my study years. This decision turned out to be wise, and allowed me to take time to travel the world.

Living the Dream

If you can dream it, you can do it.
– Walt Disney

Go confidently in the direction of your dreams.
Live the life you have imagined.
– Henry David Thoreau

I had a vision of owning my very own business, one that would allow me to pursue and live out my passions in my everyday life. Running my own modelling, photography, and creative vision agency that was once a dream is now the iCandiCre8iv Visionary Company – creating the vision for you, for me, for everyone.

With over ten years experience on both sides of the camera, I have a deep understanding of the arts from all angles, and an extensive knowledge and appreciation for the multimedia industry as a whole. With ten-plus years experience as a promoter and model under my belt too, I aim to bring my company to new heights and expand into international waters, where models and clients alike can come together to create visions. Anything is possible.

iCandiCre8iv provides unprecedented photography and design work at an extremely high standard, and is uniquely suited to serve such an array of creative genres, having myself gained years of experience in different areas. I'm a deep believer in cherishing every day like it's the last, and it's this that makes me so passionate about using all my talents to share this joy with others.

Aspiring to the quote "If you love what you do, you'll never work a day of your life," I dream it, I create it, and I live it. My positive and ambitious thoughts become my reality, thus creating a magical world around me. It is this very concept that I so passionately promote.

My passion for all things creative enables me to succeed and continue to fulfil my life dreams. As my grandad once told me, "There's nothing worse than wasted talent," and just that, I strive not to be.

Not just an artist on paper, but an artist in all aspects of life. I have a great passion for winning in work and life! I live it to the fullest with a strong aim to succeed and to help others succeed!

I now also work with Young & Wildly Successful, helping to change people's lives daily by empowering them to realise their full potential. I'm currently in Bali with the Y&WS team, delivering a phenomenal and game-changing Business Mastery, Six-Figure Speaker course to a group of inspirational leaders. After our upcoming Perth, Sydney, and Melbourne tours, we're flying to New Zealand and Queensland to deliver our business and health mastery retreats. I'm also due to fly to Ibiza in October to deliver my very own HealthyCandy message. My dreams of seeing the world and inspiring and helping people are certainly my reality.

Now an international speaker, I just recently flew to America to speak on the stage at Caesars Palace, Las Vegas, for SevenPoint2 (an Alkaline company). I shared my cancer survival story and was humbled to receive a standing ovation and floods of tears from the audience. This injected me with even more drive to continue on my mission, as I know that my message is so powerful and needs to be shared with the world.

I love life and have found it extremely therapeutic writing this chapter. I feel extremely blessed and am thankful for all life's trials and tribulations.

Our success rate for handling a bad day is 100 per cent so far, so always remember that if *I* can, *you* can handle anything. I embrace all opportunities that come my way, and I always endeavour to feel the fear and do it anyway.

Live life on your terms!

Love the life you live, and live the life you love.
– Bob Marley

Dating with Confidence

Jason Barrett

Jason Barrett is an experienced NLP and speaking coach, residing in Perth, Western Australia, who has presented and delivered seminars to both men and women on dating and confidence. He has coached men and women on the art of attracting partners and having confidence to talk to anyone. He is currently a part of Young & Wildly Successful, Australia's leading Gen Y personal development company, helping bring it to a six-figure business in less than ninety days. Jason also has experience in health and fitness supplements, as well as business. His specialties lie in helping men gain confidence; coaching women about how to attract their ideal partner, as well as avoiding who they have no interest in; and how to tell the difference. He has presented to women on identifying pick up artists, and to men on avoiding the concept of the friend zone.

———

Dating is a lost art. The days when men and women could be friends, without men claiming to have been *friend zoned* (when one person has feelings for someone, and the other doesn't feel the same), or women claiming to not be able to meet a *nice guy,* are long gone. Facebook and social media, which make people far easier to access and assess, play a big part in this. They allow people to have a peek at who you truly are, and not the personality you put on to attract someone. It's absolutely crucial in this day and age to be aware of everything we put out there about ourselves. As the saying goes, "Water seeks its own level."

I'll be sharing with you some myths around the friend zone, tips on dating, being portrayed as the person you truly wish to be seen as, and some keys to communication between men and women that are often overlooked. This is so important, especially in this day and age. Since online dating and dating apps like Tinder make meeting people that much easier, if we don't put out the right image to attract the person who's right for us, we could miss that person! No one wants to think of passing by their soulmate without knowing it.

So what we need to do is look at how we are being seen by the people we are looking to attract, male or female. If the response is negative, we need to change how the message is being communicated because the meaning of the communication is the response it elicits. So if someone is reacting negatively to our communication, it means we need to change it. The definition of insanity, as said by Einstein, is to repeat the same action expecting a different result.

I'll be going into more detail about how we apply these tools later on, including a successful strategy used by Darren Hardy, editor and CEO of *Success Magazine*. For now I want to clear up a few myths around the friend zone. I realise a lot of this content is going to seem tailored towards men, but the principles can apply just as much to women. Understanding things from the other person's point of view is one of the biggest keys to effective communication.

Myth #1: The *friend zone* is only for men.

Every man has women in his life that he doesn't see as objects of romantic pursuit. This is, in essence, the same as being in the friend zone. The number one question I ask is why? Why is this person only your friend? Could any of the reasons you have for keeping them as a friend apply to you?

We so often look at other people as the cause of our problems when it comes to relationships, when we should instead look at ourselves. It's said that the only negatives we can see in other people are the negatives which we ourselves display. What this breaks down to is looking at who is just our friend, and why we decided that. It's entirely possible that people aren't looking to date us for those exact reasons we don't date other people. A lot of time is spent chasing after people who just aren't right for us, both men and women. We have a set idea in our heads around what we would like, and pursue those people without thinking about what we would do if we ever dated them, like a dog chasing a car.

I like to use a stereotypical example from American culture to explain this – the outcast who's in love with the "popular" girl. There is a reason this relationship does not work. They are incredibly different. They value different things, such as partying versus staying in on weekends, and are fundamentally different people. If there is a conflict of values between two people, and it isn't resolved, it will cause major issues later in the relationship. The only time this trope has ever worked out is when the two realised they actually had a lot of common ground. This is why whatever we put out to the universe – we get. If we act a certain way, we will encounter more and more people who act that way. Be careful what you wish for, you just might get it!

One of the first keys I want to share with you about dating is the concept of being a *nice guy*. As the saying goes, "Nice guys finish last." Do they really? This all depends on what being a nice guy actually means. This is important, because if your definition of being a nice guy is completely different from what someone of the opposite sex views it, then there's going to be a miscommunication.

If you believe that calling someone three times a day and texting her nonstop is being nice, and she believes that it represents something different, then she isn't getting the message. As we know, the meaning of the communication is the response it elicits. So if we are to get the proper message across, we have to look at how we are communicating from the *other* person's point of view, and make adjustments.

For example, I may tell a friend that I think she looks pretty today, and she might get annoyed at me and not talk to me the rest of the day. Why? All I said was that she looked pretty! From her point of view, though, it could have had a very different meaning. She could have thought I was implying that she looked pretty *only* today, as opposed to every other day. This is why proper communication in this sense is of such importance.

By just looking at the communication from the other person's point of view, we can gain far more understanding of how we can communicate more effectively. What we need to do is remove our idea of how the world works – our map of reality – and attempt to look through theirs. We each have a map of reality that is as individual as our thumbprint. This is shaped by our beliefs, values, experiences, and memories – basically anything that's happened in our life. Once we realize this, we can test. See how different people react to different forms of communication, and speak in their language.

How this all relates to being a nice guy is simple. If it's a miscommunication that's happening, and you're a generally nice person, the conduct I've described will help people see that. If you constantly claim to be a nice guy and have to tell people that's who you are, then you aren't a nice guy. It's that simple.

I see it as a difference between being nice, and being good. Nice is a way that you act, and good is a way that you are. I've never heard someone come back from a date saying "he [or she] was really nice!" without adding a "but…" Don't be a nice guy. Be a good person.

Myth #2: They're single, which means they're available.

Something many people don't understand is that there is a difference between being single and being available. Have you ever had a time in your life where you've felt the need to be alone, with just yourself? Everyone has times like that, whether it's following a break-up, concentrating on a career, or having family issues, everyone needs to be alone. The last thing you need in such times is to have someone constantly trying to talk to you, ask you out, and then complain about being put into the friend zone. Whatever chance that person had with you is basically blown by acting this way.

Furthermore, since when did being friends with someone become a consolation prize? We should be happy that we've become friends and can continue a relationship with someone. Yet we complain that what we want isn't what the other person wants, or is ready for at the time. If you like someone who isn't ready to date anyone, be a friend. More than likely that's exactly what that one needs in a time like that. Regardless, a solid relationship cannot be founded on anything but a solid friendship. People can and do fall in and out of love constantly. By having a mutual *like* for one another, the times when you fall out of love change from being roadblocks to a great relationship to nothing more than small bumps in the road.

The next key to dating is patience. I touched on this before, but it bears repeating. Patience is a virtue, and this is no less true in dating. Often the biggest factor in people feeling uncomfortable, rejecting someone, or not progressing to a closer relationship is that it feels *rushed*. This happens at every stage of getting to know someone, from meeting, to becoming friends, to dating, to having a relationship. From friends to dating is when most of the issues with rushing arise.

Both men and women are guilty of trying to rush things. I'll give an example from my own life. I met with a woman I'd been talking to, and things were going great. She was good-looking, sweet, fun to be around, and I agreed to take her on a date the following week. During this week she talked to me constantly, dropping hints about things she wanted on the date, including flowers. To me, for a first date this was a bit much, but as I was new to dating I just rolled with it. The date came around, and everything went great. She loved the flowers. The week after the date, however, we met up again and talked, and she revealed that she was disappointed that I hadn't asked her to be my girlfriend. At mention of the word I started freaking out. *Girlfriend?* At this point I'd known her about two weeks. It felt incredibly forced and rushed. Again, being new to how everything worked, I asked her to be my girlfriend (big mistake) and she said yes. Four days into the relationship, she told me she loved me. Two days later I broke it off and haven't spoken to her since. She was a lovely girl, but the fact that she tried to rush and force something that I wasn't ready to do is what caused us to split. I hadn't had nearly enough time, in my opinion, to get to know her properly before making that decision.

The way to make sure that things aren't moving too quickly for the other person is to match the way that that one communicates with you. If you aren't getting text messages every day, don't send daily text messages yourself. Likewise with calling constantly. Another way is to have an open honest discussion, but no one should be pressured into feeling the same way. It takes time for some people to build up trust in another person. If you struggle to keep distance between you and the person you're looking to date, remember this: To create heat or friction between two people, there needs to be some tension. Imagine a rope tied between the two of you. The closer you get, the less tension there is; the further you get, the more tension. Dating is a subtle art of staying far enough away that the tension stays and the rope doesn't go slack, and close enough so the rope doesn't snap and the other person finds someone else. As the relationship grows, the rope shortens, and you can become closer without worrying about the heat or the tension.

Before I move on, I want to touch on communication one more time, as it is the basis for our interactions with each other. Men and women communicate in very different ways. Men tend to be more direct in their communications and confrontations, whereas women tend to be more emotional and indirect.

Take, for example, a couple driving down the freeway en route to a destination. The wife spots a McDonald's on the side of the road. She asks her husband, "Honey, are you thirsty?" Without looking over, the husband replies, "Nope!" and continues to drive.

As they continue the journey, the husband realizes his wife is being uncharacteristically quiet. He asks her, "What's wrong?" and she replies, "Nothing."

A few things happen in this interaction. The first and most obvious is when a woman says that *nothing* is wrong, that's 100 per cent absolutely never the case. She is being indirect in her communication. The cause of the problem is that she communicated indirectly, and he answered directly. She was thirsty herself, but asked if he was thirsty, hoping he would realize she was thirsty, and pull over for a drink. He viewed this in an entirely different way. She asked if he was thirsty, he wasn't, so he said no, and now he will be scratching his head as to why she's mad at him.

The last point I'll make before moving on is something so important that if you want to communicate with a woman effectively, *write this down!* If a woman comes to you with a problem, *do not try to solve it for her!* She more than likely already has the solution to her problem, and is looking for someone to talk to about it. Men immediately go into problem solving mode and try to offer a solution. Instead, try to ask questions regarding how she feels about the situation. She will leave feeling far better, having been listened to, which is what she wanted in the first place.

To the women reading this: Understand that men are direct in their conversations. There is almost no hidden meaning to what we are saying, so don't dig too deeply into what's said.

Myth #3: They are putting you in the friend zone on purpose.

I have a quick question for the women reading this. Do you go home after meeting someone to your whiteboard with two lists of people labelled Friend Zoned and Interested and place him in it? No? OK good, just had to clear that up.

A lot of guys feel that because a girl isn't interested right away, it must mean she knows how you feel, and doesn't feel the same way. But nine times out of ten, the woman in particular has no idea how you feel. If she doesn't know how you feel, how can she make a decision either way? The first question I ask anyone coming to me for dating advice or coaching who mentions someone he likes is: Does this person know how you feel? If not, you need to make sure she knows, even if it's as simple as "I'd like to get to know you better; would you like to catch up for a cup of coffee or dinner?" It sets much more of an intention than just asking someone to hang out. Friends hang out with each other, so if you constantly ask someone to hang out, it's hard to complain when that person assumes you're just friends!

There's a lot of nervousness involved with confessing to someone how you feel – I've been there. But if you never ask, the answer will always be no.

This is a great philosophy to take forward with dating, and life in general. If you never ask someone a question, the answer will *always* be no.

This leads me to another key I want to elaborate on: being certain and clear about what your intentions are. Imagine you are asking a woman (or man) to marry you, and you said this: "Darling, you are one of the most amazing people I've ever met, and I'm 60 per cent sure you're the one for me." Is that going to get you anything other than slapped in the face? Why not? It's over half way! OK, how about 70 per cent? Or 90 per cent? Oh come on, 99 per cent? You're saying you have to be 100 per cent committed to get a yes from that question?

That's a good point. You have to be 100 per cent committed. No one likes to be just an option. Although the example was for a relationship, the same can be applied to dating someone. If you don't go into the situation 100 per cent clear on what you want, and 100 per cent certain, then the other person will sense it. If you want something, go for it, no holds barred. It's the only way to get anywhere with others.

I want to share with you the story of Darren Hardy, publisher of *Success Magazine*. The way he attracted his wife is a fantastic way of looking at life. "Before you have, you must first do. Before you do, you must first become." What this means is to have the result, you must first become the person who performs the actions which get the result.

To attract his wife, first he had to become clear on his outcome. Steven Covey, author of *The Seven Habits of Highly Effective People*, says in the first chapter of that book to start with the end in mind. Once Hardy was clear on his outcome, finding a partner to marry, he analysed what sort of person he would want to spend his life with. He wrote out over forty pages detailing everything about his dream partner: her character, attributes, values, beliefs, personality, tastes, interests, what kind of family culture she'd come from, and of course her physical attributes.

If he had then asked, "What do I have to *do* to find and get this woman?" he might still be on that chase today. But Jim Rohn taught him:

Success is not something you pursue. What you pursue eludes you. Success is something you attract by the person you become. To have more you must first become more.

So instead, what he did was to look at the list and then look at himself and said, "What kind of a man would this woman be looking for?" He wrote out over forty pages of detail on how *he* would have to be in order to attract a woman of the calibre he was looking to spend his life with. As Les Brown said: "To achieve something you have never achieved, you must become someone you have never been."

This all seems to be leading toward changing who you are – your entire personality – but that's not the case. It's my belief that there is someone out there for everybody, and that by being yourself you will attract that person. It's about being in line with your values, and being congruent with who you say you are.

For example, I'm heavily involved in health and fitness, and a love for health and fitness is a value I look for in a partner. However, for the last few weeks I've been less than attentive to my health and going to the gym. Even though it's a high value for me, if I don't act like it, then I won't meet someone who values it.

A large divide that has shown up in recent years is the masculine and feminine energies that men and women are showing. Men, especially young men, have shifted to becoming more and more feminine. I don't mean this in a bad way, nor am I implying that men have become more girly. Both genders have masculine and feminine traits; no one is purely masculine or feminine. The divide is apparent when men are "nice guys" rather than being men. A woman wants a man, plain and simple. I'm definitely not saying change who you are to be more "manly"; I'm saying get in touch with what masculinity means for you, and simply display that side of you when looking to attract somebody.

Women, this works both ways. More and more women are becoming masculine to make up for the femininity displayed by men. Men want a woman, someone they can sweep off their feet, someone *feminine*. Men need to realise that we need to be a lover, not a brother. She has fathers, brothers, and uncles in her life for a reason. We don't need to add to that list. If all you do is please and appease her, there will be no positive sexual tension.

Women are getting used to men doing things for them and expecting something in return, another instance of where the concept of the nice guy, who's not actually nice, comes into play. If we aim to do things for people, we should be doing so without expecting them to do something for us in return. It's the idea of planting the seed of a tree, even though we won't live long enough to see the shade of it. It's doing something unselfishly for someone. That's what defines a good person compared to someone who is doing something for some kind of gain.

Personal grooming is such a big part of attracting the right person. This doesn't mean you have to change everything about how you look, but if you're looking to attract someone who looks after herself, then look after yourself. This means making sure you smell nice, your hair is done, your clothes aren't dirty, and your facial hair isn't unkempt. That's basically it for men.

Dressing for the occasion definitely comes into play when it comes to meeting someone. If you're meeting at a park or an outdoor café, you can afford to wear something more sporty or casual. If you're going out to dinner, then definitely dress to impress. Put some effort in. This is all a small part of attracting someone, but it's an important part, as it provides someone's first impression of you. Others can judge us only superficially until they get to know us, so it's important to make a great first impression.

Ladies, this section is for you. I touched on it earlier when I mentioned social media, but this is such an important point, especially in today's society. The first question you ask when someone mentions a new romance is almost invariably "What's his Facebook?" That's often where we find the first impression of someone.

You meet him on a night out, chat with him, exchange Facebook information, get home, and immediately stalk through their profile pictures and timeline. If the first thing you see is a picture of him with his shirt off, with a swarm of women commenting things like "Looking good," would you be impressed or deterred? My guess is the impression is off-putting!

And it works both ways. If the first picture a man sees of you is half-naked or with excessive cleavage, with over a hundred likes, and multiple men commenting on it, is he likely to have respect for you, or be intimidated? Speaking from experience, he'll be quite intimidated, so much so that he'll more than likely not even try to get to know you.

People can put whatever they want on social media. I'm not telling anyone to take their pictures down, or to change who they are. All I'm suggesting is if you want to start dating a guy who will treat you the way you wish to be treated, then the first thing to do is to check what you put out for the world to see. If you're tired of seeing guys who are shallow, superficial, and rude, then the first point of order is to stop putting things that attract them where others can see them, such as on social media sites.

People are free to post whatever they want. However, if a woman posts a photo of herself half-naked, I believe she forfeits the right to complain when the calibre of person she meets turns out to be creepy and shallow. The same does go for men. If you're looking for a serious relationship, but you're giving off the energy of someone who's looking for something casual, you will always get something casual.

When it comes to social media, pictures are not the only revealing part; so are status messages. If you get lonely and broadcast that fact on Facebook, it sends a certain vibe. When someone has a *need* for a relationship, it becomes unhealthy, and that person simply will not work in any relationship. If someone cannot be happy with who they are when they are single, then no one person is going to be able to fill that gap. A common misconception around dating is that two halves make a whole. A proper relationship should be one plus one makes two, three, four or more. Each person is an individual, and unless you can be comfortable and happy with who you are while you're single, then you won't be fulfilled and happy while in a relationship.

Initial Stages of Dating Advice

Some people have no problem attracting someone and getting to know that person. Where they fall down is the initial stages of dating and taking it to the next level. Sometimes the hardest part is just asking, and it's made even harder if the other person is a friend, because you don't want to risk the awkwardness of being turned down.

There's a simple way to get around this: just *do* it. As I said before, if you don't ask, the answer is always no. The importance of this is reflected in this simple statement: the pain of regret is greater than the pain of rejection. No one wants to look back on all the "I could have" or "I should have" moments in life. If you value your friendship enough, then asking someone on a date will be of no consequence if the answer is no. If someone chooses not to see you after you ask, then the friendship obviously didn't mean enough to that person, and this gives you a chance to move on and surround yourself with other potentially more fruitful choices.

I work off the philosophy that you are the average of the five people that you surround yourself with. So the more you spend time with higher quality people, the more likely you are to develop naturally to be more like them. If someone doesn't want to be your friend, that someone definitely won't be worth dating.

Women can use this to test whether a man is being genuine. If he's upset about being just friends, then he definitely is not worth pursuing in a romantic way. I'm not *recommending* that women should be testing men, or vice versa. I'm saying only that people reveal their character when they don't get what they want.

Have you ever asked someone on a date, and then had absolutely no clue where to take them? Don't worry – it happens to all of us. Personally, I'm not a big fan of dinner and a movie. When I first meet someone, the last thing I want to do is spend 80 per cent of my time with that person either not talking or attempting to talk between mouthfuls of food! The first date is the difference between a "good night" and having that *spark*. Of course, a lot of the content of the first date should be talking, getting to know each other personally. So a lot of the date will come from how much you have in common, and what you have to talk about.

But the setting can change the game completely. For example, if you date a woman you know to be a bit shy, introverted, and relaxed, she may be more at home going for a walk and having coffee, rather than dinner and a show. If she is interested in health, outdoors, and activities, she might feel more in her element going rock climbing, or playing laser tag or paintball. If someone is more social and focused on nature and animals, then bush walks, beach walks, and trips to the zoo or aquarium would be where they are happiest. If the person you're dating can see you've put effort into where you've chosen to take them, it will be an entirely different experience, trust me.

Conversation on the first date is exceptionally important. Here are a few things to stay away from talking about.

- *Your Ex:* No one likes to be compared to an ex, but the more you bring one up in conversation, no matter how you do it, the more the person you're with will feel she's being compared. Stay away from that topic entirely.
- *Yourself:* It's great getting to know every little detail about someone, but at some point you want to share as well, right? That's how people feel if you take every chance you can to talk about yourself. It doesn't impress anyone. It does the opposite: You come off conceited and egotistical. Unless that's something your date is looking for in a person (which is a red flag), then keep the conversation balanced between asking and answering questions.
- *Phone:* This should go without saying guys, but as a gentle reminder: Keep your phone off or at least on silent for the whole date, and don't touch it! In this day and age, your date will feel utterly respected and impressed if you ignore any phone call, and don't even touch your phone throughout the date.
- *Too Sexual:* One for the women. If a guy is just a bit too sexual in what he says, then you can tell what's on his mind. He could just

be horny, but either way the response is the same: Don't have sex with him. This is obvious, but time and time again I've seen people dating get sexual far too early, and the sexual tension between them goes away. More often than not, the man will leave because he has no desire to continue the relationship. Another case of what you do: you attract. You may not be someone who has sex right away, but if you do, that's all he's going to think you want, and as a result he won't have any interest in staying around. A quality guy will want to see you again regardless of whether you have sex.

Online Dating

The last part I want to cover in this chapter is online dating. There once was a stigma surrounding meeting someone online, but as our culture has progressed, we have become more open to meeting people outside of our circle of friends without relying on someone to introduce us. Besides, no one wants to be the person who constantly asks "Have you got any single friends?" So online seems to be the way to go. For women, however, the online dating sites seem to be full of creepy guys that are hell-bent on sex, sex, sex. It's hard for women to find genuine guys, whereas men are struggling to attract and connect with women. I'll offer a solution for both genders.

A lot of these problems can be solved simply by choosing the right Web service. Some free apps and sites attract men who are looking for a one-night stand. I'm not claiming that's the only type of man on them; however, they are the overwhelming majority. Women can usually spot these guys from a mile away: Shirt off in their profile picture and excessive use of the ;) emoticon are easy-to-spot red flags. There are more subtle signs that a guy is only in it for one thing. The eagerness to meet up soon, lack of substance in a conversation, wanting to meet up at night only, and the obvious one of wanting you to come around to "watch a movie." I think we all know what that means. If you meet up with a man and he's eager to kiss you early on in the night, this can be an indicator that he's interested in only one thing. In the end, each man will be unique in how he acts and what he is looking for. Any of the paid websites are for when you want to get serious. But I feel no one should have to pay to talk to a potential partner.

Men have to create a profile that is interesting to the sort of person we're trying to attract. We have to be genuine, because people too often put a mask over who they are. If you're looking to meet someone online who you really connect with, then you can't present a false identity. How would you feel if you met with a woman, expecting her to love health and fitness, bush walks, and outdoor activities, but when you got together you found out she doesn't love any of those things? The thing that initially attracted you would be gone. So be honest about what you enjoy.

Be brief. A small paragraph is best. This is something I've used in the past, and I feel works well on sites with just an About Me section.

> My name is Jason, and I'm an entrepreneur and coach. I'm passionate about what I do, and I love health, fitness, and the outdoors. I'm a very social person, interested in connecting with like-minded people."

Depending on the website, you may have to expand on that, but see how it's succinct, has a bit of intrigue and mystery, and yet gives a bit of a sense about who I am, which is passionate, social, and loving of the outdoors. A woman reading this who is interested in what I am, will at least be intrigued.

If you don't like your job, or what you do for a living, then don't mention it. No woman wants to know that you're an accountant, and it's going alright. Talk about what makes you passionate. That's what I do.

Apart from your bio, you need a high-quality photo, preferably not a mirror selfie. I personally would use a front-camera shot from a high quality smartphone.

The last tip I will give: *Read her profile!* It's staggering how many men do not do this. When you send a message that touches on something she mentions in her bio, and you include a compliment about it, your results will be incredible.

For the love of God, don't ask, "Hey, how are you?" This applies to women as well. I've had women message me with "Hey" or "Hey how are you?" and I instantly understood how they felt! No effort went into that, and I felt like a number. Women feel that way, too, when you message them pointless greetings.

The overall message I want to convey can be framed by this simple concept: If you are genuine, and you be yourself and try to connect with someone but the other person isn't interested, this is not your burden. Besides, would you really want to be with someone who didn't connect with you on a personal level? My point is that if someone is not interested, that someone isn't right for you. But if you be yourself and avoid putting on a mask of what you think someone else wants, you will find someone who will be worth the wait. Change your message, not who you are.

Afterword

Each time you reread or rehear good training material you get something different out of it. This is not because you missed something before, but because you are a different person than you were before.

And so you have come to the end of this volume of guidance and secrets to help you on your way to making the most of your opportunities for new beginnings in all areas of your life. By this stage you will have found some useful nuggets, which you are even now putting into practice. I don't know whether you've noticed the positive changes these are already making to your life, or whether you will start to realise these more slowly over time. But either way, let these be a sign that you are on the right track to a much richer and more empowering life as a result of applying the many lessons you have learned from this book.

However, this is not a book to be read once and then hidden away in pristine condition, forgotten on the shelf, never to be read again.

Oh, no.

This is a book that will amply reward and repay regular rereading.

It is a book that will bring new insights each time you read it, because you will be at a different stage in your life each time, facing different challenges and immersed in different experiences.

It is a book in which to highlight relevant sections, underline key points, and scribble inspired notes and comments profusely in every available margin. If you haven't already begun to do that, grab those highlighters and pens and get to it right away! For in the process of so doing, you gain deeper insights and unlock deeper secrets, and that means that they will continue to serve you and help you to win in life and work.

It would be lovely to hear from you regarding some of the ways in which this book has helped you. What you have learned and discovered as a result of reading this book? What changes have you made in your approach to your new beginning, and how have they made your life even more successful and enjoyable?

Please do get in touch with your success stories, your comments, and your suggestions by sending an email to comments@ WinningInLifeAndWork.com.

Thank you, and good luck in all your endeavours and journeys through life!

Keith Blakemore-Noble,

August 2014

Acknowledgements

Let Go to Begin – Keith Blakemore-Noble

I would like to thank all of my fellow experts who have each contributed a chapter to this book, for without their contributions this would be a slim volume indeed.

I'd like to thank all my current coaches and mentors for their general support and encouragement in so many ways – that's Chris Howard, Elliot Kay, Clinton Swaine, and Lucy Whittington.

A big thank you too to all my family and friends, none of whom I get to see as often as I would like these days. I hope to see each and every one of you soon.

Finally I want to acknowledge you, dear reader, for buying and reading this book – for without you, this would all have been a pointless endeavour!

Make a Fortune Making a Difference – Calvin Coyles

To the team at Young & Wildly Successful, your passion and commitment inspire me. To my partner, Cherish, I am nothing without you. To my family, thank you for your support and to all the YWS family. Live life on your terms!

The Business of Social Media – Kim Barrett

I'd like to acknowledge all the people that have trained me and mentored me along the way. It's allowed me to bring the best to the marketplace, and without them I wouldn't have any of the information I have today.

Driving Your McLaren: Autism, Formula 1, Lasting Change – Sanja Zeman

I would like to thank and acknowledge all of the wonderful and brave individuals who struggle in fitting into our world every day. Without you and your extremes of perception, our understanding of our world would be so different. I would also like to thank my family. You guys challenge me every day to be a better person and role model. Without your support, I couldn't do what I do.

Embracing Change – Michelle Armstrong

I would like to thank the following people for their help in the creation of this chapter. Without their presence in my life, this chapter simply would not be.

First, thanks to my dad, who taught and encouraged me to cast my net wide and believe I can catch whatever I want; to my beautiful mother for openly sharing her truth and beliefs and her relationship with the unseen force that lovingly guides and directs our lives; and my incredibly deep yet humble brother for his quiet, powerful, and often unspoken love that I feel every day and cherish. You have all witnessed and supported the many changes in my life. For this I am deeply grateful.

I also thank my incredible son, whose rapid growth, expansive heart, and limitless spirit remind me daily of the magic of life and the constant presence of change within it.

I wish to thank and acknowledge Amanda Rooker, my brilliant editor and a spirited soul whose presence in my life I cherish, feel thankful for, and deeply respect. Thanks also to my friend Chris Howard for re-entering my life again at the perfect time and for introducing me to Keith Blakemore-Noble, who is the creator of this fantastic book and who has been extraordinarily patient with me, above and beyond, as I sought to write this chapter while juggling many other projects.

Last but not least, I thank the loving presence of God in my life and my spiritual teacher, guide, and constant source of comfort, Jesus.

Break the Rules. Find Your Freedom. Live Your Life. – Kasia Nalepa

I acknowledge with love and respect:

All these wonderful people in my life who have touched my heart and my soul.

All these who have challenged me so I can learn and grow. Challenges that looked huge before became manageable. Challenges that have made me persevere; that's a part of what makes me successful.

All these whom I have challenged. Challenge eliminates complacency.

My wonderful advocates, who have shown their loving support for my work and who continue to be a source of inspiration for me.

All those whose hearts are opening more and more each day.

My loved ones and my dear friends around the world, who surround me with unconditional love, joy, and just plain fun.

My beloved Mum, who has always encouraged me to follow my heart, fulfil my dreams, and travel the world, and who has taught me how to be an honourable person.

All of my inspirational fellow authors for sharing this great experience with me; Keith Blakemore-Noble for putting this incredible project together and for his constant support; Chris Howard for his invitation to participate in this transformational publication; and my Inner Guide for grasping this amazing opportunity within seconds.

All people I meet on my journey who continue to teach me about the mystery of life and the majesty of living, my heartfelt appreciation and love.

Last but not least… I acknowledge with love and respect *You,* dear reader. I would love to think that I have inspired you to be a courageous person, a person who follows their heart. I hope you have enjoyed this journey of finding your *why,* your mission statement, and your purpose in life. Thank you so much for taking it with me. This is just a very beginning. The destination of being a fulfilled person and living a meaningful life is fantastic! However, do not forget to enjoy the process. "The journey's what brings us happiness, not only the destination!" Please keep in touch with me and let me know your progress.

New Country: New Life – Lourdes Katague

I would like to thank the people that accepted me as who I am. Their support and encouragement provided motivation and allowed me to express the real me. To my husband, Efren Katague, for the gift of freedom to educate myself. To Julia Stephenson and Ilse Hillermann for editing the early manuscripts and further suggestions. To Corazon Sinha for promoting my expertise. To Keith Blakemore-Noble for the invitation to participate in this publication, and for his untiring support and encouragement. Thank you to Chris Howard for his continued confidence to bring out the best of me. I am very grateful to the women who contributed their stories for this chapter. Whether they were used or not, they were well appreciated. To the rest of my family: Marie Florence, Stephanie, Dave, Louren, Angelina, and Anastasia, you are my inspiration.

Closure and New Beginning – Duda Prestes

I would like to thank everyone that collaborated with me all my life, in so many different ways, that today I am who I am.

A very special thank you to my dear kiwi friend, Janet Dougherty, who reviewed the draft of this chapter.

Can't thank enough my family, all experts in new beginnings!

They all give me wonderful examples. My sister is a great example on friendship and perseverance, my father on how to never give up, my stepfather on how to overcome losses, my mum on how to be reborn from the ashes, and my daughter-in-law on how to follow dreams!

A big especial thank you to my grandparents for the great lessons taught in a daily basis and to my son, the best example I have on how not to judge others; to Chris Howard and Johnnie Cass, for the inspiration they are to me; and to my grandkid to be, we welcome you and the amazing new beginning you will bring to our lives!

At last, but not least, I am very grateful to God, to the universe, to the force, for creating this opportunity, and to you, my dear reader!

Have fun, always!

The WoW Factor – David Jackson

I would like to acknowledge first all my fellow contributors to this book and Keith Blakemore-Noble for the vision and assistance in making this project a reality. I would like to thank John Nugent for reviewing my chapter and providing his highly valued guidance and direction. I would like to acknowledge my parents and family for always being there. I also wish to acknowledge all the mentors that have supported and guided me down through the years. I wish to acknowledge my daughter Saoirse and son Nathan for all their love and support and joy they bring to my life. I wish to acknowledge my beautiful wife and soulmate Ashling and to thank you from the bottom of my heart for your unconditional love, support, and joy that you bring to my life. Thank you one and all.

4QI – A Questionable Intelligence for Change – Patrick White

I would like to thank the following people for their help in the creation of this chapter: all the people I have coached, those who have attended my training sessions, and those who have let me consult for them, as you have taught me so much. Thanks also to my wife, Michelle, and daughter Laura, who have contributed as proofreaders and commentators.

Power Choices at Pivotal Points – Ian Crawford

Thank you to all my friends that have supported me in the development of this chapter. You know who you are, and you are sensational.

To my parents and sister for always supporting my crazy life journeys that have led me to living my dream: thank you.

To my two girls: Love seeing the world through your eyes as you grow.

Singing – Antidote to Modern Life – Colin Bennett

I would like to thank the following people for their help in the creation of this chapter:

My wife, Anne, daughters Hazel and Laura, and grandchildren Steph and Josh. Everything I do, I do for you – you are my reason for being.

To everyone who has touched my life has contributed to this work, as it reflects my interaction with them. In particular I thank all those with whom I have sung and who have helped me to sing; all those who have worked with me whilst on the board of the British Association of Barbershop Singers, both on the board and with other organisations worldwide.

To all my work colleagues who whilst being audited or trained have to hear about four-part harmony or even try it as a learning exercise, I apologise and thank you.

I would finally like to thank Keith Blakemore-Noble for his help, patience, and guidance in the formulation and completion of this work, without which it never would have seen the light of day.

From Dry Inland Australia to the Tropical North! – Heather Traeger

I would like to thank the following people for their help in the creation of this book – all of my fellow experts who've contributed a chapter; Chris Howard for introducing me to the wonderful possibilities of a world where you can significantly enrich your life; Keith Blakemore-Noble for his invitation to contribute to this book of new beginnings and be inspired by other experts.

I want to acknowledge:

My parents, Nola (Johns) and Alan Traeger, sister Lynley, and brother Keith (gone to higher duties); my sons Isaac and David for their support and loyalty; my beautiful grandchildren, Georgina, Nicholas, and India.

I want to thank all my managers for their teaching and coaching over many years, my lecturers, and other inspiring entrepreneurs, and importantly, my business and private clients who love my work and allow me to make a living.

And LinkedIn.

If I Can, You Can Handle Anything! – Candice Marie

First I would like to thank my body and the cancer it once housed. Being made aware of having a terminal illness allowed me to awaken, heal, and share my story with the world, thus saving my own life and

294

the lives of others. I would also like to thank each and every person that I have crossed paths with. I have learned great lessons from you all, and it's thanks to my life experiences that I am who I am today. I am proud of the person I have become, and I now love and care for myself like never before. It is this message that I wish to share with you all: "Love thyself and let thy food be thy medicine."

I dedicate my life to helping others and spreading the truth.

In loving memory of

Jamie Timothy Brownsmead
21 December 1977 – 11 June 2009
Frankie Marie Geraghty-Gauthier
08 November 1995–29 July 2009

and to everyone touched by cancer, especially the people who have lost their lives in the hands of the cancer industry. This is for you.

Further Reading

Rock Your World: Transform Your Life! – Christopher Howard
   Christopher Howard, *Instant Wealth: Wake Up Rich*.
   Christopher Howard, Turning Passions into Profits.

Let Go to Begin – Keith Blakemore-Noble
   Keith Blakemore-Noble et al., *Winning in Life and Work: Volume 1*.
   Deepak Chopra, Keith Blakemore-Noble, et al., *Ready, Aim, Captivate!*

Make a Fortune Making a Difference – Calvin Coyles
   http://www.youngandwildlysuccessful.com
   Napoleon Hill, *Think and Grow Rich*.
   Dale Carnegie, *How to Win Friends and Influence People*.
   Tony Robbins, *Awaken the Giant Within*.
   https://www.youtube.com/user/calvincoyles

The Business of Social Media – Kim Barrett
   Gary Vaynerchuk, *Jab, Jab, Jab, Right Hook*
   Sanja Zeman, Driving Your McLaren: Autism, Formula 1, Lasting
      Change
   Brainworx: http://www.brainworx.net/
   Empact: http://www.empact.com.au/
   Brainbodyblitz FB: https://www.facebook.com/Brainbodyblitz
   A. Jean Ayres, PhD, *Sensory Integration and the Child* (Western
      Psychological Services, 2005).
   J. Vitale, *The Key* (John Wiley & Sons, Inc., 2008).
   W. Dunn, *Living Sensationally* (Jessica Kingsley Publishers, 2009).

C. S. Kranowitz, MA, *The Out-of-Sync Child* (Perigee, Penguin Group, 2005).

L. J. Miller, *Sensational Kids* (Perigee, Penguin Group, 2006).

N. Kashman and J. Mora, *The Sensory Connection* (Sensory Resources, 2005).

Stephen R. Covey, *The Seven Habits of Highly Effective People* (Free Press, 1989).

Embracing Change – Michelle Armstrong

Michelle Armstrong, *Manage Your Mind, Master Your Life* (Mind Management, 2004).

Michelle Armstrong, *New Book* (Morgan James, 2014).

Break the Rules. Find Your Freedom. Live Your Life. – Kasia Nalepa

Adam Zamoyski, *Poland: A History*, (2009).

Norman Davies, *Heart of Europe: The Past in Poland's Present*, (2001).

Richard C. Lukas and Norman Davies, *Forgotten Holocaust: The Poles under German Occupation, 1939–44*, F (2001).

Timothy Snyder, *Bloodlands: Europe between Hitler and Stalin* (2011).

Halik Kochanski, *The Eagle Unbowed: Poland and the Poles in the Second World War* (2013).

Norman Davies, *Rising '44: The Battle for Warsaw* (2004).

Jan Karski, *Story of a Secret State: My Report to the World* (Penguin Paperback Classics, 2012).

Tymothy Garton Ash, *The Polish Revolution: Solidarity*, (1999).

Napoleon Hill and Tom Butler-Bowdon, *Think and Grow Rich*, (2009).

Robert T Kiyosaki, *Rich Dad Poor Dad*, (2011).

Mira Kirshenbaum, *Everything Happens for a Reason – Finding the True Meaning of the Events in Our Lives* (2005).

Eckhart Tolle, *The Power of Now: A Guide to Spiritual Enlightenment* (2001).

Don Miquel Ruiz, *The Four Agreements: A Practical Guide to Personal Freedom* (Toltec Wisdom, 1997).

Don Miquel Ruiz and Don Jose Ruiz, *The Fifth Agreement: A Practical Guide to Self-Mastery* (Toltec Wisdom, 2011).

Dalai Lama and Howard C. Cutler, *The Art of Happiness: A Handbook for Living*, (1999).

Thrive, http://www.thrivemovement.com

New Country: New Life – Lourdes Katague

Russell H. Conwell, *Acres of Diamonds*, http://www.ThinkAndGrowRichGifts.com.au

Michael E. Gerber 2008, *Awakening the Entrepreneur Within: How Ordinary People Can Create Extraordinary Companies* (New York: Harper Collins, 2008).

Napoleon Hill, *Think and Grow Rich* (Mt. Druitt, Little Hills Press, 2007).

Christopher Howard, *Instant Wealth – Wake up Rich: Discover the Secret of the New Entrepreneurial Mind* (Hoboken: John Wiley and Sons, 2010).

Christopher Howard, *Turning Passions into Profits: Three Steps to Wealth and Power* (Hoboken: Simon Schuster, 2004).

Robert Kiyosaki and Sharon L. Lechter, *Before You Quit Your Job: Ten Real Life Lessons Every Entrepreneur Should Know about Building a Multi-Million Dollar Business* (Scottsdale: Tech Press, 2005).

Anthony Robbins, *Awaken the Giant Within: Take Immediate Control of Your Mental, Emotional, Physical, and Financial Destiny* (London: Simon and Schuster, 2001).

Anthony Robbins, *Unlimited Power: The New Science of Personal Achievement* (London: Simon & Schuster, 1998).

Loren Slocum, *Life Tuneups: Your Personal Plan to Find Balance, Discover Your Passion, and Step into Greatness* (Guildford, GPP Life, 2009).

Wallace Wattles, *The Science of Getting Rich: Attracting Financial Success through Creative Thought* (Rochester, Destiny Books, 2007).

Closure and New Beginning – Duda Prestes

Chris Howard, *Turning Passions into Profits* (John Wiley and Sons, Inc., 2004).

Donald Walsch, *The Little Soul and the Sun* (Hampton Roads, 1998).

Conversations with God – Book 1 (Hampton Roads, 1996).

Eleanor Potter, *Pollyanna* (Scholastic Inc., 1975).

James Allen, *As a Man Thinketh* (Tribeca Books, 2011).

James Redfield, *The Celestine Prophecy* (Grand Central Publishing, 1993).

The Tenth Insight (Grand Central Publishing, 1996).

The Secret of Shambhala (Warner Brothers, 1999).

Jose Silva, *The Silva Mind Control Method* (Simon & Schuster, 1978).

Wallace Wattles, *The Science of Getting Rich* (Thrifty Books, 2009).

The Science of Being Great (Thrifty Books, 2009).

The WoW Factor – David Jackson
Napoleon Hill, *Think and Grow Rich* (Vermilion: London, 2003).

Richard Bandler, *Get The Life You Want* (Harper Element, 2008).

Richard Bandler, *Make Your Life Great* (Harper Element, 2008).

Anthony Robbins, *Awaken the Giant Within* (Pocket Books, 2001).

Anthony Robbins, *Unlimited Power* (Pocket Books, 2001).

Paul McKenna, *Change Your Life in Seven Days* (Bantam Press, 2004).

Christopher Howard, *Turning Passions Into Profits* (Wiley, 2004).

Christopher Howard, *Instant Wealth – Wake Up Rich* (Wiley, 2010)

Owen Fitzpatrick, *The Charismatic Edge* (Gill & Macmillan, 2013).

Brian Colbert, *The Happiness Habit* (Newleaf, 2010).

Kevin Kelly, *How When You Don't Know How* (On Stream, 1997).

David J. Schwartz, *The Magic of Thinking Big* (Pocket Books, 2006).

4QI – A Questionable Intelligence for Change – Patrick White

Leadership
Robert I. Sutton, *Good Boss, Bad Boss: How to Be the Best… and Learn from the Worst* (2010).

Robert I. Sutton, *The No Asshole Rule: Building a Civilised Workplace and Surviving One That Isn't* (2010).

Warren Greshes, *The Best Damn Management Book Ever* (2011).

Emotional Intelligence

Daniel Goleman, *Emotional Intelligence: Why It Can Matter More Than IQ* (2009).

Margaret Chapman, *The Emotional Intelligence Pocketbook* (2001).

Travis Bradberry, *Emotional Intelligence* (2009).

Innovation

J. Dyer, H. Gregersen, and C. M. Christensen, *The Innovators' DNA* (2011).

Entreprenership

Hannah McNamara and Patrick White, *Business Cookery: Tried and Tested Recipes for Business Success* (2011).

Ian Crawford, "Power Choices at Pivotal Points" (Australian Sports Commission).

"Volunteer Toolbox" (Audio CD).

"Seven Steps to High-Performing Organisations" (Audio CD).

Singing – Antidote to Modern Life – Colin Bennett

Alan Johnson and Harry Wells, *Twenty-Five Years: The History of British Barbershop Harmony* (2003).

Benjamin C. Ayling, "An Historical View of Barbershop Music and the Sight-Reading Methodology and Learning Practices of Early Championship Barbershop Quartet Singers, 1939–63" (International Journal of Research in Choral Singing, 2004).

Jim Henry, *The Harmonizer* (July–August 2001).

Richard Mook, *Journal of the Society for American Music* (Cambridge University Press, 2007),

Robert A. Stebbins, *The Barbershop Singer: Inside the Social World of a Musical Hobby* (Toronto: University of Toronto Press, 1996).

http://www.managingsafelytuition.com

http://www.tasteofsidmouth.co.uk

http://www.sidmouthholiday.com

http://www.singbarbershop.com

http://barbershop.org

http://www.sweetadelineintl.org
http://www.labbs.org.uk
http://www.sweetadelines.org.uk
http://worldharmonycouncil.org
http://www.getmenots.com
http://greatwesternchorus.com

From Dry Inland Australia to the Tropical North! – Heather Traeger
Brian Tracy, *Maximum Achievement* (Simon & Schuster Paperbacks, 1993).
Catherine Ponder, *Open Your Mind to Receive* (DeVorss Publications, 1983).
Christopher Howard, *Three Steps to Wealth and Power* (Chris Howard Companies, 2004).
Dale Carnegie, *How to Win Friends and Influence People* (Simon & Schuster, 1981).
Debbie Ford, *Why Good People Do Bad Things* (Harper One, 2008).
Ernest Holmes, *Creative Mind and Success* (Wilder Publications, 2007).
Heather Traeger and George Faddoul, *How to Get a Bigger Bite out of Life! – Special Edition* (Quantum Change Publishing, 2011).
Heather Traeger, George Faddoul, and Ralf Behn, *Unlocking Your Ideal Weight – Special Edition* (Quantum Change Publishing, 2014).
Dr John F. Demartini, *The Heart of Love* (Hay House, 2007).
Masaru Emoto, *The Secret Life of Water* (Pocket Books, 2006).
Napoleon Hill, *Think and Grow Rich: The Twenty-First-Century Edition, Revised and Updated* (High Roads Media, 2004).

If I Can, You Can Handle Anything! – Candice Marie
Thomas Campbell, *My Big Toe*.
Bruce Lipton, *The Biology of Belief*.
Susan Jeffers, *Feel the Fear and Do It Anyway*.
http://www.healthycandy.me
http://www.icandicre8iv.com
http://www.candice-marie.com
http://www.nutritionaloncologyresearchinstitute.com

Contact

Rock Your World: Transform Your Life! – Christopher Howard
    Web: http://www.RockHouseGlobal.com
    Facebook: http://www.facebook.com/chrishowardglobal
    LinkedIn: http://www.linkedin.com/in/chrishowardglobal

Let Go to Begin – Keith Blakemore-Noble
    Change: http://www.be-your-change.co.uk
    Confidence: http://www.TheConfidenceAlchemist.com
    Phobias: http://www.FreedomFromPhobia.com
    Personal website: http://www.Blakemore-Noble.net
    Facebook:
    http://www.facebook.com/keith.blakemorenoble
    http://www.facebook.com/TheConfidenceAlchemist
    LinkedIn: http://www.linkedin.com/in/keithblakemorenoble/
    Email: keith@be-your-change.co.uk

Make a Fortune, Making a Difference – Calvin Coyles
    http://www.youngandwildlysuccessful.com
    calvin@youngandwildlysuccessful.com
    http://facebook.com/calvincoyles
    https://www.youtube.com/user/calvincoyles

The Business of Social Media – Kim Barrett
    kim@yoursocialvoice.com.au
    kim@kbossfitness.com.au

Driving Your McLaren: Autism, Formula 1, Lasting Change – Sanja Zeman
   About me: http://about.me/sanjazeman/#
   Email: szeman@empact.com.au
   Telephone: 1300 721 944

Embracing Change – Michelle Armstrong
   The Armstrong Method: http://www.ArmstrongMethod.com
   Personal website: http://www.MichelleArmstrong.com

Break The Rules. Find Your Freedom. Live Your Life. – Kasia Nalepa
   Web: http://www.kasianalepa.com
   Email: connect@kasianalepa.com.
   LinkedIn: http://uk.linkedin.com/in/KasiaNalepa

New Country: New Life – Lourdes Katague
   Facebook: Hear Our Story
   Web: http://www.MigrantEmpowerment.com
   Skype: lkatague

Closure and New Beginning – Duda Prestes
   Mediation: http://www.b2bmediation.co.nz
   Personal Development: http://www.dudaprestes.com.br
   http://www.akademiadamente.com.br

The WoW Factor – David Jackson
   Website: http://www.chrysalisevolution.ie
   Email: info@chrysalisevolution.ie
   LinkedIn: http://ie.linkedin.com/pub/david-jackson/25/a01/25b
   Facebook: Chrysalis Evolution
   Skype: davidambrosejackson1

4QI – A Questionable Intelligence for Change – Patrick White
   Website: http://www.hrmglobal.co.uk
   Email: pwhite@hrmglobal.co.uk

Skype: white9326

LinkedIn: http://uk.linkedin.com/in/patrickwhite

Power Choices at Pivotal Points – Ian Crawford

Looking for something specific to develop yourself further?

Contact me directly and let me help you specifically.

Email: candorperformance@gmail.com

Web: http://www.candortraining.com

Facebook: http://www.facebook.com/candortraining

LinkedIn: http://au.linkedin.com/in/candortraining

Singing – Antidote to Modern Life – Colin Bennett

colin@managingsafelytuition.com

http://www.managingsafelytuition.com

From Dry Inland Australia to the Tropical North! – Heather Traeger

Staff Management:

Web: http://www.staffmanagement.com.au

Mobile: +61 421 960 317

Email: Heather@StaffManagement.com.au

Right Mind Right Body (Reaching Your Ideal Weight):

http://www.rightmindrightbody.com.au

Quit Cigarettes in 60 Minutes:

http://www.quitandlivelonger.com

RecruitLoop (saving you 80 per cent off recruitment costs):

http://recruitloop.com.au/recruiter/heathertraeger?country=
Australia

Twitter: @staffmanagement

If I Can, You Can Handle Anything! – Candice Marie

http://www.healthycandy.me

http://www.icandicre8iv.com

http://www.candice-marie.com

http://www.nutritionaloncologyresearchinstitute.com

Dating with Confidence – Jason Barrett
Telephone: (+61) 421 813 991
Email: Jason@kbossfitness.com.au
Web: http://www.YoungAndWildlySuccessful.com